FAMILY SECRETS

Galina Evangelista

Printed in the United States of America

ISBN-10: 099817310X

ISBN-13: 978-0998173108

10 9 8 7 6 5 4 3

Empire Publishing

www.empirebookpublishing.com

FAMILY SECRETS WAS ORIGINALLY WRITTEN IN THE RUSSIAN LANGUAGE AND WAS TRANSLATED TO ENGLISH TO CREATE THIS MAGNIFICENT BOOK FOR YOUR READING PLEASURE.

Table of Contents

FAMILY SECRETS

CHAPTER 1

Like an artist, the frost mysteriously painted designs of a forest on the windows of the fast moving train. The trunks of trees with curly crowns on the tops were bent to one side and were located symmetrically on both sides of the window.

She blew hot air at the middle of the glass, and with her tiny finger, made a clear dot in the steamy glass. Getting closer, she looked outside. The forest was thick and the branches of the pine trees were bent downward under the heavy blanket of fluffy white snow. "Everything is white," she thought in her mind. She tried to focus on one tree, but it ran away very fast. The white forest continued forever, and there was nothing else to see. She turned her head and saw her father reading a book, sitting with his legs up on the sofa, with big pillows supporting his back. Their eyes met.

"What is it my little one?"

"I wonder Papa, why do you look older than everyone else's papa?"

He smiled and was puzzled as to what to say to her. It is true that a child can ask a thousand questions that the wisest man cannot answer, but he knew that the time would come to answer her, and this might be the perfect time to tell his daughter the truth about the secrets of their family.

He got up and put another big pillow on the opposite side of the sofa. Little Angelica jumped on her side and pulled the soft blanket which she was sharing with her father up to her chin. She stretched her full pink lips into a broad smile and her almond shaped dark blue eyes disappeared behind thick black lashes.

"She can smile with her eyes, just like her mother. How I adore this face." Michail prolonged talking for a moment admiring his daughter, and then answered, "I look older my Angel because I lived a long life, and a lot of good and bad things have happened to me. Good things keep you young, and bad things take a part of you, piece by piece. However, I'll be with you forever my Angel; you don't need to worry; you are all I live for." He smiled back to his little daughter and slowly started his story.

"You probably don't remember that particular day. You were there with your nanny, walking into the big hall. You looked so beautiful as a flower, in your light blue dress, with blue ribbon holding the mane of gold curls which were touching your waist. You were a carbon-copy of your mother. But your mother, alone, could replace all flowers in a garden; she was such a stunning beauty. When I look into your eyes, I can see the same deep dark blue eyes with teasing sparkles under the thick lashes.

That day, the ballroom in the new skyscraper of the hotel "Moscovskaya" was lavishly decorated with fresh flowers in big porcelain vases. The crystal chandeliers sparkled; guests were arriving in evening gowns and the most fashionable tuxedos of the season, for the occasion of my fifty-fourth birthday celebration."

Angelica listened to her father with a faint sound of the repeated rhythm of the carriage wheels in the background; she entered into a mysterious realm. For a moment, she disappeared into sweet slumber and didn't hear her father's voice. Her dreamy mind was catching moments, but if she missed some of the stories, she would know about them later because history was written and remembered just as it happened.

Father and daughter were occupying one-third of the carriage in the Trans-Siberian Railroad train. This particular carriage was built and decorated for privileged people like Billionaire Michail Alexandrovich Rennin to bring them to the remote area of Siberia. Their two bodyguards, Butler and Nana, were traveling with them along with a doctor who was taken on the trip in case of emergency situations; some of them occupied the section next to the father and daughter, in the same carriage. In the second carriage were restaurant personnel and a cook.

Father continued his story, and realistic images were appearing in Angelica's mind.

~

"Oksana, I think you will look better in the silver dress because it will complement your dark hair. I will pull back your hair like this, and a diamond hair clip will hold it very well, just like this. Are you are ready. Here is the mirror so you can see the back."

"Thank you, Anna, you are a real magician."

Anna knew that Oksana, at twenty-four, was not as beautiful as her stepmother Laura, who was also twenty-four years old, but Oksana Michailovna was smart and a very generous young woman. Anna liked her for because of her quiet nature, kindness, and generosity.

When Oksana arrived at the hotel, the employees, and the guests, crowded into the large ballroom with tall rounded tables wrapped with white tablecloths, elegantly held by a wide ribbon with bow. The guests were standing in groups, drinking champagne, and socializing. The uniformed male waiters walked around with trays of appetizers. The live orchestra played soft music. People surrounded Michail, talking and laughing.

The oldest son of Michail, Vladimir, holding a glass of champagne in one hand, made a sign requesting silence with the other hand. All guests turned their heads in his direction.

"Ladies and Gentlemen, May I have your attention. Today, we are celebrating the birthday of a person well known to you who rose to triumph and glory at the height of his dreams. His achievement speaks for itself. He is not only an excellent business person but also a great person. We all love and respect him, and as it happens to be, he is my father. Happy Birthday, Papa." The orchestra played a little happy birthday hurrah tune, and everybody raised their champagne flutes, chanting Happy Birthday.

"And now," he continued in a loud voice, to overcome the music and people's voices, "we will hear a word from Vice President of Rennin Oil Corporation, Mr. Timoshenko Kiril Vasilevich."

Oksana moved to the side to let Kiril Vasilevich to pass through. Holding a glass of champagne in his hand, Kiril made a short speech, mentioning the merits of his boss, wishing him a Happy Birthday and many more Happy Birthdays ahead and he emptied his glass of champagne. The crowd enthusiastically applauded one more time. After that he returned to the spot, where Oksana was standing and toasting with her, he emptied another glass of champagne. The waiter replaced his empty glass with new flute, full of fresh bubbling champagne.

"Oksana Michailovna," he whispered in her ear, "you look magnificent today, and I wish to make a toast to your beauty." She looked at him with surprise not trusting his words. She knew that she would like to have a more beautiful face and to accept compliments like this, but hesitantly, she thanked him politely.

The sound of drums in the orchestra called attention, and everybody's head turned to the decorated gilded designed French doors. Both halves of the door opened at once, and the guests could see a table on wheels with a replica of the oil tower with surrounding buildings and figures of people. The oil tower was so tall that the table was lowered with the push of a button, almost to the floor, to make the tower pass through the door opening, and then it was returned to its original height. They rolled it into the center of the hall. All excited by the surprise, the guests were asked to step a little bit away from the table, and the sides of the table extended on all four sides.

The voices became lower until there was silence. For a second time, drums announced something special with the single beat. The fountain of dark chocolate erupted from the tower, splashing on the tower and covering the buildings and the figurines, which were also made of dark chocolate. The silence was broken with loud applause and guests got closer to the tower to see more details of this culinary masterpiece. Both sons and daughter came closer to their father and wished him a happy birthday.

"Thank you, my children; this is an excellent present from all of you.

"You are all kind to me. I want to share it with my guests and employees. You are all welcome to dip the strawberries in the chocolate oil. As many strawberries as you can eat today, I will match the number of shares of the company you will get, as my gift." This generosity was met with enthusiastic applause. He smiled, and his eyes moved to his wife.

Laura, finishing a conversation, left a group of people and slowly walked toward Michail. Watching her move across the room, he was captivated by her tall and slim silhouette. The delicate fabric of her dress hugged the curves of her young and firm, but tender body. Her face, finely carved as from an ocean pearl, long lashes hiding dark pupils. The crown of large curls shines like liquid gold framing her face. The thrill of true love went through his body. He was discovering her again, and he said to himself. "She is even more beautiful than the first time I met her. Her beauty has become deeper and refined, and at the same time, more spiritual." He saw in her a magnificent heavenly creature and likewise, she too was uncontrollably attracted him."

He stepped toward her and led her to the dance floor to enjoy the soft, slow music. He looked into her mysterious eyes which were hiding behind thick lashes and said, "You are a picture of beauty, and I will never get tired of looking at you, my Darling." She followed his steps with such lightness and grace and he felt her beautifully shaped body under a silk dress, and at that moment, her sexual power overwhelmingly enticed him.

"I am blessed with my children and now double blessed to have you and our precious Angelica in my life."

"I love you for what you are, Misha, kind, loving, and very handsome." She smiled at him with her particular contained attractive smile. The music changed to a fast beat, and they walked to see Vladimir.

"I thank you, my son, for the kind words. You are my oldest, and I'm proud of you; not often enough do I have the chance to express it to you."

Vladimir, smiling, touched his father's arm. Then he threw a short glance at Laura, not seeing her as if she was transparent and turned back to his father.

"Where is your wife, Adele, I don't see her?"

"She is with her brother, Mansur, over there, at the window. He just arrived from Grozny. There were delays because the airport in Grozny is not yet completely rebuilt."

Laura rested her hand on the arm of her husband, and together with Vladimir, they walked to see Adele and her brother.

"Mansur, I assume your flight was safe and comfortable?"

"Thank you Michail, everything went well. I wish you a Happy Birthday!" Mansur met his stretched hand, "You are having quite a party here; everything is in the tradition of Old Russian aristocrats. Moreover, you surpass all our expectations."

"I'm glad to see you Mansur and thank you for coming.

Adele, hello dear, when are you going to bring the children back to Moscow? I haven't seen them for some time. Is it dangerous to live in Chechnya these days?"

"They are very safe with our father, and I'll bring them back to Moscow very soon. I just want them to learn to speak their native language."

"Ahmed must be seven by now, and Fatima is five. I can't wait to see these mischievous black-haired children. They must be adorable."

Just then, Andrey walked over to join the family.

"What are you wearing Andrey, a short vest instead of a tuxedo? You should let your brother set an example; he's always dressed impeccably and with good taste."

"He doesn't have my free spirit father. I like a fast life and for that, I need to feel comfortable so I can run."

"Be careful my son, maybe you are moving too fast," and with a smile, he touched the shoulder of his twenty-six-year-old son. "When I was close to your age I married and soon after became a father while you don't even have a wife."

"Don't worry father, my time will come, why rush?"

Michail Alexandrovich pulled the cellular phone from his secret pocket and asked the nanny to bring his daughter to the hall.

The little blue butterfly walked with her nanny through the corridor of the adoring people like a royal princess, slowly approaching her parents and was left there by her nanny.

The waiter brought a tray with glasses and poured champagne for everyone. "Happy Birthday, Papa," Oksana joined them, and the magnificent seven raised their flutes wishing Michail Alexandrovich happy birthday, many good years of health and prosperity."

"Thank you, my children. I just remembered that the day after tomorrow is your mother's birthday. I'll be far away, but I hope you will put flowers on her grave. I wish your mother could see you now. She would be so proud of all of you. She left us too early, but what you will do? The life is going on, and we will make the best of it. I drink to success in your lives, my children. Thank you for taking time from your busy lives to join me on my birthday. I want us always be together; remember the family is the most valuable thing in life. Tomorrow I'm flying to the oil field, and if it is possible, I'll stay there for some time because the business needs my attention."

He said goodbye to his children and walked towards the door with his gorgeous young wife and beautiful daughter. The guests applauded.

"Will you take me with you, Misha, please? Don't worry about me; I will fly back myself; I just want to be with you as much as possible."

"I will be working, and there will be no time to spend together. Besides, Angelica needs you. I'll call you every day, I promise."

Holding the hands of little Angelica they left the hall and got into a limousine that was waiting for them.

~

The train was rolling, and the wheels made their typical clicks on the rails, "Ta-ta, Ta-ta..."

Michail looked at his sleeping eight-year-old daughter, "Hard to believe it was only two and a half years ago. For me, it was yesterday, for her it was almost a lifetime ago."

CHAPTER 2

Soon after Michail left the party and the liquid chocolate fountain finished its display, the crowd started to dissipate, and Mansur stopped Vladimir from leaving.

"Vladimir, I flew from Chechnya to join the family on Michail's birthday, and while I'm here, I would like to discuss some business with you. Can we meet tomorrow at your office?"

"Sure, stop by about nine in the morning; I'll make time for you."

The sign on the building where Vladimir had his business read:

Vladren

The Architectural Firm

Mansur took the elevator to the seventh floor, where Vladimir's office was located. The secretary called her boss and then walked Mansur to the door, opening it for him.

"Hello Mansur," Vladimir got up from his massive mahogany desk and stretched his hand to welcome his brother-in-law.

"How are you? Did you sleep well last night?"

"I always sleep well when I make enough money."

"Teach me how to make more money so that I can sleep well."

"That is why I'm here."

"Make yourself comfortable," Vladimir said walking to the bar and poured scotch into two crystal glasses. Handing one glass to Mansur, he sat opposite him on a soft brown leather armchair. They exchanged a few phrases about family and yesterday's event, and Mansur went straight to the business.

"Did you hear about a diamond mine near Yekaterinburg, which was recently opened by some young entrepreneur from Chechnya, his name is Ali Akmadov?"

"No, I haven't heard his name, or about the diamond mine."

"Well, a few weeks ago, I was approached by Ali Akmadov to become a partner in the business. What can be more profitable than diamonds? I thought about it a lot, but to be a partner I need to invest and I don't have enough capital to do it. Adele advised me to ask you about it. I want to propose a partnership with you in this business; a lot of green can be made.

I know from Adele, about your ambition to expand your business and that no inheritance money is expected from your father anytime soon."

"In that you are right." Vladimir sipped scotch from his glass.

"What do you expect from me in this business?"

"Please understand that it will be our business, and you will have 20% profit." Vladimir's brows moved to his nose.

"20% is not much in any joint business."

"But you don't need to do much. All I ask is for you to buy snow vehicles and heavy-duty trucks to be able to operate in the harsh winter in Siberia. You will sit in your comfortable office while I will labor for both of us."

Vladimir put his empty glass on the small table next to his armchair and folding his arms on his chest, stared at the massive gold ring on his finger, digesting with what Mansur had just said.

"What will be your role in this diamond business, Mansur?"

"My role is to provide transportation."

"What figures are we talking about?"

10

"Half a million would be about right." Vladimir put his hands on his knees and moved his torso forward looking at the black burning Mansur's eyes.

"You said 20%; let's make that 25% and we have a deal."

Now Mansur took his time to think, and a few moments later got to his feet and stretched his hand to seal the deal.

"It's a pleasure to do business with smart people."

"It's my pleasure to work with you Mansur, as our father said yesterday, 'The family is the most valuable thing in life.' "

CHAPTER 3

Two days after the birthday celebration, the chauffeur held the door of the black limousine while Michail, his young wife, and little Angelica stepped out and walked to the private jet with the engines already warmed up. The crew was on board and the only thing left was to say goodbye.

"It's too cold for you and Angelica, go to the car."

Laura hugged her husband, and then he kissed her and his little daughter and climbed aboard. At the door, he turned around and blew kisses to his beautiful ladies, then disappeared inside the plane. Laura and Angelica waved to his face in the rounded window and then the plane took off.

"When will Papa be back?

"Soon my Angel, he will be back very soon."

Inside the plane, Michail buckled himself up, and when the plane reached altitude, he started his work. It will be a long flight, almost six thousand kilometers from Moscow to Magadan, through nearly one-third of Europe and all of Asia, across Siberia to his oil fields. The jet will make two stops to refuel: One in Yekaterinburg and another in Yakutsk, which is located on a wide, deep river, called Lena. From Yakutsk, they will fly another twelve hundred kilometers to Magadan on the Sea of Okhotsk. Magadan is located on the same parallel as St. Petersburg, but this city doesn't have a warm Mexican gulf stream, and the climate there is brutal. But the land is rich in oil, and this is where Michail Alexandrovich made his fortune.

~

Returning home from the airport, Laura spent some time with Angelica and then called her chauffeur to take her to a beauty salon. Tonight will be a charity function in the Detsky Dom (Orphanage), opened by the government and supported by charity donations. The NCT television station will cover the event.

The emerald green silk suit with black trim was delivered yesterday from Paris and Laura knew she would look exquisite in it. It will complement her creamy skin and shiny gold blond. Coming back from the beauty salon, she had a light snack while looking from the window at the overcast November sky. "It must be frigid cold outside of Misha's jet."

The sky was gray and dark outside of her window, so she decided to stay at home for the rest of the day until the evening function; however, her hair stylist will arrive soon to help her dress and put on the final touches.

While Angelica sipped her warm milk which her nanny brought her, Laura finished her preparations. Angelica threw up her hands making her lips into a big puffy O.

"Mama, you look better than my porcelain doll."

Laura kissed her goodnight and before she left home the telephone rang.

"Angelica come quickly it's your Papa. He is calling from Yekaterinburg."

Laura held the telephone next to Angelica's ear.

"How is my little Angel? Did you put all your dolls to sleep already? It must be dark outside."

"Yes Papa, and I'm too going to sleep soon," and she yawned like a little kitten.

"How is your flight going Misha? Whenever you fly so far away, I can't calm myself; I'm so afraid for you."

13

"Don't worry my Love; everything will be fine. When I come back, the three of us will go on vacation to our Dacha (summer home) on the Canary Islands. Don't you like it my Swan-Princess?"

"I do, I wish the time would fly faster than your jet."

"Everything has its time. I love you both, put Angelica in bed, and be beautiful tonight at the charity function, remember you're representing our company and me, tomorrow I'll call you again."

"No Misha, call me from Yakutsk, I'll have my telephone with me. You don't go to sleep until late anyway, and it will be about nine in the evening our time."

"Stop worrying; I'll be okay. I promise I'll call you from Yakutsk."

The charity function was a success. Their donation was the biggest and Laura shined like a movie star. The business men standing next to their wives couldn't take their eyes off Laura. She was charismatic, and so strikingly beautiful, and she knew it. She fully enjoyed her youth, thinking all the time about her husband, and then the telephone buzzed. She went to the window, further away from the noise.

"Misha, I was expecting your call any minute. I held the telephone in my hand the entire time. How is the flight, I worry very much."

"Everything is going well. We just landed in Yakutsk to refuel. You can't image how much snow is here; everything is white. The snow looks like it is flying horizontally because the wind is very strong. I can barely see the building from my plane window. The snow storm is already on day two, and it looks like it will never end."

"Misha, isn't it dangerous to fly in a storm, maybe you should wait for better weather?"

"I rely on my pilot's judgment. Do you look beautiful as always my Love?"

14

"Our donation was the biggest and the television people are here, we got many compliments for our large contribution, but I don't have you here tonight for my complete happiness."

"Go home and sleep well tonight my Love and I'll take a nap also. I'll call you from Magadan tomorrow when I land. I love you, sleep in peace."

Laura was a little tired coming home from the charity function, so she took a long bubble bath. "Tomorrow I have another job, to present a check to the hospital which is in worse shape than the Children's

House," she thought while falling asleep.

CHAPTER 4

"Vera, I'm walking to my car."

"Where are you, Andrey? I'm already waiting for you to open the car door, hurry up I'm freezing."

"I'm here, let's go."

"What the hell, why doesn't it start?"

"Andrey, what happened? Start the car; we need to go."

"It doesn't start; Let me open the hood."

Vera couldn't wait. She jumped out of the BMW and stopped a passing car with her raised hand, jumped in and disappeared in a second.

"Vera, why can't you wait?" Andrey ran a couple of meters chasing her car, but Vera was already far away. "What love can do to a man? She will destroy me, this crazy woman." While Andrey figured out how to start his car, Vera already got to the Tobacco Shop and met the 'Dealers.' The store was empty of customers and two brothers, the owners of the Tobacco Shop, didn't waste time.

"Here is twenty thousand dollars cash, bring me a good AUDI this time."

"Now you are talking. Last time I was driving for you a Ford from Germany, it was shaking and rattling at 160 km/h, but an AUDI can push 200 km/h, and it rides smoothly like it's gliding on butter."

Andrey came on time to pick Vera up with his problematic BMW, and they headed to Germany. The trip will take about two to three days.

Everything was going as normal; it was not the first time they made this trip.

"Why are you never waiting for me?"

Vera didn't answer and lit up a cigarette.

"Andrey, marry me, I need to help my family. You know that the beautiful women don't wait for long."

"To afford this woman," he thought, "I need to drain the oil out of Magadan."

"You know I love you, give me a chance to prove it. I need more time to make money. My father was generous before, but lately, he cut my allowance not to spoil me. For my inheritance, I need to wait another life."

To avoid further useless conversation, he turned the music on one of his CD's and listened to it till the next stop, munching sandwiches with salami and cheese, flushing them down with Coke. He would prefer to have a beer, but he was driving, and the road patrol could appear unexpectedly.

"Andrey, why don't you buy a new car; I'm afraid your old nag won't make it to Frankfurt? I like to drive newer cars. This time, we will find the best AUDI. I know more about cars than you do."

Crossing the border into Poland, Vladimir watched from his car, how is Vera walking to the border patrol booth dressed in tight leather pants and a short to her waist black rabbit jacket, in high heel boots with tight tops reaching her knees.

"For those legs, I will lay down flat and let her walk on me."

She was walking with swinging hips in a smooth movement and disappeared behind glass doors. Andrey could see her friendly exchange of a few phrases with a young officer, who gave her the necessary documents. In three minutes she was back to the car, her friend didn't even inspect it.

After a day driving, crossing the Polish border, they rested again in a small motel and then headed to Frankfurt.

"Push your old nag, let it work for us, let's go."

She put her feet on the dashboard and lit a cigarette singing the melody of a popular song, 'Don't leave me my love'.

In Frankfurt they walked in a huge space under a roof, full of parked used cars.

"Here are all the AUDI's. Aren't they beautiful?" While Andrey was inspecting the cars, Vera already negotiated the price of the navy blue A8L. The Dealer suggested a price and Vera negotiated the numbers down. She used her fingers to help with her German, but the dealer stuck to his price, she stuck to her offer and not getting an agreement, returned.

"It won't work Andrey, they want too much money, but I know where we can find a good one." She made a couple of phone calls, and soon after, they rolled into the driveway of a nice looking two story house, hidden behind trees. The owner walked them to his garage and sitting there was a masterpiece, a shiny black AUDI S-8 with four silver rings on the grill.

The owner opened the hood. Vera, with the look of an expert, leaned over the impeccably clean engine, touched it with her finger here and there and found it in suitable condition for the money they were going to pay. The arrangement was made, money was paid, and she said to Andrey, "It's a really good deal because the mileage is low. When we get on the road, you will follow me, because I want to test the engine. "What Russian doesn't like a fast ride?'" This expression in the Russian language came from the old-time when they still rode horses.

The slippery road went through a snowy white forest. Andrey was following his wild partner. "She must be using all two hundred and seventy kilometers available on the speedometer because she disappeared. There she is, I see her slowing down, waiting for me."

On the second day, Andrey reached the Russian border; Vera was waiting for him outside the car, leaning on the door with crossed legs and smoking a cigarette. Andrey passed her car, giving her a hand sign that signified craziness, and then parked his old nag.

Together they walked to the border booth, and she hugged the young skinny border guard like an old friend. He asked them to wait a little bit because there were two cars ahead of them, which needed to be inspected. They went outside, and she again lit a cigarette. Through the smoke of her cigarette, she sees smoke coming from the engine of the AUDI. She waved her hands to clear the air and saw flames rising over the hood. Her cigarette fell on the ground, and she threw her hands up in disbelief.

"Oh, Oh," that was all that she could mutter. Her face froze. She was standing and watching the growing flames in disbelief. Suddenly, there was a massive explosion, and the whole car disappeared in a spectacular fireball. She would have fallen from her feet if Andrey didn't support her. People silently watched the dancing fire. When it was just the tires burning, they walked a little closer to see what was left of the car. The snow around it melted, and the car was still smoking and was so hot it burned their faces.

The border control officer went to the booth, came out with documents and gave them to Andrey. Holding Vera by her shoulders, Andrey walked her to his BMW. For a long time, they drove in silence still in shock from the incident.

Vera was the first to break the silence.

"I'm in deep shit. What will I say to Peter and his brother, they will kill me."

"Don't worry so much, we will face them together; we will think of something."

All the way back home they didn't talk. Each was in deep thoughts.

CHAPTER 5

Oksana was working in her office with the legal documents of her father's corporation when the secretary brought her a bouquet of pink roses wrapped in cellophane with a card attached to a pink ribbon.

"Oksana Michailovna, I am overtaken by your charm and surrender myself to your power; signed Kiril Vasilevich."

"What nonsense, what happened to him? He probably drank too much champagne last evening." She thought, trying to remember last night, but all she could remember was the toast after his speech, and said, "big deal."

She put the card in the drawer of her desk, poured water from a jug into a porcelain vase and placed the flowers in it.

Timoshenko Kiril Vasilevich joined the company not long ago, but she saw him very often on their job. It never occurred to her that he could be interested in her.

"If he is sending me flowers, it means he is not married." She pulled a small mirror with a handle from the drawer and examined her face. "Maybe I should have some plastic surgery done to my nose and to do something with my chin." Then she looked at the flowers and decided to wait for further developments.

When the day was over, Oksana got in an elevator full of people, and there in the back, she noticed a familiar face with a mustache. Her heart started to beat faster. "He is handsome, how didn't I noticed him before? "She walked to the street, where her car was brought to her from the garage and was ready for her to drive.

"Oksana," Kiril approached her with a smile, "I want to thank you for the documents I requested. In my position, being vice president of finance, everything has to be legal and mistake free."

"Thank you for the flowers Kiril, you surprised me with them today," She said in a quiet and shy voice.

"You deserve to get flowers every day," he smiled, looking with his beautiful brown eyes at her, "If you are not tired, would you like to go to a restaurant and have dinner together."

"Thank you Kiril, but not today."

"Then maybe tomorrow, it's Saturday. I'll wait for you in the Restaurant Beriozka, it's close to your home," and he looked at her with a begging expression. She kept him waiting.

"All right tomorrow at 7 o'clock, I'll meet you at Beriozka." He opened the car door for her and kissed her hand. "He is such an unusual gentlemen," she thought, putting the key in the ignition, starting the car, and drove away looking through the rear view mirror at the man who just touched her heart.

Oksana had boyfriends when she was a student at the University, studying law, but she didn't have a serious relationship. Since she completed her education three years ago, she started to work in her father's company and sometimes went out with girls. She had girlfriends in the University and like any girl was waiting for prince charming to show up. She was conscious of the way she looked, and that made her a shy person.

"Wait and hope and he will come," her friends told her, "Someday he will come, you'll see."

On Saturday, for this special occasion, she put on her new navy blue wool dress with a turtle neck and a single strand of pearls on her neck. Her hair pulled back in a single knot. She didn't use any makeup since her skin looked fresh and natural.

Walking into the restaurant Beriozka, she checked her fur coat and mentioning her party's name; she saw him getting up from his chair. The restaurant was full of people looking festive and busy. He greeted her and held the chair for her to sit down.

"Oksana, thank you for coming, I was looking forward to seeing you in an unofficial atmosphere."

They sat at a table for two with a white table cloth, in the center of a big hall, with colorful stained glass windows. The stained glass was lit up with lights behind it and colored the room with red, yellow, orange and violet. It made the atmosphere happy and sunny, on this cold autumn evening.

He stretched his hand to greet her, and she responded. Their hands met over a wide vase with red roses cut short and crammed. Then they sat comfortably in their chairs.

"Since I joined the company, I have been trying to read the secret in your eyes," he started, "what is hiding behind the shy look?"

She lowered her head avoiding his attentive eyes and didn't say anything. He chose the wine and then they ordered dinner. Kiril was talking about business, about the brilliant mind of Michail, how happy he was to join this big company and finally mentioned that she caught his eye and that lately he had sleepless nights. He also admitted that he couldn't hold his emotions in anymore, and wanted to share them with the person of his admiration. She didn't say much, just listened to him and watched his attractive face and thought that his mustache made him very desirable.

On the way home, she thought about the roses he sent her the other day and felt like one of the buds, with tight petals, losing its grip and moving away from each other to make the flower open its body. At home, she couldn't keep herself from thinking about the evening, the warmth and comfort inhabited in her mind.

Going to bed, she thought that she needed to have a good night sleep so that she would look fresh tomorrow.

Kiril opened the door of his apartment and was met by his children.

"Look, Papa, Mama, shot some videotape, watch how Masha will jump and fall." Kiril sat on the sofa next to Masha and looked at the television screen. "That must hurt, do you have a bruise?"

"I injured my knee," and seven-year-old Masha showed Papa her scratched knee.

"Children leave your father alone; he needs some rest."

After having dinner with the children, Tania cleaned up the table, finished scrubbing the kitchen pots, and walked into the living room.

"Kiril, I hope you will eat with us on the weekends."

"Sorry Tania, I must have a dinner tomorrow with our banker. She is a woman, not attractive at all; you should see her nose. When Michail is out of town, I have my responsibility to keep the company finances in good shape. But on Sunday we will take the children to the circus, I can get tickets without any problem, how about it?"

"That would be wonderful," Tania smiled.

"We used to go to the theater and lately you are working so much; I hardly see you anymore. It's hard for me to work full time teaching children in school, and after my job, drive Masha to figure skating twice a week and Oleg to his music school. I don't get any help from you."

"I know Tania, but this is a new job for me, and I need to prove myself if I am worthy of this position, and after all, I make good money, so we can afford the children's schools and move to a better apartment. Please give me some time! Go to sleep; I need to work a little bit; I'll come to bed soon." When he finally came, Tania was peacefully sleeping.

CHAPTER 6

The next morning, Laura opened her eyes at seven o'clock and stretched her body on the fine sheets of their wide soft bed. She touched Misha's pillow and threw off the goose down blanket. "Misha must be already in Magadan and will call me soon. Or maybe, like always, he will call a little later, because he thinks I'm still sleeping and he doesn't want to wake me up."

She put her light colored lavender plush robe over her long silk nightgown and went to the kitchen. The coffee was already made by Angelica's nanny. Nana didn't mind doing some chores like this not only for Angelica, but for her mama also. After all, she was paid very well and lived with them in a luxurious apartment, which occupied a whole floor of the penthouse. There was a housekeeper who did not live with them, but came every day to do her work and to manage the cleaning crew, the cook, and the helpers, who took care of ladies clothes, as well as the other chores.

Laura took a sweet pastry with her coffee while looking at a fashion magazine. Tonight, I will wear the light blue suit which will be perfect for the hospital's charity event. Then she took a shower and with her towel twisted like a turban on her head, she turned on TV and watched it until Angelica walked into the room and climbed on her lap.

"Did you sleep well my Angel?" and they cuddled together in a big soft armchair. "Soon your Papa will call from Magadan. Go to the kitchen and Nana will give you your breakfast."

"Come with me Mama, we will eat together" and she pulled her mama by the hand. The morning time passed slowly; it was only nine o'clock.

"Maybe Misha will call now. There is nothing worse than to wait. I need to be patient." She was trying to calm herself. But he didn't call. She waited another hour, trying to occupy herself by reading the same magazine, over and over not able to concentrate on anything; her eyes constantly checked the clock, but he didn't call. "He arrived in Magadan last night our time, it was daytime over there and, now it is nine PM. Why doesn't he call, maybe there are some problems and, he is very busy?" In her mind, she was talking to him, walking from room to room. "Misha what happened, soon it's time for you to go to bed? I'll wait for another hour, till ten o'clock and then will call the office. No, I better call now; surely they heard from him by now."

She was ready to dial the office number when telephone rang.

"Larisa Alekseevna, this is Executive Administrator Stepanov Dmitry Borisovich calling. Did you hear from Michail Alexandrovich, he didn't call to the office yet? His cell phone is not answering. We called to the Aviation Administration, and they said that he is late according to his flight plan."

"How late, how many hours is he late?" Her heart was beating faster.

"Many hours," there was silence on both sides.

"Did you call the Magadan's office?"

"Yes, they spoke with him when he was in Yakutsk, and they were expecting him on time."

"Something is wrong." Restive doubts crept in her heart. "He would have called me by now. I know something has happened." She was speaking in a shaky voice, pacing from side to side in the room.

"Don't worry Larisa, it is not clear yet, what is keeping him from calling. We'll put all our resources to find the answer, and you'll be the first one to know, I promise," said Dmitry with assurance in his voice.

She put the phone in its cradle and sat where she was standing in an armchair, covering her face with both hands, "No, please not that." Troubled thoughts flooded her mind, but she pushed them away, "He will call, I know he will call."

Another hour passed, and nobody called. She got dressed, put her cell phone in her purse, and drove to the company headquarters. Walking from the elevator, on her way to Executive Administrator's office, she greeted the receptionist, nodding her head. In the office, all of the high-level employees were gathered together, some sitting and some standing; they looked like they were waiting for the news, because all heads turned to the door when she walked in. Dmitry rushed to her and greeted her with both his hands.

"We don't know yet, what is keeping him from calling, but everything will be alright we hope," and he walked Laura over to the group of employees.

They were guessing and speculating what might have happened and how different aircraft are affected by strong winds.

Another hour passed, maybe even more and they got news from the Aviation Administration that at a certain time, the plane had disappeared from the radar screen. The snow storm is so big that it's too dangerous and practically impossible to send out a search crew. It should be possible to fly a search plane in about 24 hours.

"That's it; this is the end. The plane disappeared from radar, and that must mean it crashed. No, No, No, it can't be true, he is alive; he must be alive." She could see his face clearly, could hear his voice; he can't just disappear from her life.

Many people were walking in and out of the room, and nothing was happening. She turned her head to anyone who walked into the room, but there was no news. Then the time came, and lunch was served in a small conference room. A few executives and Laura sat at the table, but she couldn't eat, and after they had finished with food, she decided to go back home.

"We will inform you right away if we hear anything about the plane."

Laura was so upset that Dmitry arranged for the company car and chauffeur to drive her home.

The troubling thoughts didn't leave her mind for a minute.

"In Magadan, it's about midnight now. Within twenty-four hours as expected, the storm calmed down, and it was possible to fly a search plane, but then," she thought, "it will be midnight again and in Siberia daylight in November is very short. It's not possible to find a small white plane covered with snow!"

She knew there was very little chance of finding it. "If they located the plane, they won't find anyone alive, even if by some miracle anyone had survived, they would freeze to death in the brutal Siberian freezing temperature."

Laura was sitting on her favorite chair, and the world wasn't the same anymore. She was still wearing her coat, not moving from the chair, and was troubled beyond imagination.

"Did I lose him, did I lose my Misha?"

She couldn't accept it. The shock was so disturbing that she wasn't even able to cry. She was just sitting and trying to comprehend what happened, what to do next, and couldn't concentrate on anything else.

The last scene at the airport was all she could remember, when he walked up the steps to the plane, turned around and blew her kisses. Then he was gone.

"If I knew that I would never see him again, I would have gone with him so we could die together, but it seems like it was his will for me to stay alive."

Then she heard her daughter's voice; the nanny had brought Angelica from the kindergarten for privileged children. Angelica ran into the room still wearing her white fur hat.

"Angelica, wait. Give me your gloves and hat, funny girl." Nana was running after her.

They found Laura sitting in her fur coat next to the window. Behind the window the day was gray, and a veil of fine rain enveloped the city like a dirt shroud. Calling them both to come closer she hugged her daughter not knowing how to tell them. Then she bit her lower lip, trying not to give away her emotions and to scare them.

"What is it, Larisa? Why are you still wearing your coat and your face is so pale, what happened?"

With a low pensive voice, slowly pronouncing the words, she told them the news.

"Something happened with the plane in Siberia. The plane got lost in a big snow storm and didn't arrive in Magadan." Nana covered her mouth with hand in shock.

"Did it crash?"

Looking down at the floor, Laura said in a trembling voice, "I don't know, and nobody knows yet, but I'm afraid that a crash has taken place."

Six-year-old Angelica, seeing her mother upset, put her little head on Mama's knees and wrapped them with her small hands. Laura was stroking her daughter's curls and didn't say anything more. She remembered the hospital charity function that she has to attend tonight, but the secretary in headquarters must have canceled it.

"They will find them alive. What can you do? Don't worry too much." Nana rushed to the kitchen to share the news with the cook and household lady. Then she came back to take Angelica to her room.

Laura was left alone with her thoughts, "I can't give up hope."

At nine o'clock in the evening, Laura thought about the possibility of starting a search if the storm calmed. "It's eight o'clock in the morning in Magadan right now." She felt such fatigue that she went to put her head on the pillow of the sofa. She got up a few times and went back again to the same spot. She couldn't sleep and couldn't get up. Spending most of the night this way, and when it was almost morning, she fell asleep.

At six o'clock in the morning, she was jolted awake by the ring of the telephone.

"Larisa Alekseevna, The rescue crew just returned to the base, and it's not good news, they couldn't locate the plane. They will continue the search, but they have feeling that there is little chance for anyone to survive in such frigid temperatures, it was minus forty degrees Celsius there."

The phone slipped from her hand; she couldn't say a word, falling back on the pillow she closed her eyes. Her mind and soul sank into darkness like in a grave.

Exhausted by the sleepless night she still couldn't sleep, put the TV on, and within a few minutes, heard the news.

"The TND channel is announcing the news of the hour from Moscow.

The aircraft belonging to the Magnate of the oil empire Rennin, with Michail Alexandrovich Rennin on board, disappeared from the radar screen yesterday at 10 pm, Moscow time. Our correspondent from Magadan reported a big snow storm in that area at that time, and officials are assuming the plane crashed in the mountain range of Suntar-Hajata. The rescue crew from Magadan was trying to locate the plane but didn't have success. The location of the aircraft crash is unknown at this time, but, as the Magadan's local officials informed us, the search for the missing plane will continue."

"If it was officially announced on television, it means it is true," Laura dropped herself on her bed crying in a pillow until she was told that the Executive Administrator of Rennin Corporation Dmitry Borisovich was here to visit her.

He was escorted to her bedroom by the household staff, and there he found her dressed lying stretched out on the bed with her face buried in a pillow. She raised her tearful, sorrowful eyes and dropped her head back down.

She heard his sympathetically voice, say that the search will be continued, but it didn't matter anymore because her Misha couldn't possibly be found alive.

She hid in the bedroom for many long hours, trying to understand and absorb the news, and couldn't accept it.

Later she got a call from Oksana, and they shared the terrible news. They were of the same age and could relate to each other more than two brothers. Vladimir had too big of an ego and was too proud to bring himself down to a small creature like Laura. He hated her because his father loved her.

Laura and Oksana couldn't say much on the phone because they both were devastated by the news.

CHAPTER 7

Mariya was standing next to the door so she could open it for Ivan and close it fast, not to let the cold wind into the house.

"Umm...," the wind was making a scary noise outside of the house and down through the chimney. The strong wind was picking up dry, light snow from the surface and together with the falling snow, clouded the air with zero visibility.

"Sasha sweetheart, stay away from the door while Papa is bringing in firewood. We will make our home warm and cozy. The weather is so bad, and I don't know when it will end."

"Mariya," Ivan called his wife rushing into the house and dropping the firewood where he stood, "please quickly close the door."

"I just heard something like a plane engine. It was very loud one moment, and then the noise stopped. I looked at the sky, and I saw through the snow that something was moving. It happened so fast. I think the plane fell from the sky."

"What are you saying?"

"It's true, I was carrying the firewood from the shed, and I heard and saw it. It came from nowhere and glided very fast to the ground."

"Oh dear God, did you hear an explosion or see black smoke or anything?"

"No, it was descending very fast and low like it was going to land, but it couldn't land anywhere. There is no flat ground for many kilometers. I didn't hear an explosion, so it might just be laying somewhere in the snow."

"How far do you think it is from here?"

"I think maybe a kilometer or less, it's somewhere behind the hill. I'm going to take a look to see what is left of it."

"Vania, it's a blizzard outside, at least wait for the wind to calm down."

"The storm will last for a week and maybe will never stop. If there was no explosion, perhaps there are survivors who need help."

Nodding in agreement, "I'll go with you."

"No, no, you are so light, the wind will just pick you up and throw you somewhere, and I'll have to look for you. I'll go alone, don't worry, I'll be okay. I survived much worse than this storm."

8-years-old Sasha's eyes were wide open, and he stood and listened to the news with his mouth open. "Sasha, give these gloves to your father."

"Vania, take the sled with you, tie yourself to it and it may hold you on the ground. Who knows, maybe something useful fell from the sky just for us."

"I'll come back before lunch, Mariya." Ivan put on his sheepskin coat with a hood and his snowshoes and left for the forest with the sled and the big sack Mariya gave him to gather anything that he may find. He walked very slowly against the blizzard blowing in his eyes which making it impossible to see. The wind was so strong that it knocked him off his feet a few times. He was bending almost to the ground to cut the wind. "Maybe Mariya was right, not to challenge the storm, perhaps I should go back? But I must be closer to the plane than to my home by now."

He continued to walk, struggling to climb the hill, pulling his sled by a rope tied around his waist. The snow was blinding him, and the cold wind made his face numb. "One more step to grab that tree and rest a little bit. What an inclement weather." He leaned on the trunk of a tree and covered his face with his hands to blow hot air on his face.

Then he took a few more steps to reach another tree.

"A little bit more, just a few more steps," he was telling himself. Finally, he reached the highest point of the hill. He looked around, but the snow was melting in his eyes and the snow filled air was blending with the ground. He started to descend the other side, and now it was easier to walk downhill. He would use the sled if there were not so many trees in his way and the snow wasn't so loose. Finally, he was at the foot of the hill, and he stopped to look around.

"It should be somewhere here close to this place," but all he could see was white snow, white trees, and white air. He walked a little more and suddenly out of the corner of his eye, he noticed some dark spots on the snow.

"That must be the plane; I found it!" He moved faster, got a bit closer and could see a huge white object covered with snow.

Ivan got closer, and it seemed as the plane was as big as his house. The wing of the plane was missing and instead of a door, there was a hole, covered with snow. The hole was located closer to the top of the fuselage; the plane was lying almost on its side. The tail of the aircraft was high in the air, and the nose was buried in the snow.

Fighting the wind and snow, he flattened the snow next to the door with his snowshoes, which he took off, and pulled the sled closer to him. Using the sled as a ladder, he climbed to the top of the snow pile, used his hands to remove the snow from the entrance door, and climbed inside of the fuselage.

Now he could see better without the snow in his eyes. He stood for a moment to catch his breath and adjust his eyes.

"Oh God, how beautiful it is inside, just like in a king's palace. Must be important people to fly in such comfort."

Because the plane was lying almost on its side, he could barely hold his balance since he did not have the floor to stand on. He got on his knees, cleaned more of the snow away to see better inside. Then he slowly got back on his feet, carefully stepping on the debris and furniture, walked down to the front of the plane. He reached the cockpit door and opened it. The pilot and co-pilot were still in their seats bending forward. He couldn't reach them from his place.

"Are you alive?" He called them. But they didn't respond.

"They must be dead."

He looked back inside the plane and in the distance behind the white leather armchair he saw a person, just his back. He rushed to climb over and saw a man covered with debris. He removed the broken table top from the man and saw one of his legs was bent the wrong way, and an arm was twisted as well. The other leg and arm were under his body. The torso was folded in half. He couldn't see the head behind some papers, so he moved them out of the way and saw a black head of hair with a touch of gray over the ear. The man's head was bent to his chest. He took off his glove and touched the man's neck under his sweater's collar that seemed to be warm.

"He is alive, oh, almighty God, he still is alive." Ivan touched the man's face, but he didn't move.

"If he is alive, he will freeze to death soon in this frigid temperature. I need to move him fast." Placing his hands under the man's armpit, Ivan slowly pulled him toward the door. The floor which was almost at a forty-five-degree angle made it more difficult to drag the heavy man.

Ivan climbed backward to his ladder and pulled the man closer to the door opening.

"I need to find something to cover him with or he will freeze to death if he is still alive."

Ivan quickly climbed back to the plane but didn't see any cloth. Then he climbed further back. There was a wall with a black screen attached to it and behind this wall was another section with a wide bed. At the feet of the bed was a sliding door, "It must be the closets." He reached the door and opened it. A large fur hat fell into his hands. At the same time, a bunch of blankets fell on his head.

"Good they have everything I need." A few fur coats were there also. He grabbed one with thick fur inside. Then he grabbed some things including a scarf and mittens. He tried to work as fast as he could because the man wasn't dressed warm enough and could freeze to death.

In a short time, he was at the door.

He spread the coat on the slanted floor and rolled the man onto it. He took one of the man's hands to put on the mitten, but the hand was broken. "I had better do without the mittens."

He wrapped the coat very tight around the man's body with arms together and tied it up with a scarf around his waist. He put on the fur hat, called 'Yshanka,' designed to cover the ears on the man's head. He quickly tied a knot under the man's chin to hold the hat in place and put the hood over his head.

"This way you will be warm."

His hands were so cold that he didn't feel the fingers. Putting his gloves back on, he threw four blankets on the snow and started to climb down on his improvised ladder, using all his strength, dragging the heavy man until he was on the ground. Then, fighting the wind and snow, he arranged one blanket on the sled; not an easy task because the strong wind was blowing it away, but he managed to place the man on it. He wrapped the man's legs with two other blankets, and with the fourth one, covered the rest of his body and face, and secured the cover. The last thing was to put his snowshoes on, and he was ready to go.

35

He moved a few meters and thought, "I didn't check if there were more people on the plane, but there is no way that I can manage to pull two people, so at least I'll save one."

Climbing the hill was incredibly difficult. If not for the wind, which was now blowing at his back, he wouldn't be able to pull all the weight. Slowly, step by step, he climbed up the hill. Fortunately, this side of the hill wasn't as steep as the other. Resting every four or five steps, he continued to pull the sled. Finally, he made it to the top.

His body was warm from the physical output, and now it was easy to pull the sled; sometimes he even had to hold it from sliding into the trunks of the trees.

After walking in the blizzard for more than an hour, he saw his house. "I hope I was not carrying a corpse all this way."

Mariya opened the door for Ivan, and the strong wind blew the snow inside.

"Sonny, stay away from the door it's very cold."

"Vania, thank God you came back alive. You brought something with you. Let me get my coat and help you."

"I found a man, and I think he is still alive. I pulled him from the plane."

"Oh my God, you found the plane that fell from the sky and the man is somehow still alive?"

"Mariya, help me, he is so heavy. We need to move fast."

Both of them grabbed the four corners of the blanket, brought the man inside, and put him on the floor. Mariya untied the scarf and put her hand on his neck while Ivan opened his coat. Mariya listened for a heartbeat with her ear. I don't see or hear much life, but he is warm. "Thank God."

"Be careful he has broken bones."

They cut his sweater with scissors and carefully together carried him to a small room and put him on the bed. They

36

examined his body. He was unconscious. Ivan was checking his legs after he cut his trousers from the bottom up.

Mariya went to the kitchen to warm up water and get the remedies for the wounds.

"Oh, look at this," Ivan threw up his hands when he pulled aside the cut trousers.

"His right leg is broken in two places; both bones are sticking out of the flesh." Mariya came to see how bad it is.

"Oh, my Goodness," she gasped covering her mouth and shaking her head.

"If he lives, he has a long recovery time ahead of him."

Ivan carefully examined the other leg.

"Looks like that this leg is broken in many places. The clavicle is broken, as well as both of his arms." He examined the ribs and found that two of them were broken.

"Let's hope his organs are not damaged by the broken ribs. And what if he has internal bleeding? He needs to be in a hospital with these severe injuries."

"I hope that the spine and the neck are not broken because his head was bent to the chest when I found him."

"Good gracious, he is all bruised, and all his bones are broken. How he didn't freeze to death in this frost?"

"Though the door was ripped off, the snow was covering the doorway, and it was warmer inside than outside."

"Oh, Vania, I was worried, when you left, asking myself if I will see you alive? Thank God you are both alive."

Mariya made the sign of the cross with her hand.

She moved fast to make her remedies to clean the wounds of the unconscious man.

"I found two pilots on the plane, but they were already dead. When the storm is over, I'll go back to the plane and take a better look, and when spring comes, I'll bury them like good Christians to free their souls.

"Vania, Vania," Mariya was whispering loudly. "His eyes are rolling under his lids."

Ivan got closer. His anxiety replaced the weak hope that the man will live. It's true the eyes were moving under his eyelids, but they didn't open. Mariya soaked a small piece of fabric in cranberry juice and gently touched the man's lips. The sour juice got into the man's mouth, and his lips moved like he was testing it, then he opened the eyes. Mariya smiled at him, and the man just looked at her and closed his eyes again.

"Thank God he is alive, Vania, he is alive."

So they got busy moving around quickly. Even little Sasha was helping his mother.

"This blizzard will never stop, and the man's bones can't wait. I need to stabilize them before he regains consciousness. I'll go to the shed to find some wooden planks to secure his broken legs.

"Vania, when you come back, kill a chicken, and I'll make chicken soup, this is the best remedy for a sick man."

"Little Sasha, stay away from the door sweetheart, you better go to the kitchen; the wind is too strong."

Ivan pushed the door, and the wind slammed the door back into his face. Fighting the fierce wind and snow on the ground, he managed to get behind the door.

Struggling to walk through the snow, he reached the shed where he found pieces of wood planks suitable to use as splints to support the broken legs and arms and keep them from moving.

Mariya was busy with the remedies in the kitchen preparing special food for the injured man.

Ivan went to the back of the house where the door to the stable with the animals was and brought the freshly killed chicken to the kitchen.

"Sasha, my little one, I need your help to pull the feathers from the chicken. I already scalded it with boiling water to loosen them."

Ivan carefully connected the broken bones on one leg and using the portion of the bed's sheet, wrapped the leg with the clean fabric attaching the wooden plank. He did the same with the other leg and both arms.

"It's better that he is unconscious with his broken bones because he would be in unbearable pain."

A few hours passed, but the man was still unconscious. They ate their dinner and Ivan said.

"Maybe more people were inside the plane, and I didn't check for them. Maybe somebody else was alive?"

"Vania you can't go back, I'll not let you go, wait until the storm is over, after all, there can't be two miracles after this accident."

"I guess you are right, even if somebody survived the crash, they are dead by now in this frost."

With this, they turned their concerns back to the man who was still alive.

CHAPTER 8

Andrey drove Vera to her apartment and promised to face the Dealers together with her.

"$20,000 has gone up in smoke." Vera dropped herself on the bed and laid there for a long time thinking about whose fault it was. The doorbell rang and interrupted her thoughts.

"Sorry to bother you, but do you know the people who live across from your apartment?" A tall, handsome blond man, looking like a big bear was standing in front of her.

"Yes, my friend Leda lives there."

"Leda Kruglova, and I am her brother Lev Kruglov. I just arrived from Tula, and I have been waiting for her for an hour already. Do you know where she can be?"

"Come inside; you can wait for her here."

Lev walked into the tiny entrance hall and put his canvas suitcase on the floor.

"Come, come inside," Vera walked ahead of him into a small living room.

"Have a seat. Would you like a beer?"

"That would be nice."

He looked around while sipping his beer and didn't talk much.

"Visiting your sister? Oh, by the way, I'm Vera.

"It's nice to meet you, Vera. Thank you for inviting me. I just arrived in Moscow to see my sister and I think I'll stay here for a while."

"What are you going to do here?"

"I don't know yet."

"It's interesting," she thought. "He came from nowhere to do nothing, but he is very handsome."

"Thank you for the beer," he put the empty bottle on the table and said, "I'll go to see if my sister has come home."

He went back a couple more times to check to see if his sister had returned. Meanwhile, Vera put some food out on the table and invited the surprise guest to eat.

"Looks like my sister won't be coming home tonight."

"She must be at work flying today, and I don't know if she will be back tomorrow. You don't have much luck today, me neither, but I have just the right medicine to fix it," and she brought a bottle of Stolichnaya Vodka from the kitchen.

"This will heal our wounds," their glasses clinked, and she emptied her glass down her throat all at once.

"I needed that; I had a bad day today and tomorrow will be even worse, but you Lev don't need to know why. Just pour this good medicine in our glasses and let's forget about everything. This medicine on an empty stomach will heal the soul in an instant."

"You have to eat something," and Lev put a piece of smoked sausage in her mouth.

Now it was easy to drink more vodka; it just went down by itself. And then the natural aftermath took place. After they had spent all their physical power, their naked bodies were lying across the bed sideways, and they slept like this throughout the night.

The ringing telephone woke her up. She covered the naked butt of her surprise guest and grabbed her robe on her way to pick up the phone in the kitchen.

"Hey Vera, guess what, I found the money. Tomorrow I'll have all $20,000."

"Andrey, you are a genius," she said lighting a cigarette, "I knew you would find a way to save us."

"Will you come to the Disco tonight? I want to see you."

"Yes, of course, I'll come."

"Great, then I'll see you tonight, bye."

That night Vera didn't show up, and Andrey was busy all evening solving small problems. The next morning a briefcase with money was on Andrey's desk. The man who brought money wanted to have the Disco Club as collateral.

"If you don't return the money in three weeks, the Club is mine and not yours anymore, do you understand what I am saying here? It will belong to me." The spunky looking business man was warning Andrey, poking his finger in his chest.

"Yes, I understand", Andrey nodded his head, closing the briefcase.

"Then sign here."

Reading the agreement, he thought, "Three weeks is not too much time to find $20,000. I will ask Vladimir to lend me money, to pay this lender; my brother can wait longer for me to pay him back. I am sure my brother won't refuse me this small amount of money."

And without hesitation, he signed the agreement. Right away he called Vera to tell her the good news and interrupted the lovemaking with her surprise guest.

Close to noon, Lev's sister arrived home from her trip. She worked as a flight attendant and was gone for four days. Lev collected his small suitcase and moved next door to his sister's place.

In an hour Andrey picked up Vera outside of her building and they drove to the Tobacco Shop to deliver the money.

The two brothers, of course, knew about the car that was lost in the fire and was happy to see their money brought back.

The older brother Peter slapped the hand of his younger brother to stop him from playing with money and pushed the briefcase back to Vera and said: "I need you to do something else this time. Buy a BMW in Germany, only don't burn it to the ground this time. On the way back across the Polish border, drive till you see the 140-kilometer mark and take the first exit to the left. Drive on that unpaved road until you see a red brick unoccupied structure, stop there and wait.

You should be there at noon. Take this money back and I'll give you another $25,000."

He put another briefcase on the counter and pushed both of them to Vera.

"Here, take this cellular phone with you, this is a one-way telephone. When you reach the brick building, sit in the car and wait for a call.

A car will arrive, they will put a child in your car, and you will give money to the two men, then you will drive to Moscow, to this address, and deliver the child. Here is the amount of money you will get if everything goes smoothly and Peter wrote the numbers on a piece of paper.

Vera bit her lower lip, "Deal," and closed both briefcases. Peter pulled $500 out from under the counter and handed it to Vera, "This will cover your travel expenses."

Andrey dropped Vera at her apartment and drove to his Club.

He just stepped into the Club as the bartender called him. "Andrey, hurry up, listen to the news, something has happened.

"...Rennin, with Michail Alexandrovich Rennin on board, disappeared from the radar screen at 10 pm Moscow time, yesterday..." Andrey couldn't react right away; then he sat on a stool and froze in disbelief. He sat with his head down for a few minutes then called Vladimir.

"Did you hear the news; there was a plane crash with our father on the board?" It was somewhere in the mountains and crashed in the bad weather. I don't think anyone could survive a crash like that."

"Yes, I heard. Our father must be dead. I just spoke with Oksana. The locals were searching for the plane but came up empty handed. They will continue the search until they find where it went down."

"I can't believe it, we just celebrated his birthday and now he...," he couldn't finish his sentence.

"Andrey, Oksana and I will meet you at the cemetery at 2 pm today, and we will talk."

Andrey thought; "I need to call Vera and tell her that I can't go with her to Frankfurt, I'm sure she will understand." But his mind switched to the bad news, and he forgot about Vera. He got in the car and drove to the Vagankovskoe Cemetery.

His Mother had died nine years ago from heart failure, and she was buried there. They had a tradition of visiting her grave on her birthday and had been doing this for the last nine years.

He was walking through the cemetery on a thin layer of dry snow thinking that now it looks like he doesn't have his father also and now they will come to the cemetery on the same day - only now, for two parents.

"Her grave is on the left side of the main alley. It's a different world here; it's a city of the dead. As big as this city is, every stone was at one time, a person. Some are small stones, and some are great monuments. Now not only are old people buried here, as it perhaps should be but many young people who have died prematurely.

There is too much crime in our country. Life has lost its meaning and value. And not only crime and illness claim human life, but people die in plane crashes and other accidents. Is my father dead or alive?"

On the way to his mother's grave, he remembered seeing the "Big People" memorials. On the right side of the main alley were buried "Big Persona" and their graves were secured from the eyes of strangers. Andrey with his friends wanted to see these monuments with bigger than life size sculptures. These last tributes were done for the "elite-the biggest criminals of society."

With his friend, using the passages cut through wire fence by earlier intruders, they got into the granite world. This solid granite from Karelia, guaranteed to stand for more than a hundred years, it is the most expensive granite available in the world. The walk-in mausoleum, with stairs and sculptures, cost more than $300,000. In here, you will find buried, the crème de la crème, the highest society of criminals.

He heard that at the funeral of "Big Persona" where live music is played and where opera singers perform sorrowful songs from Italian operas. He also heard that coffins of the elite are masterpieces made of redwood with antique bronze handles, lights, air conditioners, stereo music systems and decorated with reproductions of paintings from famous masters.

Especially popular are the "Senator's" - the top two coffins. In addition to the other features, it is equipped with an elevator, which raises and lowers the body. Their funerals were real spectacles. At the end of the burial, the grave was covered with fresh flowers, wreaths and firework specialists shot air rockets with black sparkling stars.

Further into the cemetery, he remembers seeing an Armenian section where there are the monuments to thieves. They looked so big and impressive that reminded him of the memorials to the Russian poet Pushkin, on Tverskaya, or to Minin and Pozarsky on Red Square.

On the right side was a man sitting comfortably in an antique bronze chair. Carved on a granite stone, his name was Roganov, one of the most famous thieves of all time. On his left side was sitting comfortably on a cushioned bronze bench his younger brother. They had the highest positions in the criminal hierarchy, and for that, they paid the highest price, their lives.

He reached the place where his mother was buried, approaching closer he could see Vladimir and Oksana holding red flowers, standing at their mother's grave. He heard Oksana saying.

"Mama was only forty-four years old, and now Papa is gone at fifty-four."

"Why did he have to marry this bimbo just two years after Mother's death, at almost thirty years his junior?"

"Don't talk like that about your father, Vladimir."

"Don't talk like that;" Vladimir mimicked Oksana's words. "We will soon see how the inheritance is divided amongst the three of us, and there will be a fourth portion for his Bimbo and her Angelica."

Oksana gave Vladimir a dirty look and placed two bouquets of red flowers in front of the black granite stone, one for each parent.

"The second bouquet is for our father, isn't it? Do you think that he is dead?"

"I think we lost our father, Andrey."

The November wind was cold, and they didn't spend much time at the grave site.

"Happy Birthday, Mama. Goodbye, Papa." They said in one voice, then turned around and left the cemetery.

On the way home from the Cemetery, Oksana thought about what Vladimir had said about their father and Laura.

"Father loved our mama, but she died, and it is better to be lost in new love than to live with an empty heart. He fell in love again so soon because when the heart is still young, there remains a passion, and a person is more ready to receive a new love than

46

when he is already entirely healed. I remember reading that somewhere."

CHAPTER 9

While Mariya was crushing dried plants in a mortar cup and transferring it to small glasses where she mixed it with water to prepare the mixture, Ivan was wiping the man's face with a damp cloth soaked in warm water.

"Wake up. Wake up you can't die on us. We will make you better; just open your eyes, and wake up."

The man heard Ivan's voice and opened his eyes.

"Oh, good, you are coming back. Hello. You will be okay, just stay with me. I'm Ivan, and this is my wife, Mariya. Can you tell me, what your name is?"

The man tried to move his lips, but his face grimaced in pain, then with a strenuous effort, and barely recognizable, he uttered, "Michail."

"Good, you have a name Michail, Misha."

Ivan got up and rubbed the palms of his hands and squeezed them tightly with excitement.

"We will take good care of you, Michail." "Mariya," he called, "give me the medicine for pain."

Ivan sat on a stool and with a small spoon, put the liquid in Michail's mouth, then another spoon, and then another. Mariya was watching and smiled at him. She noticed tears rolling from the corners of both eyes and disappearing into his hair. She took a cloth and dried the tears.

"Thank God you are alive. God sent you to us right out of the sky. You must have a guardian angel because you are the one who survived the crash. "

Ivan looked at the door where his son was standing and saw a smile on Sasha's face.

"He is alive, Sasha."

Michail's face twisted into a grimace. He groaned again and again from the intolerable pain.

"Try not to move; you have too many broken bones: broken legs, arms and ribs, I'll help you if you need something, just be patient a little bit more and let the medicine take your pain away."

Ivan continued to give medicine little by little.

"You see, we live far away from any village or city; there are just mountains around us, and your plane crashed close to our home. But don't worry, Mariya is as good as a doctor, she'll make your wounds heal nicely."

Ivan was sitting next to Michail waiting for the medicine to take the pain away. Mariya was working in the kitchen pulling stock from the chicken soup and mashing it with a fork, then adding some bullion and brought it to Ivan.

"Looks like the pain diminished. Try to eat a little bit. This chicken soup will give you strength to recover faster."

He held Michail's head with one hand and with the other hand fed him. The first spoon was difficult to swallow, the second one too, but the next few went down better, and when he finished the last spoon full, Ivan wiped Michail's mouth.

The exhaustive effort of eating took all the energy of the injured man, and he fell asleep or went unconscious again, it wasn't clear, but at least he didn't feel pain anymore. Ivan was watching his patient, in case he woke up. In a couple of hours, Michail opened his eyes again.

"You slept a little, and that's good because the body is healing when it rests. You must want and need to relieve yourself, I thought of a way to help you, without disturbing your body," and Ivan did it only as a professional nurse could manage. When Ivan again covered Michail with a blanket, up to his chin, Michail closed and opened his eyes a few times, and they filled with tears.

"That's better," Ivan said with a smile while drying wet Michail's eyes.

~

The days in November are very short and at five o'clock in the evening, it is pitch dark outside. Michail's room was lit by a fire from the fireplace from another room, which provided warmth for the whole house. Mariya prepared food and the three of them ate and fed their patient. Ivan continued checking his condition throughout the night.

"He is breathing calmly, and the sleep must be providing some comfort. Thanks to your wonderful soup, it's helping." Ivan was whispering in Mariya's ear while falling asleep himself.

The next morning, they both waited for Michail to wake up while preparing breakfast and warming the house with a new fire.

"Good morning," Ivan quietly walked into the small room and saw Michail's eyes open.

"How are you feeling?"

Not expecting to hear response Ivan continued, "First let me give you some of Mariya's miracle mixture and then we will have breakfast."

He again raised Michail's head on a small pillow and gave him medicine. Then he fed him scrambled eggs and bacon, cut into tiny pieces, and herb tea. For the first time since Ivan learned his name, Michail said in a quiet voice.

"Thank you." Ivan again saw the moisture in his red eyes. Ivan stretched his lips in a smile and couldn't hold back his tears, which were filling his eyes.

"Everything will be alright Misha."

Ivan again helped Michail relieve himself and with warm water cleaned and gently dried his bruised body.

"The snow storm was still raging outside. The snow covered half of the windows, and when Ivan tried to open the door to go outside, it didn't move a bit.

When Ivan built the house, he thought of everything. He made a sliding door on the roof to get out. He used it this time.

He climbed a ladder in a closet in the back of the house and got into the space between the ceiling and roof and using a hammer, opened the sliding piece of the roof. It moved slowly, a centimeter at a time, with each strike of the hammer. The snow was falling inside through the opening in the roof and finally there was enough room for a body to pass through.

The wind was strong, and the snow was blinding. While standing on the ladder, Ivan was throwing the snow from the roof, cleaning the way for himself. Then he managed to get out on the roof and clean it as much as he could, to take the weight of the snow off the roof to help avoid the possibility of the roof collapsing.

He jumped down into the fluffy snow and slowly took steps sinking into the dry snow which was almost up to his waist, he got to the front door and cleaned the snow from the entrance. Exhausted he came back into the house, fed the animals, sat at the table and Mariya brought him some hot tea. The entire day passed unnoticed with the routine chores of every day. They tended to their patient the best way they could, and it was late evening again.

"Looks like the storm is losing it strength," Ivan walked into the small room, where Michail was just waking.

From his bed, Michail could see that the snow half covered his small window. Only through the small spot, where there was no frost on the glass, Michail could see the snowflakes as they were dancing around, touching the glass.

51

"I will shovel the snow for you so that you can see the sky and daylight. In late spring it will be green and beautiful outside."

He didn't get any response from his patient yet, figuring out that he must be in excruciating pain from so many broken bones.

"We will make you better Misha; very soon you will feel much better." And he went outside to clean up the snow.

Soon it was dark outside again, so Ivan placed more wood in the fireplace and the house lit up with an orange color of the fire, emitting a wonderful smell of burning wood. Ivan then set on a stool next to Michail.

"Tomorrow, if the weather permits, I'll go take another look at the plane, perhaps I can find something that you need, from your belongings."

Michail just blinked with his eyes; it must have been painful for him even to say one word, Ivan understood.

He brought warm water to clean Michail's face and noticed that his face was burning hot.

"Mariya he has a fever, he needs your medicine to break it. Where is our thermometer?"

Mariya rushed to the room and brought the thermometer which needed to be put under the armpit to measure his temperature. It would be impossible to do it with both his arms broken, so he held it next to Michail's neck. The mercury rose in a few seconds up to number 42 degrees centigrade and beyond, to the top of the scale, when normal body temperature would be 36.6.

"You are not going to die, Misha, you will go on living."

Ivan could hear the noise of the doors of the kitchen closets when Mariya was preparing the medicine; she always made it fresh from dry plants which she collected in the summer. While she was making it, Ivan soaked a small towel in cold water and held it on Michail's forehead refreshing it and keeping it cool.

"We are not going to lose you, Misha; we will cure you."

Then, spoon by spoon, he put the medicine in Michail's mouth. He was changing the cold towels on Michail's forehead. From time to time he wiped his whole face and neck, to dry away the sweat. Michail was breathing all night very heavily and was making noises like he was trying to talk, only without using words.

"He is delirious."

Ivan did everything that was in his power to help Michail, but there was no progress for better. He looked up at the ceiling and begged God for help.

"Go to sleep Mariya. I will stay with him all night. I'll wake you up, if I need you, we all need strength for tomorrow."

All night long he didn't take his eyes off of Michail's face changing the cold towels on his forehead. Close to morning, Michail's breathing got quieter, and his temperature started to come down. Ivan again raised his eyes to the ceiling and thanked God for this miracle.

When it was again light outside, Michail opened his eyes and saw Ivan's face. His lips slightly stretched in the suggestion of a smile.

"That's better, the crisis is over, and you will go on living."

Ivan looked out the window where the morning was quiet; the wind calmed down, and it was not snowing anymore.

"Vania, go take a nap, you didn't sleep all night. I'll watch Michail."

Ivan just hit the pillow and fell asleep instantly. In four hours he got up and said that he rested enough.

"I'd better go to the plane now so that I can get back before dark."

He checked on Michail, who was peacefully sleeping. He put on his snowshoes, took the sled and the sack that he didn't use the first time and left toward the plane.

This time, the journey to the plane without wind was easy, and he made it in a pretty good time. He found the plane and climbed in, the same way as he did the first time.

Finding spots to put the foot he climbed to the tail of the plane. There was another section divided by a wall.

On the right side on a white leather sofa, he saw a man. He must have slid down and hit the wall when the plane crashed. His head was over his body, and the body was in fetal position. Ivan, of course, didn't see him behind the wall in the first visit. He didn't expect the man to be alive. He touched him and saw that he was frozen in that position as a solid block.

"I'll come in the spring to bury you the proper way," he promised the man.

Ivan looked around and didn't see any more bodies. There was a door at the tail of the plane, and he climbed towards it. The door opened easily by pulling the handle, and inside was luggage, a few suitcases, and some carton boxes.

Ivan pulled the eight suitcases to the front door, one at a time. It will be impossible to take all of them at once, so he threw four of them in the snow, climbed down and placed them in the sled. Then he covered them with the sack and tied them up with a rope. Returning the same way, he carried the suitcases to the house.

"We will open them tomorrow, I'm tired now, and we have done enough for today. How is Michail? Is he in pain, did he eat?"

"Don't worry, I did everything for him, and now he needs your help, you know. If he doesn't have a fever tomorrow, we will need to wash him somehow."

"Yes, we will do that tomorrow."

"Did you find somebody else?"

"I found one more man on the plane, and he is frozen. He must have broken his neck and died instantly hitting the wall with his head.

Now there are three dead bodies. They will have to wait for the spring to be buried.

There are more suitcases in the plane and also some boxes. It will take me another two days to bring everything here."

After they gave Michail his pain killer and fed him, they ate their dinner and soon it was time to relax.

Ivan placed his hand on Michail's head and found it to be normal. He kissed his forehead and said goodnight to him. During the night he got up twice, and Michail seemed to be alright.

The night passed, and it was a new day again. Ivan opened the suite cases and found clean and fresh men's clothes, but they were useless right now because Michail was not movable.

Ivan put more wood in the fire and Mariya gave more and stronger pain reliever to Michail. Then together they managed to put a waterproof tarp under Michail and washed his body with homemade soap. The soap smelled good, like wildflowers, then they gently dried Michail with a soft worn out towel and covered him with freshly washed sheets and a blanket. The sheets were freeze-dried in the frost and smelled incredibly fresh. Michail was groaning from time to time, but apparently, the medicine was helping him a lot. Then Ivan shaved Michail with the shaving gear he found in the suitcases. Finishing with bathing, he fed Michail pieces of cooked fish, then half a cooked egg and some herb tea.

"That's good, and now you are feeling better. I'm going to the plane again to bring more things, no reason to leave them, being used by no one. I hope you will soon be able to talk, believe me I know about suffering, I know."

Ivan made the trip to the plane again and brought back more of the suitcases. The next day he made another trip to retrieve the boxes. Two of them were very heavy, so Ivan decided not to take them. He found that both boxes contained two drilling bits, each very large. "We don't need these. There is no use for them." On this trip, he collected everything that he could take with him including a bunch of documents and books. The day passed very fast, and it was nighttime again.

"Maybe tomorrow Michail will be able to talk," Ivan said to Mariya, as they fell asleep.

CHAPTER 10

"Vladimir," Adele put a cup of coffee in front of her husband, "I know it's a very difficult time for you to concentrate on anything right now, but Mansur needs to fly home to Chechnya, and he asked me if he can see you tomorrow?"

"Oh, yes tell him to come to my office tomorrow morning at ten."

The next day, Mansur walked into Vladimir's office and stretched his hand.

"I'm so sorry, Vladimir. I'm upset indeed shocked, just four days ago we all celebrated the birthday of Michail Alexandrovich and it is hard to believe that he is gone. You must be feeling awful losing your father so unexpectedly. I'm so sorry that they even can't find the plane."

"Yes it's a big loss for the whole family and now we need to adjust to a new life without our father."

Looking at the motionless face of the son who just lost his father,

"Startling calmness," on the spur of the moment Mansur thought about Vladimir, "as if not his father died."

"Have a seat, Mansur," Vladimir went to the bar and brought two glasses and some whiskey.

"I made some arrangements, and $500,000 will be in your bank account in a few days. Are the banks in Grozny safe right now after the city was destroyed?"

"It's my city, and I'll make it safe."

"Then you have to sign some documents. My secretary will provide them on the way out. I believe it will be some time before I'll see any profit, but I understand any business arrangement like this takes time."

"Don't worry, you will have your 25% return, you will see, it will be a very profitable business."

"I believe you."

They talk more about family, kids and then Mansur left with relief that he got the money. The next day he flew to Grozny, the capital of Chechnya and from there went by car to his home, which is located just west of Grozny in the Caucasus Mountains.

While sitting on the plane, he figured out how to proceed further. The diamond business is just a cover up, but the money will be used differently. They will sell the raw diamonds in the future, but for now, it's only a camouflage for his real business. It is as profitable as the diamond business but much different; his "diamonds" are much larger in size.

In four days, he flew to the Ural Maintains to transfer the money from Grozny to a new account that he opened in his name at the bank of Yekaterinburg. He met with Ali Akmadov, and it took them much longer to find the right vehicles than to get the money. After that, some adjustments will need to be made to the inside of the vehicles.

While Mansur was doing his part, Ali put together the working team. He didn't have any problem with that because the unemployment in Chechnya was 75%. The country was inundated with Chechens, and many of them were looking for jobs anywhere in Russia.

Now the last thing to be done is to bring the "tools" and ammunition for the job, from Chechnya. Mansur's job was to find the weapons in Chechnya and deliver them to Yekaterinburg. For that, he flew back to Grozny.

This business wasn't new for him. In Chechnya, Mansur worked for a similar business, and after he had gained enough experience, he decided to work for himself, with Akmadov only, using Vladimir's money.

"How convenient to have a brother-in-law like Vladimir, because now he became wealthier after his father's death," Mansur said to Ali. "This is only the beginning. He will help us with further expansion of our business. You will see."

"You are lucky to have a relative this rich. Our business now will go smooth as soft butter. Not much left to do."

"It will take a little more than a week to deliver the merchandise to Grozny; that's not so bad, right? Soon we will start the operation," and he rubbed his hands together like he was washing them, only without water, tasting the success.

CHAPTER 11

Returning from the cemetery, Andrey decided to go with Vera to Frankfurt. He had to drive her because she made a commitment to the Dealers. He picked her up in front of her building. Vera heard the news about Andrey's father on the morning TV news.

"I'm so sorry, Andrey." Vera hugged him and held him for a while in her arms. "I know that they looked for your father's plane and didn't find it, I'm so sorry, and I'm grateful to you for coming with me in this difficult time."

"Since I can't help my father, at least I can help you," and he looked in her eyes, with thick black lashes caked with heavy mascara.

She brought with her two briefcases with $45,000.00 and her medium sized sports bag.

"There must be some food for both of us inside the bag. What a thoughtful girl," Andrey thought. They got into his BMW and were on their way first to Poland and then to Frankfurt, Germany.

Vera fastened her seat belt and pulled from her sports bag a small purse and refreshed her lipstick. Then she rubbed her upper and lower lips together and thought about Lev Kruglov, her attractive lover.

"Of course he is much more handsome than Andrey, but Andrey is rich, and now that his father is dead, he will inherit a sizeable fortune. I need to love him more." And the fantasy took her to London and Paris.

"I'll take Lev with me for love and Andrey for money; I will have my own car and everything a girl like me deserves. Enough of working and risking my life, I'll be smart now", and she sang a melody, just a murmur without words, "Oh, Paris, ta-ta-ta...." and in her ears, the sound of an accordion accompanied her melody.

They drove many hours a day, snacking all the way stopping to sleep in motels until they were in Frankfurt. After a shower, she put on a white lace, half transparent, lingerie robe and then set the table with the food they bought: a delicious looking loaf of bread, smoked sausages, cheese, hard boiled eggs, pickles and a bottle of Stolichnaya Vodka, they brought from Moscow.

"Smells good, I'm starving."

"First we need to drink to your father, maybe he is alive and will be found."

"I don't think so since his plane crashed in freezing Siberia, but I'll drink to him nonetheless. For my Papa," and they emptied their glasses to the last drop. The food went fast and the vodka also. Then Andrey enjoyed his delicious desert with legs to die for, fighting with the white lacy lingerie.

The next morning, they woke up at nine and by eleven they were again under that same football field size roof, which covered the parked cars. They purchased a shiny navy blue, almost new, BMW for $20,000.00. One briefcase was gone, so now they had to drive in separate cars to make the exchange of money, for a child. Like always Andrey followed Vera's BMW and like always, she quickly disappeared from his site.

Finally, they met at the Polish/Russian border and again Vera took off.

On the second day driving, she noticed that a Mercedes was following her for some time.

"What is that driver is doing, speeding like a lunatic; he will crash into me if I don't drive faster." She pushed on the gas pedal, and the car took off like a bullet. The Mercedes was gone from her rear view, but soon it appeared again, and the distance between them was closing.

In her rearview mirror, she saw two people in the front seats.

"They are thieves, and they are going to take my car. I'm not going to lose another one," and she pushed the gas pedal to the limit. Suddenly, from out of nowhere, a highway patrol car was after her with sirens blasting and flashing lights on the roof. She slowed down and stopped, waiting for the patrol officer.

"You were driving at a very high speed and exceed the speed limit, your documents, please." the officer said, holding his paperwork and a pen.

"The people in the Mercedes behind me are thieves and were chasing me from the Polish border. You had better arrest them."

"What is in that briefcase?" The officer pointed to the briefcase on the passenger seat.

"A million dollars," she smiled with her gorgeous smile.

"Do you want to pay cash, or . . ."

"I'll pay cash," she took her wallet out from her sports bag and gave the officer forty dollars. He gave her a receipt and waved his hand for her to go.

"Andrey must be close by now, but I better disappear before the Mercedes shows up again."

She sped up, but it wasn't long before they were behind her again. They were chasing after her and weren't going to let her go this time. A few times they were so close that they almost pushed her off the road. She maneuvered her car to the left and the right and sped up again.

The road curved to the left, and she couldn't see the chasing car. A little further she sees a narrow unpaved road crossing the main road past an intersection. She quickly turned to the right, dropped down and stopped her car near the trees on the right side of the road.

"Let them pass; they won't notice me here."

In her rearview mirror, she saw a truck with lumber approaching the intersection where she sat. The very next moment she saw the Mercedes, going at full speed crash into the truck. The car flew high in the air over the lumber and dropped on its roof.

"Oh, eyes. You got what you deserve damned tiffs."

She drove to the other side of the truck and saw the roof of Mercedes was smashed down, almost to the floor of the car.

"They are dead of course. I had better take off faster before the car gets in flames", and she drove back to the main road.

Soon will be the 140's kilometer sign where she is to turn left and drive until she sees the brick structure. There she will wait.

"I need to wait for Andrey now" and she drove slowly, relaxing after the chase. Andrey showed up, and they continued to drive close together until she saw the 140-kilometer post and turned onto the road, following the sign. They drove about two hundred meters and saw the two-story unfinished brick structure. Vera got out of her car.

"Andrey, you better wait for me behind the building. I believe they don't want to have witnesses."

"Did you see the crash?"

"Of course, those thieves were chasing me from the Polish border. They got what they deserve."

"Well, well, 'you are lucky, nobody is chasing me."

"Of course not, look what you are driving? Who needs your junk pile?"

Andrey drove behind the structure, thinking; "One day I'm going to lose this crazy girl one way or another. She should have been born as a boy, but what can I do? I like her as a woman."

In twenty minutes the telephone Peter gave her buzzed, and a man's voice said that they are arriving with the delivery.

Another ten minutes passed and a car drove closer and stopped within two meters of Vera's car.

A man sitting in the car opened his window and made a hand signal for Vera to do the same.

"Show the money," he commanded.

Vera opened the briefcase and showed it to him.

"Bring the child."

The man opened the back door and pulled an eight-year-old boy out of the car.

"Put him in my car, in the back seat and I will give you the money."

The boy was in her car, and she handed the briefcase to the man. She waited for the car to leave then drove behind the building, got out and fastened the seat belt for the boy.

"What's your name?"

"Oleg," the boy said quietly.

"Okay Oleg, until we get to your home, you are my son, and you call me mama, then I'll bring you to your mama." The boy nodded his head in agreement.

"Let's go, Andrey, follow me."

They drove a couple of kilometers and again a car got between her and Andrey. It got so close that Vera couldn't even see the front wheels of the chasing car.

"Oleg, sit lower so that the people from the car behind us can't see you," Vera commanded.

"What the hell is going on again? She swore. "I have been chased now for the second time in one day. This time, my cargo is more precious than money. Are they after the car, or after the boy? If after the boy, they will snatch him again.

Either way, I need to run, or his parents will lose their child" and she pressed the gas with all her power. The BMW tore off ahead so fast that the smoke flew out from under the back wheels, and she didn't see the car behind her anymore, but not for long; soon it was on her tail again.

"Dammit," she swore again, "I'll show you," and she pressed the gas pedal to the floor again.

But the Volvo wasn't going to let her go. They were pushing her from the road with the side of their car so she sped up again.

They were so close on her tail now that they were almost touching her bumper. She still was pressing the gas pedal to the limit. The road slightly turned to the left. Suddenly behind the curve, she saw a car directly in front of her and almost crashed into it.

She made a sharp turn to avoid a collision, and then she heard a loud "bang" and saw the Volvo was pushing the car in front of it, and both cars did a 360-degree turn and rolled over a few times.

Vera stopped and looked in her rear view mirror as the fire was engulfing the Volvo. She saw a huge explosion and an orange monster-fire, consumed the entire area along with the Volvo and the other car. Then she looked at her back seat where the poor child's head was crouched down inside his chest, but he didn't cry.

"Oh, what a day," she said with a sigh. "Do you like to ride fast?" Vera asked him. When she saw Andrey's car approaching from the rear, she didn't wait for him to arrive, but took off, this time not speeding so fast.

Soon they arrived in the city and drove to the address where they would deliver the child. She dialed the number, which Peter gave her while on her way to the delivery address and when they came closer to the building, she saw a man rushing toward her car. She stopped, and the man opened the back door, unfastened the seatbelt and grabbing the child in his arms, he said to Vera, "Thank you for bringing me my son; I'll call Peter," and then he disappeared inside of the building.

Andrey walked to Vera's car and said: "What a day! The tiffs are guarding the road. They must be driving the same cars that we are bringing from Frankfurt because they are all German cars."

"So you think that I'm in the wrong business?" Vera quickly replied.

"It looks like it to me. You need to hurry up to deliver the car right away before being chased again, or even worse it will explode. I'll follow you like always and then drop you at your house."

"Okay, follow me." And she took off.

Chapter 12

On the fourth day after the plane crashed with Michail Alexandrovich on board, which disappeared from the radar screen and was assumed to go down somewhere in the mountains between Yakutsk and Magadan, came the news from Magadan that there was little hope of finding anyone alive. It is impossible to spot the plane from the air due to the rising snow fall. The search is to be continued when the snow melts, which may be late Spring or early Summer at best. Because the snow is high in the mountains, it often melts later in the summer if at all. Six days after the crash, the official death certificates were issued by the coroner, for all four missing people, even though no bodies had been recovered.

A group of three Vice Presidents got together to form the Office of the President until the Board appoints a new President.

To stabilize a company of this size takes time. A meeting for all two hundred fifty employees of the Moscow headquarters was made and on Monday, they officially announced that Michail Alexandrovich had died and a new President will be appointed.

There was sadness among the people and concerns of losing jobs, but the temporary Administration promised that there would be no changes in the company and there was no need to panic.

One of the three Vice Presidents was Timoshenko Kiril Vasilevich. Though he was the newest Vice President of the company, he felt very confident and powerful; he is the one who manages the finances.

He didn't see Oksana for some time.

"She must be grieving at home. As soon as she comes back to work, I will help her to heal."

Seven days after the crash, she came rushing into the office with her head down.

That afternoon, Kiril Vasilevich decided to personally express his condolences to the grieving daughter of a dead Billionaire.

He knocked on her door and slowly opened it, pushing his head in the doorway.

"Am I intruding?"

"Kiril Vasilevich? Oksana looked at him and invited him in. "Come in, please."

He walked to her desk and stretched both his hands to meet hers and gently squeezed them.

"My deepest condolences to you Oksana, we were all shocked by the sad news of the death of Michail. I'm very sorry you lost such a young father."

She only said, "Thank you, Kiril."

He said nothing for a moment allowing his words to have impact and meaning. It's a sore point to continue to repeat the same words that he decided if she allows him to help her, he will.

"Oksana, if you are feeling sad and lonely and wish to have a respite from grieving, I would like to offer you my company. May I take you somewhere that is a bit lighter place to help take your mind from your sadness? Life goes on, and you need to recover from the shock."

"How sensitive he is." She quietly held her head, lowered her eyes and rolled them over to look at him. She took a deep breath, closed her eyes and nodded in agreement.

"Then we will go to eat together. After work, I will pick you up outside of our building, and we will go to a restaurant called, 'Tabor' on the bank of the Moscow River. It's famous for its food, and it's a very Russian nostalgic place."

"No Kiril, I think I will better take my car and meet you there at seven."

He leaned over the desk, took her hand and kissed them.

"See you at seven," and he walked out, quietly closing the door behind him.

The restaurant Tabor was an exciting and popular place. It was famous for its atmosphere and the gypsy ensemble with their dancing and singing.

The restaurant's interior was totally lit with red lights and was full of noisy people. The male host walked them to a private booth, handed Kiril the beeper, and closed the heavy burgundy velvet curtains that allow privacy for privileged guests.

The spacious booth was lit only by a candle in a small red glass vase in the center of the table providing an intimate atmosphere.

There were three wide soft cushioned seats covered in burgundy velvet with several pillows; that sat around the table with a white starch tablecloth. The candle light in the red vase made the whole booth look red, and sultry.

Oksana was sitting quietly, and Kiril ordered a bottle of wine and food, after consulting with her. The waiter gave Kiril a taste of the wine and after his approval filled the glasses.

The crystal glasses met, and the first toast was to her father. The food was on the table, and Oksana picked a little bit from her plate.

"I hope you feel a little bit better now; you need to have some nourishment," Kiril said with a soft voice, looking in Oksana's eyes. She felt relaxed, and it was easy to look in his eyes in the dimly lit booth.

The red lighting, the fast and exciting gypsy's music and the wine, took the pressure off and made her forget her troubles for a while.

Kiril filled the crystal glasses a couple more times and after the third glass, he found an intolerable desire to have her. He moved closer to Oksana, and he wrapped his hand around her waist. Oksana in impulse pushed him away. He didn't lose his grip on her. Oksana froze; he pulled her closer to him. First, he gently tasted her lips and then their lips met for a long time. Her soft body pressed close to him, and he felt passion for her. They kissed more passionately with each kiss longer and deeper, holding her tightly around her waist with one hand and with his other hand moving around her body. He gently lowered her back on the cushion. Oksana felt that her resistance was weakening, she suddenly found herself surrendering to his masculine power and by the call of desire she voluntarily gave herself to him in trembling passion.

The relief felt so good that all troubles and pressure disappeared in her mind, and her body was fully relaxed. He gently pulled her back into a sitting position so that she could straighten her clothes and they sat quietly for a while.

They sat quietly holding hands and from time to time turned their heads to look into each other's eyes, each of them reviewing their actions.

"It happened so fast, I didn't have a chance to think," having a modest nature; she justified her action, feeling how the blood was warming her face. "It's good thing that in this red lighting he can't see my burning cheeks blushing."

Something big just happened in her life, and this is as big as life and death. This new feeling mentally and physically was changing her life and taking her to an unknown direction. "I guess I was waiting for this for a very long time, and it happened, and I'm not sorry."

"I'm her first man; I didn't expect that. I hope she doesn't feel that I took advantage of her. I was too impatient, and now it's imperative, that I prove my honesty to win her trust."

70

"Now I'm a woman, and it feels sensational."

"She gave me more than I had hoped and it feels great."

When their heads were clear enough for driving, they left the restaurant in their respective cars. Oksana's sorrow of losing her father stepped aside giving space to a new dramatic change.

"I'm falling in love for the first time," she thought driving home. "What is that desire of life I have always longed and hoped for?" And her heart answered her clearly, "It's love. I'm twenty-four and waited for him to come into my life for a long time. Papa would be happy for me because he approved Kiril for a high position in the company, and he would also approve Kiril for me. If there is anything better than to be loved, it is to love" she thought, "I lost my father and the best cure for my sorrow is love."

The vogue of presentiment of this event which took place confirmed to her that she is in love and loved back. The streets she was driving through transformed into the beauty of nature, music, poetry and art and all inextricably bound up with the feeling of love. Her sadness of losing father softened up with the rising not known to her before this feeling.

Kiril, on his way home, was deep in thought.

"She is not as attractive as I would like, but there is something about her that attracts me. She has a soft body, and her face is invisible in the dark; she is the daughter of a Billionaire, and that makes her beautiful."

~

"Hi Honey," Kiril yelled to his wife taking off his coat."

"You are late again for dinner; the kids don't see you anymore." she said.

"Tania, you know what recently happened on my job, I have more responsibility now than before. I think that I'm one of the candidates for the President of the company. Think about it, the President of the Rennin Corporation, Timoshenko Kiril Vasilevich and you are his wife."

Tania didn't say anything and went to the children's room to check on them. "They are sleeping."

She put on her new white silk nightgown which she just purchased and stood in the doorway of the living room leaning on the door. He looked at her and said,

"Go to bed Tania, I'll be there shortly; I just need to look at some documents which I brought home."

Tania walked over to him and pulled him by the hand.

"You'll see them later." But he took his hand back.

"I'll see you in a minute. Go to bed and wait for me."

When he came to the bedroom, Tania was already sleeping.

~

In a week, the family lawyer scheduled the reading of the Will left by Michail.

The three children and Laura were sitting in one room of the lawyer's office and silently listened to his reading.

After mentioning all assets and all related to it important sentences they heard:

"Each of my four children: Vladimir, Oksana, Andrey, Angelica and my wife Larisa, together all five will have 20% of the assets." Then followed the details and in the end things were mentioned of what he left to the people outside of his family.

After the reading had been concluded, they walked out separately. Vladimir joined Andrey on the staircase.

"Did you listen and understood everything?"

"Why are you asking?"

"I saw you were playing with your cell phone when the lawyer was reading the Will."

"I was listening," he exclaimed.

"Did you hear that the Bimbo with her 'extension' (the half-sister, Angelica) will have 40% of the company? I was expecting 20% for the child, but he left the same money for Bimbo. I can't believe it! She is not even part of our family. This is an indefensible act done by our father. We can't allow it to happen."

"But Angelica is also our father's daughter and that makes four of us plus Laura. Andrey shrugged his shoulders. "She is his legal wife. It's father's Will, do you want it, or not."

"That still needs to be proven, Andrey. She got what she was after, our father's money. We need to do something to stop it. I'll call you when I figure out what to do."

Andrey threw an indifferent glance at his opinionated brother and left with the feeling that Vladimir is too greedy. Andrey wasn't that ambitious and creative like his brother, and it was easy to influence him either way.

Chapter 13

It was November the thirteenth and more snow fell on the ground throughout the night. It was still dark outside, and Michail's eyes were closed. Ivan dressed warmly and went outside to clean up the snow. Then he brought wood for the fireplace and the stove so that Mariya could cook breakfast. Mariya got up too, but Sasha was still sleeping.

First of all, Mariya made medicine for Michail and then breakfast for everyone. Seeing that Michail's eyes were open, Ivan got closer and said.

"Good morning Michail, how are you feeling?"

Ivan walking in Michail's room greeted him every morning with the same sentence.

"Good morning Ivan."

"Ooh," Ivan stretched his words in excitement. "What a good morning! You can talk, this is wonderful. Do you have pain? Shall I give you medicine first?"

"That helps."

"Mariya, bring the medicine, Michail said good morning to me. Looks like he is much stronger now and the pain diminished."

Mariya walked to the room carrying a cup with her mixture and a small spoon.

"Good morning Mariya," Michail said and smiled. Mariya made the sign of the cross on herself and glanced at the ceiling.

"It's really a good morning to see you smiling and talking. Now you will be better and better every day. Thank you Lord" and she crossed herself again.

Ivan, with the skills of a professional nurse, raised Michail's head, put a small pillow and helped him to drink the mixture from the cup.

"You are making good progress, and soon you will walk again."

"Maybe never again; maybe my spine is broken?"

"You will, you will, because your spine is in one piece, I'm sure of it. Your legs show the presence of life, and it means that one day when your bones heal, you will walk again. Now let's have breakfast and then we will have all day together."

"Sasha, come closer; don't just stand there in the doorway. This is our son Sasha; he is 8."

"Hello Sasha, I can't give you my hand, because both of them are broken."

"Did you fall from the sky?" Sasha asked in a shy quiet voice.

"I did, and your papa found me, brought me to your home and your mama makes medicine for me to get better." Sasha smiled and walked out in childlike embarrassment.

"What a handsome son you have, Ivan. I have a small daughter at home; she is 6-years-old, but I have three older children as well. My first wife died from heart failure, and she was only forty-four years old. I remarried again, to a younger woman and six years ago she gave me a daughter, Angelica. She is also beautiful like your son." He paused, traveling back in his memory.

"When did I see her last? At the airport", he answered to himself.

"Where are we, Ivan?"

"Vania, call me Vania, that's much simpler."

"Call me Misha; I would like that also."

75

"Vania, how far are we from any city or village? Maybe I'll go to the hospital, you and Mariya did enough for me saving my life, and I will never forget it, I promise."

"Mm," Ivan made a sound, slightly grimacing, "we live in the mountains deep in Taiga and very far away from any civilization. We don't have electricity, radio, telephone, or even a horse to travel with." Everything we need, we make ourselves. It's not an easy life, but we prefer it this way."

There was some sadness in Ivan's voice, and Michail decided not to ask any more questions. But seeing that Ivan was not leaving, he continued.

"I work for a big oil corporation. The headquarters of our company is in Moscow, and all of my family lives there. By profession, I'm a geologist and engineer in an oil industry and was flying to the fields in Magadan, where we are pumping oil. There was another engineer flying with me. Did you see him at the crash site? What about the two pilots and why did I survive?"

"Your plane didn't fall, it landed, although the wing is missing, maybe both wings. The nose of the plane is buried in deep snow, but the tail is up in the air. All three people, you asked about, are dead. I saw their stiff frozen bodies on the plane. They have to wait until spring, to be buried."

"Did they die instantly?"

"I think so. I saw the plane coming down, and then it crashed behind the hill, about one kilometer from our home. There was no explosion, and I thought maybe someone survived and needed help. The weather was bad from a big snow storm. I went to the plane right away and found you still alive. So I carried you on a sled and brought you here. You were unconscious for a few days so that I could fix your broken legs and arms. Mariya is a good healer and always has been taking care of the three of us. She will put you on your feet also."

"Vania help me to move this bucket, it's a little bit heavy for me."

"We will talk later Misha."

"I wish I could help."

"What are you thinking about? Your only business is to recover."

Ivan came back with an improvised basin, a small wash basin and a towel.

"Don't be embarrassed; it's not the first time for me to help you. Just close your eyes and relieve yourself, I'll leave you alone behind the closed door and then will clean you up."

He did it as a professional nurse and covered Michail with a blanket.

"See you in a little bit, I need to do some chores around the house," and he closed the door behind him. Then he came back to clean him up.

Later that afternoon Ivan and Mariya gave him a bath - if it can be called that and Ivan put a folded blanket under one side of Michail's body to make the weight shift to one side and give a little rest to his back. Later, he did the same thing with the other side. After dinner they relaxed, it was enough activity for one day for Michail and everyone else. Tomorrow will be another day.

The next day Michail was feeling good enough to talk and after all the necessary things were done, like shaving, feeding Michail and house chores, Ivan sat on the chair next to Michail's bed and a conversation began.

"Everybody has a story to tell, particularly after living as long as we have. I know that you are younger than me."

"I'm forty-eight now," Ivan said with a smile.

"I'm older, fifty-four. My oldest son, Vladimir is twenty-nine". Michail named all members of his family. "Tell me about your life, Vania. I think there is a story here."

"Yes, there is a story," Ivan took a deep breath. "I never thought I'd have a chance to tell it to anyone except to my son, but God sent you to us, and now you will hear it." Sasha's head was half pushed into the doorway.

"Sasha, come in, sonny. It would be interesting for you to hear the story of your parents, while I'm telling it to Michail." Sasha walked into the room and knelt putting his head on father's knees to listen, and the story began.

"By the time I was nineteen, both my parents had passed away from illness, and I lived alone in Okhotsk, a city right on the Sea of Okhotsk. I was part of the crew on a fishing boat, and we went to sea to catch cod, salmon, and crab to deliver to the coast.

On my days at home, I liked to hunt in Taiga. The animal life here is abundant and varied. Forest-tundra includes animals such as snow sheep, wild reindeer, moose, brown bears, arctic and red fox and wolves. The fur keeps you warm in our brutal winter when the temperature including the wind chill, drops to -60 Celsius or below.

The valley between the Kolyma River and the Okhotsk coast is the Taiga (evergreen forest) zone. In the summer, in July, which is the hottest month, the temperature rises to 15 degrees Celsius, and it's just beautiful. There grow medical plants including valerian, which Mariya gives you every day to calm you down and reduce pain. There are also ferns, juniper, lingberry, dandelion, wild rose, mountain ash and honeysuckle, all the herbs Mariya uses to heal your wounds.

You said that you are drilling for oil in the Magadan area. I know more about gold than oil. The Magadan Region is considered one of the world richest mining areas. Gold is the main natural resource. The probable gold reserves are estimated at 4,000 tons and silver some 14,800 tons. I remember it from my geography class in school. I saw in the Museum of Magadan, the biggest native gold stone in the world. Go little Sasha; Mama is calling you."

Now Michail got into the conversation.

"This is not an easy place in which to live with the climate that cold, but it's a very rich part of Russia.

Since I worked for the oil company, I have been to Magadan many times. I know that the population is 150,000, and the city is not built for beauty; most of the buildings are typical Russian architecture and very basic. But I saw that Magadan had everything that a Regional Center should have: five research institutes, three higher education institutes, schools of medicine and art, seven polytechnic universities, health facilities, cultural centers, libraries, hotels, stores, museums and theaters, they have everything.

But it is difficult to do business when there is no railroad and a very poorly developed infrastructure. Transportation connections are made by motor vehicles, sea, and air transport. There is only one 1400-km Kolyma highway, the main freight delivery route to various parts of the region.

We drilled and sank oil wells into the frozen ground, and that was the diamond drill bits you found on the plane. I was carrying them to the fields."

"Aaa, that is, what I saw. "Oh," Ivan took a deep breath. "Magadan is a reminder of the past." "I don't know if you are interested in history, but it's always good to know what human beings had to live through."

Ivan felt that he has to share with this person from far away the truth about his native land.

"The history of the Magadan Region is closely tied to the Gulag Period."

"You are talking about Stalin's time."

"Yes, everybody read the book of Solzhenitsyn 'The Gulag Archipelago.' He published his book despite that the Soviet State Security forbade him to do it."

"Yes, I know, at that time the entire territory was one vast corrective labor camp."

"So you know that near the city Butugulag, there is the Gulag prison, one of the gloomiest spots in all of Magadan. A road constructed by prisoner's leads from Magadan to the remnants of the Gulag."

"Have you been there?" Ivan asked.

"No, but I should."

"When you visit that place, there you can see the ruins of the barracks. The place is frightening, with horrible silence. It frightens you especially if you imagine that prisoner's pickaxes created all of it at minus fifty degrees. They worked for 200 grams of bread per day and those who were dying were just thrown into mines."

Ivan lowered his eyes and paused for a moment. Michail noticed how Ivan was affected by his words like he was one of them.

"The words "Magadan" and "Kolyma" Ivan continued, "have been associated in the recent past, with human grief, humiliation, and terror. Everything that had been made and built in Magadan; roads, mines, and houses were built mostly by prisoners. It's an area of everlasting mourning, and it will always remain a vivid monument to history, which people should never forget."

"You are right Vania people will never forget that bright, intelligent men and women were accused of crimes they did not commit."

"I'm sure of it. Let's hope that this time in history will never be repeated."

The men were silent for a minute, like they were paying respect to the vanished people and then Michail continued:

"Like all Siberia, this area has its riches. Twenty-nine zones of oil and gas accumulations have been identified on the Okhotsk shelf. Total reserves are estimated at 3.5 billion tons of equivalent fuel, including 1.2 billion tons of oil and 1.5 billion metric tons of gas. It was a good place for me as a geologist, to look for oil and we found it in abundance."

"That is enough talking for the morning; it's time for breakfast," Mariya announced from the kitchen.

"I see that the clavicle didn't hurt as much as before, but your legs and arms still give you a lot of pain." Ivan was talking, putting two pillows behind Michail's back to support him in a sitting position.

"The body is still bruised with dark purple and orange and green color. But despite that, there is visible progress, at least with your general condition. And that is good."

Mariya pulled a glazed simmering duck with sauce out of the stove and cut it into bite-sized pieces for Michail. She also served cooked barley on the side and walked into the room with the tray.

Ivan fed his patient with a spoon and afterward gave him hot tea and cleaned up his mouth. Michail said.

"Thank you, Vania, and thank Mariya for the delicious food," and he closed his eyes.

"The time will come, and I'll pay you back. It never occurred to me before that poor people could be so kind and giving. I see how hard it is for them to live here and what kind souls they are to share everything they have with a total stranger. I'll never forget it, and when the time comes, I'll pay them back the best way I can."

That afternoon Ivan was doing chores and feeding the animals.

In the back of the house that he and Mariya built when they came to live in the mountains, they built a double log structure for animals to live. The back of the old fashion Russian stove was open to the shed so the animals would be warm enough to survive six months of brutal winter. They kept four snow sheep to use their wool for making clothing, four goats to have milk, two pigs for meat and fat, and three dozen chickens. The chickens lived in the same shed with the animals.

It was a big job to prepare food to feed the animals as well as for themselves, so in the short summer, they would grow barley, oats, and wheat. Mariya collected mushrooms and berries to make preserves and also harvested the right plants for medicinal purposes. Ivan hunted for ducks and other birds and fished in the Ohta River for trout and salmon. They kept the fish and birds frozen to have food through the long winter.

The afternoon passed faster than the morning.

"Another day passed, and that's enough for today. Tomorrow will be another day," Ivan said walking into Michail's room to see if he needed anything.

And the next day came. Ivan was busy all day and only in the late evening they continued their conversation.

"I would like to hear more of your story, Vania." So Ivan continued.

"My parents were gone, but I was never alone, I had my sweetheart Mariya. We have been friends since the seventh grade. When I was 20, and Mariya 18, we got married. I knew that Mariya loved me and would marry me if I would ask her.

Then when I asked her, she said yes, I promised her that I would love her forever and take her to paradise. I meant for us to have a good life together. That time we were too young to have children and Mariya was working in a hospital as a nurse helper and attending evening classes at an institute, to become a school teacher."

Ivan turned his head to the door and back to Michail.

"Those were the happiest years of our life, we were very much in love, and still are." He laughed a little.

"Mariya's parents didn't live long either, so we were left alone, but we had each other. Mariya was a beautiful woman, and she is the most cherished thing in my life. I was content because I had everything I wanted in life. Often, I went to the sea, and when I came back home we spent treasured time together. Those days, when I wasn't at sea, I would go to Taiga, hunting with my friends. In the winter we hunted for white fox and elk. In the summer, for red fox and moose we went to the lakes for the geese, and duck.

On one of these hunting trips I shot a couple of ducks and smaller birds, and I knew that my friends were not far from me, so I made the sound of a bird to communicate with them. Just then, two men came running towards me who weren't my friends. They hit me in the head and tied my hands behind my back with rope. I screamed, but they hit me again, and I lost consciousness and didn't remember anything after that.

When I gained consciousness, I was lying on the floor in a moving truck without windows in full darkness. My hands were untied, and I touched my nose which was bleeding, and the salty blood leaked into my mouth. I held my head back, to stop bleeding. My head was buzzing and in the dark, I could see nothing, but I could hear the noise of the track's engine.

In my mind I was talking to myself: "Who are they and where are they taking me? I thought about Mariya, if I don't come home at the time I promised, she will panic and wonder, what happened to me in the forest? I didn't even have a chance to see my friends, so they don't know where I disappeared to. All I knew was that some bandits violated my freedom and now I'm a prisoner. All I could think about was Mariya, and that I couldn't live without her. How will she live without me and what will happen to us?"

Mariya heard her name and said.

"Vania, let Michail rest, it's late, we all need to sleep."

"Sleep Misha; later I'll tell you more. We will have plenty of time together, sleep well," and he fixed the pillows, pulled the blanket up for Michail, then left the room.

Michail couldn't sleep that night for a long time. Ivan's last words disturbed him greatly.

"This kind man must have had a worse experience, then me; I need to know what happened to him."

Then he thought about his love with Mariya and how she would feel if Ivan was injured as he is now, remembering his beautiful Laura, who must also be suffering at the loss of her husband. How he wanted to turn the time back and exclude this entire nightmare from his life. He lay without sleep for a long time, his body was very tired from not moving, and the pain was terrible. But he couldn't disturb his friend, who also needed to have his rest. After a few long hours, he finally fell asleep.

CHAPTER 14

One month passed since the plane crash, and Laura started to realize, that her Misha will not come home and that he was lost forever. Nothing was the same anymore.

"Today is December the second, exactly one month since it happened." Laura imagined herself in the aircraft since she flew many times with Misha to many places including the Canary Islands where they had a Mansion on the Atlantic Ocean, not far from Morocco. The brilliant hot sun, the deep green cypresses and palms, the bright flowers, which perfumed the air, the turquoise water, all of this, Misha won't see anymore. There is only darkness in his world as in hers.

"Did he feel pain when he died, did he die instantly?" Laura imagined herself sitting with Misha in the plane at the moment of the crash and saw herself hugging him and falling to a cold grave together. Tears gushed from her eyes, and she hid her face in the pillow. Her whole body was shaking from crying.

"Misha, Misha, Angelica won't have her father anymore, why did this happen to us? My Angel has the same fate as I because I grew up without a father. The three of us were so happy together, why did you leave us?

I can't say goodbye to you, not yet" and she squeezed her pillow, which had become wet from tears and pressed her face into it, crying and sobbing.

Now, she spends all her days at home lost in her grief, remembering their life together from the start to the end. She was seventeen when they met. At forty-seven, Misha was something more than just a charming, nice looking man; he was like a father to her. He was replacing her father, she never knew. Her father died soon after she was born and she knows how handsome he was only by the black and white photographs her mama treasured. Her mother was working as a nurse in the hospital on the outskirt of Moscow where they lived in a small apartment.

Just graduated from high school, Laura met Michail in The Tretyakov Gallery at the Museum of Russian Artists. She was looking at a painting by Michail Vrubel, "The Swan-Princess" when she heard a voice behind her, "You must have been the model for the artist; this crowned swan-princess is a copy of you, only her hair is dark."

"I couldn't have lived in nineteen century," she turned her face just like the princess on the painting and Michail saw her huge dark-blue eyes with thick black lashes. But she was more beautiful than the woman the artist had in the picture, much more beautiful, she was life itself. Glaring at her, he said, "Your beauty is the one, who deserves the crown." She gave a little smile, showing her sparkling white teeth. Michail wasn't surprised to hear her melodic voice; it could belong only to such a stunning beauty.

Michail thought, "The artist's wife was an opera singer. Did she have the same beauty as this young divine creature?"

She was going to leave the room, but he couldn't let her go.

"My name is Michail. What is your name, Swan-Princess?"

"Laura."

"Laura Rennin" flashed in his mind. "She will be Laura Rennin."

Two months later, they got married. Michail quickly found that her personality matched her beauty. Many times, Misha repeated the story of their first meeting to her.

She remembers every moment they spend together. "I was so happy and now I'm left alone without my Misha. I lost my 'swan

86

wings', I will never fly again and my diamond tiara, which Misha put on my head when we were married, will never crown my head anymore." She thought as she sobbed on her pillow.

~

On the other side of the river, in Moscow, at the architectural firm Vladren, Vladimir Michailovich Rennin didn't cry about his father.

"Our father is gone, and I am the head of the family now, and I need to take care of them."

As soon as this thought came to his mind, it was drilling in his head day and night. "The money must stay in the family."

His ambitious and greedy mind was working in one direction. How to take not only 20% but 40% from this Bimbo who is nobody to the family? This thought didn't leave his mind for a moment and was eating him alive. This is not a small business; we are talking about billions of dollars."

"If only she was alone, but she has her 'extension.' What do I do with her child? I need to be careful with strangers and not to give out any of my thoughts. It should be our family secret. I will ask Andrey. He meets different kinds of people in his Disco Club, maybe he can find some needy-greedy specialist in the "wetwork" business. Good thought.

Then, I need to call my detective, Tihonov, to find where this Swan, as father called her, flies in the evenings."

He had it all figured out, and the machine started rolling.

"The longer I hesitate, the more doubt there will be." He called Andrey right away, "I need to talk to you about something important. I'll stop by to see you tonight at your club."

Not wasting any time, he stepped into the dark, sparkling with lights mirrored Disco hall. He walked between young bodies moving like snakes, girls dressed in tight miniskirts and fellows in brightly colors shirts and trousers. They all jerked their hips and the other parts of their bodies with their arms thrown in the air to a rhythmical beat of the awfully loud music.

Walking to Andrey's office between pierced and tattooed bodies, he thought. "I think I'm in the right place."

After being in his tastefully decorated office, his brother's office looked trashy, and Andrey himself was dressed to fit this place, wearing a sweater without a shirt and headband with stripes on his forehead.

"Hey Andrey, nice place you have here, only the music is too loud."

Andrey, upon seeing his brother, moved his legs from the table and sat upright in his chair.

"Don't worry, stay where you are. I came to discuss a particular matter with you."

"What brought you here brother? You never visited me before. Have a seat."

"I think that you might agree with me," Vladimir went right to the point, "that our father made a very foolish mistake to share our family money with a stranger half of his age. He left to her and her 'extension' 40% of our inheritance. Do you want to give a stranger a billion dollars, when each of us will only receive $500,000,000?"

Andrey opened his eyes wide and pulled his jaw down,
"No."

"Then we need to do something about it, right?"

"You are right," and his jaw moved back into place. "I didn't know that our father had so much money."

"You are living in a small space and disconnected from reality, Andrey. I watched you at the reading of the Will. You were playing with your telephone and missed everything. But now you know, and you don't want to give away this big money, right?"

Andrey calculated in his mind how wealthy his father was.

In his mind, father still was alive; he just couldn't let him go. He hadn't thought about inheritance, not even if or when he will get the inheritance. He needs money right now. His problem with debt was tormenting him.

Andrey thought, "In two days, I have to return the money that I borrowed for Vera when the AUDI went up in smoke, and if I don't return it on time, I will lose my Disco. I didn't know how to ask Vladimir for money and here is my salvation. What a fortune!"

He asked, "What do you want me to do, to kill her?"

"No, not you, but I need you to find someone who will."

A troubling thought flashed in his mind, "This is a "wet" business, and I don't want to be involved in it, but I'll lose my Disco."

"I'll find for you someone who can do it, I know some dealers." he thought about the dealers at the Tobacco Shop, they know this kind of people.

"Give me their names, address, and telephone."

"Here are their business cards, but if I help you, I need your help also. I need $20,000 cash, no later than tomorrow at noon."

"Deal," Vladimir even didn't ask his brother why he needed the money.

"The money will be delivered to you tonight."

"Great, my Disco is safe," Andrey thought.

"There's one more favor I need to ask you, Andrey. I know how easy it is to influence you, so I want to ask you not to marry anyone without consulting with me. We already have one mistake in our family; let's not create another one, promise?"

"Promise, I wasn't going to marry anytime soon anyway."

Vladimir threw a warning glance at his brother and wrote down the telephone of his detective, Tihonov.

"Keep this telephone number safe. Your people will need it later to work close with him. See that not one soul on Earth knows about it. This is big secret and should stay in our family. Do you understand?"

"Yeah, don't worry."

Vladimir was still worried because he didn't trust his frivolous brother. He left Disco thinking about the 'extension.'

"I need to make some sort of document claiming that this Angelica is not my father's daughter. And I have a brilliant idea."

That evening, Andrey went to see Dealers. They easily found a way to understand each other because money was doing the talking. "You pay, I deliver."

There was no need to explain much, Andrey just said, "Peter, I need a 'wet man' to take care of someone. Here is the telephone of the detective you will work with; he will explain you everything. Don't worry he is reliable. "

Dealers didn't need to look for clients; they come to them every day.

"No problem, 'wet business masters' are standing in line waiting."

Andrey wrote down detective Tihonov's phone and left with a smile. "Good deal. $20.000 just for asking others to do the job."

On the way to his office, Vladimir called Private Detective Tihonov's agency, and it just so happened to be a good time for a meeting; he drove directly over to see the detective.

Vladimir gave him the Dealer's phone and said that they would work together. It didn't take long for Vladimir to explain to detective what need to be done.

"All you have to do is to follow the Swan-bird," as Vladimir named her, "to know where she goes or drives."

"No problem, all I need from you is her photograph and address."

"I'll bring it to you myself. And I need you to do one more thing related to this business. I need you to find me a doctor, who can produce a document with blood type; do you have someone who can do it?"

"Yes, I know exactly the person we need. His name is doctor Reznik from Psychiatric Clinic #1."

"Is he a reliable person? This has to be done in strict secret. You know how reporters are hunting for anything related to our family."

"I'm sure we can trust him. He did a similar document for me before, and I can ask him. What is it about?"

"I need to prove that the small child in our family is not my father's child as he thought. My father is dead, and nobody will be interested in his blood anymore, so we need to produce a document with a different type of blood than father's and replaced it with the existing one in his doctor's file."

"I'm sure we can handle it."

"Good, make doctor Reznik produce the document for you and have your people replace the existing document. I think I've paid you enough to do this for me."

"Of course, Vladimir, I'm satisfied with my pay, but I need to pay the others to help me."

"Don't worry about them; they also will be paid well for their job. Can you trust these people? Remember this is a big secret."

"They are loyal to me as I'm to you."

It didn't take much time for Dealers to contact the right people. Everything was arranged, and the 'wet man' was standing by, waiting for detective Tihonov's command.

Detective Tihonov did his job very well and after three days, he met with Vladimir and said that this morning the Swan-bird was a passenger in Mercedes and went to Detsky Mir (Children's World, the largest children's department store in Moscow) and

91

shopped with a female child in the toy and clothing departments, and then her driver drove her home.

"Very good, continue your job, and if you see her driving by herself, let me know immediately. Also, I want you to install bugs in all the telephones in her penthouse; it won't be difficult to do because many people are serving in there."

For a month, the chauffeur drove Laura everywhere.

"We can't wait for a special occasion. We need to act now," Vladimir was becoming impatient as if the money was already slipping away from his hands.

CHAPTER 15

It was always a lot of work to keep the Disco running, and Andrey couldn't see Vera often. When he wanted to see her, she couldn't make it.

"So, it's better that I don't see her, or like usual, I might lose my head with her and could give away the secret about my business with Vladimir."

While Andrey was busy in his club and with his new assignment, Vera was busy with her new attraction. She was paid $50,000 for the child she delivered safely and was spending it on her new penniless lover. They ate in expensive restaurants and shopped for her and him. Soon it will be a New Year, and she needs a lot of new things.

Lev's sister worked as a flight attendant; she was absent all the time and made it easy for Vera to sleep at Lev's sister's apartment. She slept there for safety reasons in case Andrey unexpectedly stopped by.

One day, she was observant, "I think I'm late, and I have nausea every morning. What if I'm pregnant?" She started to worry.

"If I am, it is definitely Lev's child, but he won't know about it, and I will tell Andrey it is his child. He will marry me, and then we all go to Paris. I'll have two lovers, and then I will tell Lev the truth." She had it all figured out, so she made the decision not to have an abortion. "I'm sure I'm pregnant, and I'm keeping the child."

Vera could easily fool both lovers because they both were in love with her and it is not their business to tell her what to do. She called Andrey.

"Where are you hiding, Andrey, I need to see you, I miss you, let's meet at the Singers Café at six this evening. Don't be late; you know I don't like to wait."

The winter frost made Vera's cheeks pink, and her lips red like summer cherries.

"You look so radiant, what happened?"

"I'm just happy to see you. Let me see, last time I saw you is when we made love a month ago. It's not good to be so busy; your child will grow up, and you won't notice it."

"What, you just said, my child?" Andrey stretched his neck and froze in this position.

"Aren't you happy, isn't what all men do to their women?"

"I just don't know how to react. I guess that I'm happy. Yes, I'm happy."

"He or she will be a beauty."

"I agree with you on that. Let's celebrate the occasion. To tell the truth, I didn't think it would happen so soon."

"I hope now, we will get married, won't we?"

"Yes, of course, we will, but I just lost my father and it won't be appropriate to rush into marriage, but we will. I will begin making plans for it."

"You must have an advantage being so beautiful; you always get what you want."

"Let's have another drink while I can" and their crystal glasses met making bell sound."

~

At a different restaurant in Hotel Russia, two other crystal glasses made same bell sound.

94

"We have to celebrate your new position in the company. All the Executive Vice Presidents on the board approved you. You got my vote as well, so here is a toast to the new President of Rennin Corporation, Timoshenko Kiril Vasilevich," and they emptied their glasses to the bottom.

The Hotel Russia was an International hotel for the foreign guests only, but for high-profile persons like Kiril Vasilevich, all doors were open.

"Shall we go to a more comfortable atmosphere, without any witnesses my dear Oksana? I prefer only your eyes now and forever."

They walked to the empty elevator, and he pulled her closer, kissing her on her neck and unbuttoning her blouse. Good wine made the blood boil, and they couldn't wait for the intimate union. Behind the closed doors in the room, Oksana performed a striptease and Kiril looked at the firm, supple shape of her breasts, teasing her, seductively caressing and kissing her slim body. She felt herself melting like ice, wet and slippery, and a flake of snow disappearing into eternity, only the sweet sensation of delight reminded her that she was alive.

"I will love you forever, Kirusha," she whispered in his ear and made even his name sound sweet.

After the intoxicating effect of wine was gone, common sense reminded Kiril that it was time to go home to his Tania, who has been complaining when he comes home late.

"I need to work using my mind on both fields, and I will."

"Where're you going Kirusha, let's stay here tonight."

"I would like to, my Love, but tomorrow I have an early morning meeting, and I can't show up in a wrinkled shirt and wearing the same tie from yesterday."

"I understand," and she got dressed thinking she will never have enough of him. To have Kiril in her life right now compensated for the loss of her father and she needed that desperately.

Kiril's home situation got tense; Tania didn't say a word when he hung his new fur coat and walked into the room like there was nothing unusual.

"Are kids in bed?"

She didn't answer.

"Tania, you are the first Lady of the President of Billion Dollar Corporation, what else do you want?"

"Nothing anymore; I'm going to my parent's house in Yaroslavl, and I'm taking the kids with me."

"In the middle of the school year? That is not a smart move."

"Sounds like you don't even care about it."

"Do what you want. I'm tired of you being not appreciative for what I do for the family," and he took his pillow, to sleep in the living room on a sofa.

~

Vladimir wasn't home much either. He had so much on his mind in the morning when he wakes up. Adele brought him coffee in bed, and said, "Vladimir, what do you think if I go visit my father? He is alone there, and I believe that it would be good for the children to take a trip and to play in nature. The weather is warm right now in the mountains and in two more months Moscow will be cold. I'm tired of this. It would be nice if we all lived there together."

"You know it's impossible for me to leave the company. Who will work then? You go and enjoy yourself. I have important business to take care of here."

Adele left to Grozny with children, Ahmed and Fatima, to see her father. Now Vladimir's had his hands untaught to do the important things.

From time to time, Adele called to talk about the children and their progress in learning a new language.

"It's so nice here, Vladimir, I wish you would be with us. I think that I and children will stay in Grozny this coming summer and for the remainder of the school period. Many schools have been restored, but I don't think you'd mind if I hire a teacher, for now, to teach them at home, especially when they need to learn their native language."

"I don't mind it at all and agree with you about the weather," he was saying, but thought. "It would be even better for me that she won't be in my way to achieving my goals."

She mentioned that Mansur is in Yekaterinburg and his diamond business is progressing well.

~

A few weeks passed, and Detective Tihonov reported to Vladimir that the chauffeur takes Laura everywhere and always waits for her to take her home.

"Are you listening, who is calling her and where is she calling?"

She is talking with business people in the corporation. She has been asked to attend the charity functions, but she refuses every time. Most of the time she spends at home."

"Continue your job and report back to me."

"The time will come; I'd better not rush," he was laughing to himself. What did father call her? A Swan-Princess? She will never be a princess, but she is a swan who needs to be caught. Sooner or later you will be in my net Swan, and there is no papa to protect you."

CHAPTER 16

Some time had passed before Michail got to hear more about Ivan's misfortune.

"Where are they taking me and who are these kidnappers? Anxiety was crushing my chest. My soul was glum; it tossed and turned and wanted to be free. They hit me in my head so badly that I had an excruciating headache. On my knees, in the darkness of a moving truck, I rummaged around the floor with my hand and found a mattress stuffed with straw and sat on it, wrapping my arms around my legs. I had to keep my head up because my nose was bleeding. My jaw and my head were aching from the powerful hit.

The truck was moving all the time, jolting on an uneven road, driving through the forest. It must have been night time when it stopped. The back of the truck was opened, and something was pushed in. It was dark, so I couldn't see what happened. But I felt a human presence.

"Who are you?" I asked, and I heard a child's quiet cry. I reached out with my hand and pulled the child closer to me.

"Don't cry; I'm not going to hurt you. I'm Ivan, what's your name?"

"Kostia," he said sniffling. I comforted him as I could in these circumstances. I wrapped my arm around his small body I pulled him close to me.

Our bodies were shifting to the left and the right and back again from the truck bouncing on the rough road. Kostia was still weeping when the truck stopped, the door was opened, and one more person was shoved inside.

"My God, what is going on? Are they are hunting for people?"

Kostia stopped crying and pressed his body closer to me. I fell the presence of a person, but couldn't see who it was.

"My name is Ivan and Kostia is here, who are you?"

In complete darkness, I couldn't see even my hands.

"Come here and sit with us on the mattress. Are your hands tied?"

I barely hear a woman's voice say, "No, they just took my robe off."

"Don't be afraid of us, what's your name?"

"Lena," she said, "Where are they taking us?"

"I don't know. I was hunting with my friends in the forest when I was hit in my head and was knocked unconscious, then I found myself in this truck, after that they threw Kostia in the truck, he is a child, and now you. I don't know where they are taking us and what is going on. How old are you?"

"I had my 17th birthday yesterday. They grabbed me on the empty street when I was walking to the bus station. I was coming home from visiting my Grandma; she lives in the outskirt of the city."

"Seventeen, and how old are you, Kostia?"

"I'm ten."

"I'm twenty-two; they must be hunting for the young people."

Michail interrupted Ivan and said, "This is unbelievable, Vania, who were they? I've never heard of anything like this. I can't believe things like this could happen in our country. What happened after that?"

"But it happened, Misha, "It happened to us."

99

Finally, the truck stopped and was sat idle for a long time. All three of us were exhausted, and we fell asleep. The noise of the door opening woke me up. It was dark outside, and all I could see through open door was the back of a building without doors and windows.

"Hey, come down," I heard the man's voice speaking with an accent. I never heard that accent before and thought that they are foreigners.

"Hurry up; we don't have all night."

I jumped onto the ground, and then helped Kostia out of the truck. He was a small child and very light weight. Lena jumped down. The three of us stood close together waiting while they closed the tailgate door of the truck. The familiar smell of sea water made me think that we are close to a coast. I looked around and assumed that we were in Marine Port, and not where the fishing boats are, but in the place where the ships are loaded with the containers. A man command, "Move over there and follow that man, if you try to run, I'll kill you."

I couldn't see who the kidnapper was; it was too dark, and I could see only their dark silhouettes. Kostia gave me his hand and Lena was following us. Tagging along behind her was another man. We walked down a path between tall metal containers. Some of them were one on the top of the others. Turning right and left for a long time finally we stopped at one container. One man opened the door on the narrow side of the container, and another man pushed us in.

"Keep quiet, or I'll kill you."

It was completely dark and quiet inside. We could only hear the noise from our feet against the metal floor.

I made two small steps, holding Kostia's hand, stretching my hand, like a blind man and touched the metal wall of the container. Then I walked forward again making a few small steps,

100

keeping my hand on the wall. Suddenly I felt some human presence. I heard as the door behind us was closed and locked.

"Who is here?" I whispered.

A man's voice said, "There are more people here. We are right next to you."

I made two more small steps forward until my foot touched something.

The man said, "We are here, sit on the floor.

I said, "There are three of us, a woman, a child, and myself. How many of you are here?"

"We are six adults and four children."

I asked, "How long have you been here?"

"They brought us here about three hours ago," and man was silent again. Suddenly, I heard the noise of a match igniting and a small light lit the inside for a few seconds, and I could see the group of people. I saw the man holding the match. The man was holding the match and men, women, and children sitting on the floor. They all were looking at us. Then the light was gone.

In complete darkness, I felt the presence of other people. I saw them for a moment, but I was alone with myself in this darkness. Fear came over me that I'm trapped and for how long, I didn't know. It's not natural for a person to be in captivity and I couldn't accept that this nightmare will continue.

I saw in my mind's eye the faces of my friends, the green forest, and the ducks I recently had in my hands. I could see our home, Mariya walking in the house, and the two of us are sitting at our table eating dinner, which Mariya cooked. I could see the fishing boat and my friends who I was just working and hunting with.

I wanted to run away, but I was locked up against my will. I was sitting on a metal floor, leaning against a wall and my head fell downwards from time to time. My closed my eyes, but too many thoughts were scrambling in my head. I was nodding out

101

for a few moments, but I couldn't fall asleep. In a half dreaming stage, I saw the beauty of my bleak region covered with snow, evergreen Taiga, the warmth of my home. I felt that I'm only here temporarily; something bad happened, and when this nightmare comes to the end, I'll go back home.

A few hours passed and we heard noises outside. It must be morning, and the port is waking up. I heard machine engines working somewhere and the sound of grinding metal against metal, even human voices faintly in the distance.

Then the noises outside got closer and our container must be hanging in the air by a crane because it started to swing from side to side. We were sitting very close to each other on the floor. There was nothing to hold onto and were sliding from one side to another, crashing into each other. Then we started to descend, and our container made a loud bang when it dropped onto a surface.

We must have been placed in the belly of the ship, I thought. Then the door was open, and the light blinded me. I squinted my eyes for a few seconds so I could see the people that were with me. I noticed that they all were young, about my age, and there were four more children, one more boy, and three girls. One woman was holding a child on her lap. All children were looking at us with wide open scared eyes.

Two men with black mustaches made signs with their hands telling us to walk out. We were in the cargo hold of a ship. One man went ahead, and we followed him. The other man walked behind us.

We walked through a narrow path between metal containers to a tiny room with just barely enough space to sit and stretched our legs. The door behind us was closed and locked. There was a dim light on the ceiling provided by small flashlight light bulb, and that's all there was in the tiny cabin. There were no chairs or boxes, so people had to sit on the hard wooden floor. I was standing and able to count the people. With me was four men,

102

four women, two boys and three girls, altogether there were thirteen people. Nobody cried or talked; they must have been warned not to. I felt a gnawing hunger and my stomach was roaring. I just was swallowing saliva to keep it quiet.

Mariya interrupted, "Do you want to take a break, the tea is boiling, and I baked a delicious pie with Chernika (wild blueberries)?"

"That would be nice, Mariya, people are starving," Ivan smiled.

After tea, Michail couldn't wait to here, what happened next.

Ivan continued, "After maybe an hour, a tray with boiled fish and loaf of black bread was pushed through an opening below the door that was just big enough for the tray to slide through. Then an aluminum can with cold water and the aluminum mug with handle was slid inside. The food was not that good, but it calmed down our hunger.

When the empty tray was taken out the same way it came in, a big bucket with one-third of water in it was pushed inside. A man figured out that it was a bucket to be used as a toilet. The children couldn't wait and then all adults turned their backs to shield each person from embarrassment. That was the most humiliating thing a person could experience. That was an indescribable indignity. We were not people to our captors. We were getting treated like caged animals.

Now you see Misha, after that experience, natural needs like that don't embarrass me anymore. I lived through it. After a half an hour, the bucket was taken out through the small opening in the door.

After a few hours, we heard the loud noise of the ship engine. We were leaving our homes and were be taken to an unknown place for an unknown future.

The children were quietly listening to what the adults were talking about in low voices. I was alone with myself.

103

I was too young to know much about humankind. What kind of people inhabits the Earth? Do all people have a conscious and live by it? How do they justify their actions? The protest inside me was mixed with anger and fear. I felt that I was trapped in a small space with a boa constrictor that was squeezing my throat and chest, and it doesn't let me breathe. I felt panic. Cold sweat covered my body. I had my freedom violated. What could it be worth?

When the first wave of fear and sadness stepped aside, the possibility of escape entered my mind. We are inside the belly of a ship in deep waters. We can't walk on water, so there is no possible way to escape. I tried to calm myself. A chance for escape may present itself and I don't want to miss it. I will be free.

The monotone noise of the engine was making it hard to think; it irritated me. I couldn't wait to get somewhere where I can think.

I had my watch with me and is the only thing remaining from my previous life. We were stuffed in the confined quarters for almost four days.

When we arrived at a port, they opened the door, and fresh air got into the cramped room and made me dizzy. I saw same men with black mustaches, and we commanded to follow one. It was nighttime and pitch dark. They walked us to a ladder, and one by one, we followed the men upstairs and got on the deck of the big ship.

The man walked us to the side of the ship where there was a gangway. We were hurried to walk faster to the dock and then pushed to run. I looked at the building, and I read the sign Vladivostok. There was a lot of shipping containers around.

It was the Port of Vladivostok. I wanted to scream for help but remembered the words "I'll kill you." We reached the road where a truck similar to the one in the forest was waiting for us. They kept us in the truck for a couple of hours. It was still dark outside when they had us walk in a single file line to another truck, and we were moving again.

All we could hear was the noise of the truck's engine. When the truck stopped, and the door was open, I saw a train with cargo carriages and a forest behind us.

"They brought us to Vladivostok to transfer somewhere far from home by railroad," and I thought I need to escape, to run from them right now because if I get into the carriage, it will be too late.

But the distance between the truck and train carriage was too short, and I didn't have a chance to escape because we were heavily guarded. One guard climbed into the carriage and pulled one of our men inside. One by one, we put the children in first, and then all of us climbed in.

They put us in an empty section of the cargo carriage with a straw on the floor. The other portion of the carriage was barricaded with wooden planks. We sat on the straw and stretched our legs, and walk in circles from time to time. They fed us boiled potatoes and very salty fish. The next meal was sour kraut and black bread. Eating so much salt, I was always thirsty, but water was only given to us when we ate. They gave us food twice a day, and it was the same routine days.

The train was traveling fast, but there were so many stops that we were tormented in the train carriage for two weeks. There were no windows in our section, and we couldn't see anything outside. The poor children were trapped in a cage at their tender age. All of them were like paralyzed small people not crying and not talking at all. It was painful to watch them.

During the day, there was some light coming through the sliding doors of our carriage. It was stuffy in our small space and very hot.

I managed to hide my father's wrist watch in my boot and regularly checked to make sure it was still there. That is all I had

105

left from my father; I treasured it and never was apart from it. With my watch, I could know what time of a day was and could count the days. However, time seems to have stopped.

It was July, and in this heat, the children were suffering from heat exhausted. One girl, Svetlana was only five years old, and twenty-year-old Leda was comforting her like mother, holding her on her lap and stroking her hair.

We share stories about how we got abducted, and their stories were the same as mine. They knocked them out hitting them in the head and stuffed them in a truck without windows. All these children lived with their parents in villages and were taken from the streets where they were playing.

Throughout the first week, we learned about each other. There was nothing else to do.

There were four of us man, four women and five children. The other two men were young, Sasha was twenty-two, Sergey was twenty-one, and one man, Gregory was thirty-five, and they all were abducted in the forest while hunting.

In this cargo carriage, the girls and children were sitting on one side and the men on the other. Kostia often sat with nine-year-old Kolia, but most of the time he was sitting with me.

"What's going to happen to us Uncle Vania," Kostia asked me.

What could I say to him? There was a chain of questions in my own mind.

"I would tell you, Kostia, if I only knew myself."

Sasha, who was same age of twenty-two as me, he was a smart, handsome, and vibrant young man. He was a pilot and could fly a helicopter. I liked him a lot. He was also married and we talked about our wives. There were two more girls, Katia and Mila. Mila reminded me of Mariya. She had the same brown curly hair, and just like Mariya, she wore them tied into a ponytail.

106

Despite our awful condition, I noticed that Sergey was looking at Lena more than at the other two girls.

Rocking under monotonies beat of the carriage wheels on the railroad track, I was thinking, "Right now, it looks like my life will be changing for a long time, maybe forever, I am a prisoner, kidnapped by organized crime bandits. Trucks, ship, train, everything is premeditated, coordinated and ran smoothly. There is no way to escape. 'If you try to run, I'll kill you,' I remembered the warning, and I believed they would kill us because they had guns; it was evident to me that we are not the first ones to be kidnapped. The kidnappers speak Russian like foreigners with an accent, are they taking us abroad? I shared my thoughts with Sasha and with the others.

"We are on Trance-Siberian Railway," Gregory got into conversation. "Only this railroad train can run for a long time. The railway starts in Vladivostok then runs through Khabarovsk, Ulan-Ude and Irkutsk on Lake Baikal, and then the next major city will be Krasnoyarsk, and the next is Yekaterinburg in the Ural Mountains."

"And after Ural Mountains where does it go?' Kostia asked.

"That will be the end of Siberia. Europe begins and the train will stop in Moscow."

"Are we going to Moscow?"

"No Kolia, I don't think so."

"Do you think they are taking us to a prison?" Sergey asked Gregory.

"I don't know,' and very quietly said so the kids couldn't hear, I added, "I think they are going to turn us into slaves. I know about Arabs, they were always among the world's most prominent slave traders and its one of the few cultures worldwide where this is still practiced and accepted."

"Arabs?" Sergey asked. "Are they Arabs?"

"I think they are from Dagestan, or Georgia, or Chechnya, but I'm fairly certain they are from southern from the Caucasus Mountains."

The kids even didn't know who Georgians or Chechens were; all they knew is that they wanted to go home to their parents.

"When the train stops and they bring food to us, we need to try to rush the sliding door when it's opened and try to escape. I'm not going to be a slave."

"They will kill you, Sasha."

"They will kill us anyway, Sergey."

"What about the girls, what they will do with them? Will they make them serve them dinner?"

"No Sergey, they will violate them and maybe take them as second wives, or sell to prostitution. By Islamic logic, if the Koran is the unchangeable word of Allah, then women will always be legitimately subjugated as subservient temptresses. They are doing it to all of us because we are Christians, and we always will be dogs and a legitimate target of contemptuous ridicule and mockery, and death."

I noticed as Sasha's face distorted after those words.

"They don't respect women as we do. In their Koran, it is written that woman must obey the man."

"What they will do with the children?" Leda asked, "I'm twenty-years-old, and I have a one-year-old daughter at home, I need to go back," and she started to cry.

"Nobody knows what will happen to the children and why they were abducted at such a tender age, may be for adoption, or for future prostitution, or for sale to make a profit. Their life is in ruins before they know what life is. It's much easy to abduct children than adults; they will find the way to use them. "

We were listening to Gregory in silence, and the feeling of horror overcame me, understanding that my life was in the process of being drastically changed. With every minute, I'm further and further from home, and it will be hard to get back from so far away.

"I'm a prisoner, a slave, Mariya. Oh my Mariya, I will never see you again." That realization magnified my suffering. And for the first time in my adult life, I cried and shed tears.

It was hot inside the carriage. The smell of sweating bodies made the air almost impossible to breathe.

It was in the afternoon when the train stopped; the sliding door slowly opened, and food in a cardboard box was pushed inside on the floor. Sasha took the box and gave everybody a piece of bread and tore the curved stick of sausage into small pieces, then a can with drinking water was pushed in.

After a few minutes, the sliding door opened again to slide the bucket of water inside. Sasha pushed the sliding door and used his shoulders to try to get through and shoved himself into the man on the other side, knocking the bucket with water on that man and both of them fell onto the gravel in a stranglehold.

We leaped up to our feet, and I saw them rolling on the stone incline, punching each other with their fists, and pushing the gravel with their feet. Each one of them tried to take the position on the top. They rolled and punched each other again and again, letting out grunting sounds. If not for the children who were blocking the doorway, I would have thrown myself to save him, but everything happened so unexpectedly and fast, that I couldn't react in time. A sickening wave of fear rolled inside me. He will kill him.

One moment Sasha was on the top of the bandit, holding his collar tight around his neck and punching the in his face, but not for long. A bigger man appeared from the side and joined them. The big man took over and beat Sasha on his head. He beat him with his fist until blood covered Sasha's face. He beat the life out of Sasha. Then this wild animal, with the roaring sound, picked up Sasha over his head and threw him onto the floor of carriage with such force, that Sasha hit the other side of the carriage, and then he closed the sliding door with a screeched sound of metal bar and locked it.

Sasha's face was covered with blood, and he didn't move. Mila crossed the floor on her knees, reached Sasha and with her skirt soaked with drinking water from the can and wiped the blood from his face, but blood was pouring from his injured head, and there was a puddle of blood on the floor. His pulse was barely recognizable and looked like he stopped breathing.

One girl took off her under dress slip and gave it to me. I wrapped Sasha's head to stop the bleeding, but in a matter of seconds, the white cloth was red with blood. Trying to suppress rising nausea from smelling human blood, I put Sasha's head on my lap and held him for the rest of the day and all of the night.

I couldn't sleep, traumatized by my bleeding friend, but finally, I must have passed out. When I woke up, Sasha was looking at me with wide open eyes. "Sasha!" His stare remained indifferent and dull. It looks like his eyes stopped on me. There was no trace of regret in his eyes. I touched his face, "Sasha, are you?...," but the words stuck in my throat. I called him by name; he looked at me disinterested. "He is dead; he died in my hands." I put my hand, red with his blood, on his eyes and closed them.

"That is how people die. One moment he was alive with the future ahead of him, and next moment, he no longer exists. Where is his soul? Can he hear me? What is death?

"You didn't live yet. How could I fall asleep and let you die?" I cried. "You will never leave me, I promise it to you, Sasha, you will always be with me," and I cried like never before in my life. "You will never leave me, Sasha." Then, after I cried and couldn't cry anymore, I said to myself. "I know that no evil can happen to a good man, after death."

When the food was brought to us, we had to give up his body; it was too hot to keep him inside. All of us were silent most

110

of the day after the horrific incident. My soul was crying. I couldn't sleep most of the night; I think only children slept.

The train moved fast at times and slowed at other times, stopping very often for ten minutes or half an hour. We couldn't talk much; everybody was lost in their own thoughts. "There is no chance to be free. There is no police around to call for help."

So much already happened, and I had a feeling that I left my previous life a long time ago.

My world with Mariya, fishing, and hunting with friends was fading away like I was standing in the middle of a narrow corridor in darkness. In front of me was a window with milky glass and not much light around. On both sides of the corridor were shelves and the moments of my life were like items lying on those shelves; they were moving behind my back, and I could sense that Mariya and my home was the last item on the shelf on the back of corridor.

"My Mariya," I cried inside without sound or tears.

Mariya heard her name and rushed into the small room, drying her hands with an apron.

"Are you calling me, Vania?"

"Always Mariya, I'm always calling you." Mariya smiled and went to the kitchen.

Michail said, "I'm overwhelmed by your horrible story, Vania. To kidnap people, children, and to sell them to slavery. Is it possible in our time in our country?"

"It happened to me twenty-four years ago and to many other people in early eighties, and maybe later, I don't know."

"You were twenty-two and it was in 1983, I was thirty at that time, and I was studying the area with a group of other geologists near the city of Chelyabinsk on the river Ob. That area has the largest oil deposits in Russia, and I often worked alone and far from the sight of other people, and I could have easily been kidnapped, but it happened to you, my friend."

111

Michail closed his eyes and said. "I know what physical pain is, but I never experienced emotional pain. I think that soul's pain is worse than physical."

He felt with all his heart and soul the pain of this man. "If it weren't for my broken hands, I would take Vania in my arms and hold him for a long time and kiss his head as he kissed mine."

"Vania," Michail cried gulping and shaking his head. "How can you bury that?"

"It's only the beginning, my friend, only the beginning."

After a dinner, Michail was left alone thinking about what he heard.

"While Ivan was suffering, I had a good life. I always had good life, growing up and living in Moscow. Even people not as lucky as me, not only never experienced, but never heard of anything like this. How can humans be so cruel to another human in our country? I'm blessed that my family is protected from evil like this, my Angel and Laura are safe, and my adult children have a good life."

Ivan's voice interrupted his thoughts, "Your arms look like healing faster than your legs, and your fingers are moving, maybe soon we'll take the splints off, and you will be able to use your hands, but let's not rush and wait another week."

"Thank you, my friend; I thank you from my heart."

Ivan waved his hand like he was saying, "No thanks needed at all," and left the room for the night.

"Vania lost his Mariya, and he was suffering from losing his love. My little Angel and my lovely Laura, I miss you so much", he thought falling asleep.

CHAPTER 17

"Hello," Laura answered the phone; she was always close to the telephone in case of the news about Misha.

"Laura it's me, Viktor Petrovich," she heard her stepfather's voice, "Don't panic, but your mama is in a hospital because of her diabetes. When I woke up this morning, she was in bed unconscious. I immediately called an ambulance, and she was taken to the Minsky hospital. They stabilized her, and she is awake, will you...?"

"You don't need to ask me, Viktor, I'll drive there right away."

A moment later, Vladimir got a phone call from his detective, "The Bird is leaving the new nest and flying to the old nest."

Vladimir dials to Tobacco Shop, "Peter, get your team ready to catch the Bird on the road, it's flying toward..."

Detective Tihonov was already on location waiting for Laura's white Mercedes to leave the garage. Making sure that it was the beautiful blond Swan, which was not hard to confirm, he called Vladimir to inform that the Bird just left the new nest.

Laura drove through the city and was soon on an empty road. The snow had melted, and the road was surrounded by a forest with trenches full of water on both sides of the road. The road had only one lane in both directions.

"It seems like an eternity since I lost my Misha, but at the same time, it feels like it was just yesterday, and now my mama; I can't lose her as well. She's been in a coma so many times, and I thought I'd never see her again," Laura pressed the gas pedal to the floor. "I'll be all alone with my daughter if mama dies."

She was deep in her thoughts. The road was empty and its been a long time since she's seen another car. All of a sudden, a car quickly approached her from behind. The car got behind her and then sped up to pass her on the left side, but then it swerved into her and started to push her toward the edge of the road.

"What are they doing, they are going to kill me," she pressed the gas pedal to its limit. The tires made a screeching sound, and her car pulled ahead of the white car.

The pursuing vehicle lined with her left side again and hit her Mercedes. She heard the scratching sound of metal as the back end of her car swung side to side. The other car slowed down and dropped some distance behind her as she got control of her car.

Again, she pressed the gas pedal to the floor to speed up. The road curved, and the turn made her slow down. After the curve, she continued to gain the speed, but not for long. The chasing car was at her side again, and this time, it hit her car with such force that her car flew into the air.

She screamed, flying over the trench. Her car hit the trees and landed on its roof. Her scream was the last song of a beautiful swan. In her song she called her Misha and her little Angelica seeing them in her mind in bright light, and then it was just darkness.

The moment of death is like the evening twilight: it makes all objects appear lovelier to the dying. Her voice was faint in the air as she took her last breath; the voice of an Angels sang, "She was so young." As poet Menander, who lived about 350 B.C. said, "He, whom the gods love, dies young."

It was reported to Vladimir that the Bird didn't reach the old nest.

The location of the accident was discovered in very short time by Detective Tihonov's people, and the road was cleaned not leaving any trace of the crash. No police were involved, no report was made, and no investigation was performed.

Laura's body was taken directly to Danilovskoe Cemetery and buried on the same day. Vladimir and Detective Tihonov were standing by the freshly dug pit and watched the coffin as it was lowered to the bottom of the grave. A small gray granite stone that was prepared in advance with her name with the dates of birth and death on it marked her grave.

On the way from the cemetery, Vladimir was sure that money will take care of everything.

"Father is dead, Oksana never was interested in Laura's life, and Andrey lives in his own world, and he will keep quiet because he is the one who made it happen."

"Good, now I need to take care of 'extension,'" thought Vladimir.

It is astonishing how soon the conscience begins to unravel when a single stitch is removed. One single sin indulged in makes a hole that you could put your head through, and the greediness takes over man's consciousness. If a man has made up his mind that a particular wrong course is the right one, the more he follows his conscience, the more hopeless he is as a wrongdoer.

In a couple of days, two women, the social workers, equipped with a letter from a lawyer, came to Angelica's home, and with no parents alive, took her to Detsky Dom (Orphanage). The furniture and all belongings were sold at an auction, and the money was given to the same Detsky Dom where Angelica was placed. Not one publication printed the news; it was taking care off.

~

Vladimir was always on a tight schedule because of his architectural firm Vladren. He was buying old apartment buildings around the Capital, mostly in the center of Moscow, then remodeling and converting them in luxuries condos and selling them for a big profit. He was constructing new buildings for housing. Also, was involved in a big project developing a large piece of land to build a new hotel with shops, pool and a winter garden under one roof.

Vladimir was ambitious and wanted to get richer than his father. His obsession with money made him do cruel things. He knew its wrong, but as Shakespeare said, "I charge thee, fling away ambition:

By that sin fell the angels. How can man then, the image of his maker, hope to win by it?" Now with his father death, the road to achieving his goals was open. He desperately wanted to climb up, to expand his business, and take over the construction in Moscow. His father's success was an inspiration to him, and he wanted to be like his father to feel and taste the power that money gives. He even thought that he looks like his father with his distinguished appearance. He was successful in his business, but it would take a lifetime to reach his father's status, but he wanted it now.

He didn't feel guilty about killing a person, but still his conscious wasn't leaving him alone. What was irritating him was father's marriage He was mad at his father for marrying a blond sex-bomb so soon after their mother died.

"It's ridiculous that my step mother was younger than me."

He wasn't sure if he mad at his father for marrying or that he just hated blonds. He didn't know which it was, but he put it in his mind from the beginning to oppose his father marriage.

Adele, the Chechen girl he met at a party, he married her because she had black hair, black eyes, and darker skin. That was his taste in women.

Anyway, one obstacle was removed, and he became a little bit richer. He paid good money to take care of 'extension' and will continue to contribute to Detsky Dom, where she belonged, and where he arranged for her to stay.

With the death of Laura, Vladimir became the head of his father's business. Because Laura, who usually presented the checks to the charity and represented the Rennin Corporation was no longer alive, Oksana was now attending the functions. Money and the striking beauty of Laura were playing a significant role in the promotion of the company.

Vladimir didn't attend the charity functions when Laura presented the checks, but he decided to attend this one when Oksana took over to see the reaction of people when the saw a new person representing the company. He felt that he has to be on the top of everything to know what is going on in the family business.

For Oksana, there were many reasons to correct the flaw that nature made creating her face. First of all, she thought, "I want to be attractive for my lover, Kiril, second for the charity functions and for all people at my job, friends, and mostly for myself to feel good about myself, to be confident, and for my father when representing him. He was a kind and generous man, and I will continue his legacy."

An appointment with the best plastic surgery specialist in the region was made, and the procedures were done. The result was not even close to Laura's beauty, but it was a huge improvement to her face. A smaller nose made Oksana's eyes larger, more lashes were implanted to make them thicker, and she had a chin implant to balance the overall proportions of the face.

Oksana was very pleased with the result. She wasn't interested in designer clothes before, but her new face motivated her to shop for a new wardrobe.

The employees were turning their heads the first time they saw her after surgery. As she was their boss's daughter, they respected her position, and when it was appropriate, they express their opinion in very positive way.

Sitting at her desk, from time to time, she pulled out a mirror from her drawer and examined her face. Beauty is important to every woman and at last, she was happy with herself.

Attending a charity function at the cancer hospital, Vladimir first didn't recognize his sister until she took the podium to present a check.

She was more confident and secure in her new appearance, and she started her speech with words her father often used, which was a saying from German philosopher Immanuel Kant, "Beneficence is a duty; and he who frequently practices it, and sees his benevolent intentions realized comes, at length, really to love him to whom he has done good."

Oksana announced, "I quoted that for my father because he is no longer with us. But his legacy will live because he was a man who felt the pain and suffering of others and shared his fortune with less fortuned people."

Not being a religious woman, she still respected all religions and used the words of a Muslim Profit. "As Muhammad said, "Your smiling in your brother's face is charity an exhortation of your fellow man to virtuous deeds is equal to alms giving, you're putting a wanderer on the right road is charity, your assisting the blind is charity your removing stones and thorns and other obstructions from the road is charity your giving water to the thirsty is charity." A man's true wealth hereafter is the good he does in this world to his fellow-man. When he does, people will say: 'What property has he left behind him?' but the angels will ask, 'What good deeds has he said before him.'

"My father was a Christian, and he thought that public charities for the gratuitous relief of every species of distress are peculiar to Christianity. No other system of civil or religious has originated them; they from its highest praise and characteristic

118

feature. My father also thought that we gain only as we give. So today....," she continued her speech with love and affection as her father would do if he were alive.

After her beautiful and touching speech, she presented a check for a million rubles check to the cancer hospital, which was met with a standing ovation.

After the presentation was over, Vladimir approached Oksana.

"You gave a very impressive speech about charity. At first, I didn't recognize you. What did you do with your nose Oksana, it's not you anymore."

"You have to get used to it, my brother. I'm a new woman and not only outside."

"What you mean new woman?"

"You weren't interested in my life before, why suddenly?"

"There is something behind this new face, and I need to find out," he thought but kept to himself.

"You look great, and the speech was good, so, congratulations."

There were no more words exchanged, nothing about Laura and Angelica. Oksana knew that Laura died in car accident. That chapter was closed along with their father who was gone from their lives.

On the way home, Vladimir's mind focused on Oksana.

"I better call to my detective. I need to know everything about the private life of Oksana Michailovna. Why the sudden change and what she meant when she said that she is a new woman and not only outside."

After his father's death, as the oldest in the family, he felt like he stepped into his father's shoes and he is now in charge of checking on everyone. It was important for him to protect the fortune their father left for them.

Vladimir wasted no time and called Detective Tihonov, who was on a salary and paid very well by him. He arranged to meet him in a restaurant to talk business.

"I have another job for you," Vladimir told his detective. "I need to know everything about my sister. She been behaving very unusual lately and I need to know what is going on. Find out, where she goes in the evenings, who are the people she spends her time with, and what is going in her life in general."

The loyal detective immediately put his people to work, and he was on the top of the operation.

Invisible eyes followed Oksana everywhere she went, and it didn't take long to find out who she spends her time with. She was spending a lot of time with the new president of Rennin Corporation, Timoshenko Kiril Vasilevich who was married with two children.

Every new discovery was reported to Vladimir.

"Hmmm, interesting, nobody dated Oksana when our father was alive. As soon he is gone, she suddenly became attractive. Of course, it's not her face that has attracted Timoshenko, but her fortune, but she thinks it is love. What a stupid woman my sister, that is why she changed her face. Everything is falling into its place." Vladimir figured out the puzzle.

"It's good that he is married so he is not a danger the twenty percent of my sister's inheritance. But still, what does she mean by saying, "new inside?" Is she madly in love with this Timoshenko and do they have plans for future?"

Vladimir couldn't accept that their family money will be shared with people like Timoshenko, a married man because money will seep to his children. "That is not acceptable. I'm the oldest now in the family, and I will protect our family fortune."

After removing two obstacles, Laura and her 'extension' from his way, and their 40% were divided between three of them, his appetite grew bigger because greed increased with the acquired pile of gold.

Vladimir's mind was preoccupied with his sister's life.

"Oksana made a bad choice; she is making a wrong move that will waste money, and she's so stupid not to know that this man is married. It's even worse if she knows and doesn't care. She is crazy. That's right, she is crazy, and she needs help."

~

Coming home from the charity function at the cancer hospital, Oksana didn't feel well. She threw up all the food she ate.

"I must have eaten something bad." The next morning, she couldn't eat her breakfast.

"I got some poisoning in my system, and I better go to see a doctor." When the doctor heard the symptoms, she brought Oksana to the examining room. After doctor took off the rubber gloves and washed her hands, she said, "You are pregnant."

Oksana repeated, "Pregnant?"

"Yes, you are going to have a baby."

Oksana's world changed in an instant.

"That explains all your symptoms. There's nothing to worry about; it's very common when a woman is pregnant."

"How long have I been pregnant?"

"It's been about six weeks, and you might feel nauseated in five or six weeks, and after that, you will be able to enjoy your pregnancy; you will feel physically and emotionally better."

The doctor gave her some advice on how to manage morning sickness, and Oksana drove home thinking about the big changes in her life that are about to take place. She was surprised and excited. She had a glowing feeling inside of her, and she needed to share it with her loving partner.

"Before the child is born, I want to get married to Kiril, so my child will have the father's name."

The Detective spotted her visiting the clinic. It was easy for the detective to find out what doctor at the clinic she was seeing.

"Vladimir, Oksana is pregnant, and we assume it is Kiril Vasilevich's child because she is only seeing him and spends all her available evenings with him."

"She is crazy mad," he was repeating himself, and these words led him to an idea to deem her crazy as in she lost her mind.

"What a stupid woman. She needs to be put into a madhouse where she belongs; I won't let her waste my family money."

"If it's true," he said to his detective, "I need you to complete the job you started. My sister is mad, and she needs to be institutionalized. Be creative and keep the secret under control. Extra money will be in your account for the expenses."

Detective Tihonov got right to work and was very creative. He obtained an ambulance that wasn't registered to any hospital and made a call to Psychiatric Clinic #1.

"Doctor Reznik, this is Detective Tihonov. I have a favor to ask you. Of course, as usual, you will be paid very well. I'll meet you in the cafe on the corner next to your clinic at 9 am tomorrow morning."

Doctor Reznik often wrote drug prescriptions for him when he needed it and received payment for his discretion.

"Hey, doctor," the detective greeted him as an old friend, and they walked to a table in the corner of the hall so nobody could hear their conversation. They shook hands. The detective ordered coffee, and while they were waiting to be served, he started with, "I know you very well and trust you because we both are not clean, and it puts us both on the same scale."

Doctor's Reznik's body jerked from the words "not clean," but he composed himself. His eyes were examining his friend in

122

crime and conspiracy; they shifted from side to side and from top to bottom of the detective's face, not stopping for a moment.

"This man with his small head on a long neck looked more patient than a doctor," Tihonov thought. "I believe that to spend your life with mentally sick people you can lose your own mind."

"So," he started, "a very high-profile woman needs help in your clinic. You understand me, right?"

By asking this question, he wanted the doctor to understand that the business is not legitimate.

"She needs to be diagnosed with a mental disorder, or some sort of it."

"Can you tell me who this woman is?"

"It's a dead billionaire's daughter, Oksana Michailovna Rennin."

"This is afamous family. The Newspapers write about them almost every day." The doctor's eyes stopped shifting and froze on the detective's face.

"Yes, and that is why I'm asking you and not somebody else. I know I can trust you."

"She is a highly visible person, and it will cost accordingly."

"You don't need to worry. I think it will be enough for you to retire and live somewhere in a warm place."

"It would be nice to retire ten years earlier," the doctor's mind was spinning.

"How will she get to the clinic?"

"Very simple, in an ambulance; everything is taken care of. All you need to do is diagnose her with an illness and to keep her locked up for life in the clinic. After she is diagnosed once, it will stay with her all her life. This is the cleanest way to get rid of somebody."

"But who needs to get rid of her?"

"That is not your concern and the less you know about it, the better for you."

"Yes, you are right."

"She is pregnant, and that needs to be taken care of as well."

"Pregnant, oh, it will be two people, not one," he thought, but said, "There will be no questions about that with our policy."

"Then we've reached an agreement. As soon as she arrives at your clinic, keep her safe, and for life."

They shook hands and parted were both satisfied with their deal. A conscience didn't bother people like them to do a deal with the devil. What does the devil have to do with it? They both are working for money.

~

Tania and the children were gone to Yaroslavl, and Kiril Vasilevich didn't have a problem seeing Oksana more often. As usual, they met at the hotel Russia in their suite where they spent the nights together.

Kiril's romance with Oksana started with a different thought in his mind, she was a daughter of a billionaire, and she was free. He just wanted to have an adventure in his life, and like many men, to have a variety of sexual experiences. Despite her not having an attractive face, she had a nice figure, smooth skin, and there was a visible presence of sharp mind in this young woman. Her shy and protective behavior made him want to conquer this untouched virginity. She was more desirable to him than his more attractive wife.

He was attracted to Oksana from the first moment he met her, but he was hesitant to approach her. There was a less possibility for him to date her when her father was alive, but his death made it easy to approach her.

After their first experience together that evening in the restaurant, it changed his inclination; he felt that she is more than

124

what he initially thought about her. He felt that he wanted to be with her all the time or that he might be falling in love with her.

It was easy for him to let Tania leave him because Oksana now occupied all the space in his heart. With the help of plastic surgery, she a more desirable woman.

Now there was no question in his mind that he will divorce Tania and marry Oksana as soon as it is appropriate for their positions. Now his feelings and his words for her were genuine.

In the restaurant at the dinner, he took Oksana's hands in his over the table and said, "You look so beautiful, my Darling, that I can't wait to take you in my arms."

Oksana tried to smile, but her expression made it look insincere.

"What's wrong, you didn't eat much?"

"I'm pregnant," she blurted out.

"You are? That is fantastic news," Kiril exclaimed in surprise, stretching his hands over the table to touch hers.

"Why didn't you tell me before?"

"I saw a doctor and found out myself."

Kiril knew that he can't marry her right now because he is still married and she knew that she shouldn't marry so soon after her father's death. They both worked in the same company, and it would not look so good, so they didn't bring the subject out in the open for the moment.

After making love, they went to their separate homes, and Oksana felt relieved that Kiril knew about the baby. That night she fell asleep happy and full of excitement.

In the morning, she felt very nauseated but decided to go to work. "Maybe my work will take my attention away from feeling so miserable."

At lunch, Oksana went to a milk café and remembered that doctor advised her to stay away from meats for now, and forced herself to eat cottage cheese with yogurt. Then she went to the park behind her building to breathe some fresh air.

Invisible eyes were following her everywhere and watched her every move.

Some people brought their lunches with them to eat in the park, and the strong smell of onions made her sick. She was feeling the food she ate rise to her throat. She was going to leave the bench and lean over to get up. The move made her dizzy. She sat back on the bench and supported herself to keep from falling onto her side.

The detective was sitting almost in front of her on opposite side of the park road. When he saw that Oksana was leaning on the side of the bench, he rushed across the park road to her dialing the emergency ambulance number.

The ambulance was already parked next to the gates of the park where Oksana was sitting. Two men in white medical uniforms rushed with a stretcher to her bench.

She bent over in excruciating pain. Cottage cheese and rice ran out the side of her mouth. Her head was spinning for a moment, and she had a temporary blackout.

The medical man gave her a shot in her arm. She was placed on the stretcher, carried to the ambulance, and taken to the hospital.

Nothing seemed unusual to the people gathering around the scene. A woman just became unconscious and collapsed. The medical people took her to the ambulance.

Next morning, when she opened her eyes, she saw a doctor standing at her bed. She wanted to get up, but the doctor made a gesture with his hand signifying not to do it.

"You need to stay in bed, Oksana. Right now you are in no condition to walk."

"What happened, where am I?"

"Don't worry, we will help you, and everything will be all right."

She lay back on her pillow and closed her eyes for a moment. The doctor instructed the nurse who was standing at the door to come in.

Oksana opened her eyes and saw a nurse standing next to her bed with the pill in her hand and a plastic cup of water to flush it down. Oksana swallowed the pill and almost immediately felt that she couldn't hold it in her stomach.

Her condition was so unpleasant that she lay down on her bed, and the doctor and nurse walked out. She was so nauseous that she rushed to the bathroom to vomit, but her stomach was almost empty, and only little came out. On the way back to her bed, she noticed that the room was spacious with white walls and her bed was in the corner next to the window and a wall.

She was lying on her back and looked around. There were no pictures on the walls, no curtains on the windows, nothing else in the room, only her bed and a table with one chair. She was alone in her room.

"They must know who I am, because usually rooms in hospitals are always crowded with beds, sometimes up to 20 beds in one room.

"Why do I feel so sleepy and sick? Where am I, why are there metal bars on the windows? Is it a hospital or I am in jail? Maybe they think I'm crazy and put me in a mental institution. But, did I get here in the first place? I need to talk to a doctor".

She got up from her bed, feeling dizzy, and she couldn't walk a straight line.

"What's wrong with me, why am I wearing this hospital robe?" Walking like being drunk, she managed to get to the door, but it was locked. At eye level, there was a small hole in the center of the door, but she couldn't see anything through it, it was for the people to see inside the room only.

Looking at the windows with metal bars, she thought, "They locked the door and the bars on the windows, I am not in a regular hospital." In a panic, she jumped from the bed and rushed to the door. She pounded on the door with her hand, but the door didn't open.

"Open the door," she screamed, "Let me out of here I'm not that sick," but it was silent on the other side of the door, and nobody came to open it. With the bitter realization that she is locked in, she slowly walked back to her bed and dropped her head down on a pillow.

A few minutes later, a skinny nurse with pursed lips walked in with food on a tray and put it on the table, "Eat your breakfast, dear." She walked out and closed the door.

Oksana's stomach was empty, and she felt light headed. She managed to walk to the table and tried to move the chair, but it was attached to the floor, and the table also was not movable.

"They secure everything in this place."

The tray, plates, and the cup were made of a rubber-like material. Feeling angry that she is locked in and nobody is hearing her, she threw the tray with food and it flew to the floor.

"Damn it, what is this place? What happened and who put me here?"

She tried to remember where she was before she found herself here.

"I ate lunch in milk café and then that awful smell of onions made me sick. I am pregnant. Do all pregnant women feel this way?"

She walked around the room, supporting herself with her hand against the wall, and dropped onto the bed. Squeezing the pillow with both hands, she wrapped it around her head and tears gushed from her eyes. She was crying until the door opened a the nurse who didn't say a word, collected everything from the floor.

"I want to see a doctor," Oksana yelled when the nurse was walking out, but she didn't get a response.

At lunch time, the same nurse brought a carrot cake with milk. Oksana ate some cake, but the smell of boiled milk made her sick, and she returned to her bed. A little later, the nurse came back to pick up the tray.

"The doctor will see you tomorrow," and she walked out with untouched food on the tray and locked the door. Later, she brought the evening pills and more food but took it back untouched.

After the morning pills and barely touching her breakfast, Oksana was escorted to the doctor's office.

A tall and skinny man with a small face and pin-head on his long neck was sitting at the desk.

"Where is the other doctor whom I saw before? Oksana asked.

"I'm your doctor, Oksana."

"I was brought here by mistake, and I need to get out of here."

"We understand and will do everything to help you."

"I'm not crazy, and I don't belong here."

"You need to eat Oksana or we have to feed you intravenously."

"Oh, please, not that."

"Then, will you eat?"

"Yes," she nodded her head.

The meeting ended and she was escorted by the silent nurse back to her room.

Every day was the same thing. "There is nothing to do and nothing to read. If I don't do something soon, I will lose my mind in this place. Even if I asked for books and got them, at night the light is turned off anyway."

When she was awake, she thought, "I can't eat, and these pills make me sleepy. All I do is sleep all day and at night. When I'm awake, there is no light, and it's miserable to spend nights like this. Tomorrow the nurse will wake me up to give me another pill to put me to sleep. No pills anymore," she decided. This pin-head doctor will poison me.

'Pin-head,' she remembered she saw push pins holding papers on the cork board in his office and some of them were without papers. "Next time I'm in his office, I need to get one of this pins. Nothing else is sharp, even my nails are cut short; they must be cutting them when I'm sleeping."

A few more days passed and she didn't have a choice but to swallow the pills because the nurse was checking her mouth. The pills made her drowsy, so she slept most of the night and most of the day.

"I can't continue this way, and it's time to see the doctor again to find out who made the decision to bring me here."

Two days later, she was sitting in the pin-head doctor's office. The cork board was on her right, but all the push pins were being used to hold papers.

The doctor didn't volunteer to start talking, so Oksana asked the same question as before, "How did I get here, who brought me here, and who gave you the right to keep me here? Do you know who I am? I need to make one phone call, and I'll be out of here."

"Sorry, but our policy is not to allow patients use of the phone."

She got the same answer that she was picked up in the park unconscious with white secretion like foam in the corners of her mouth that is an indication known in psychiatry as a symptom, and he named it with a long Latin name.

Oksana didn't say anything, her mind was focused on the push pins, but they all were used to hold the papers, and it was impossible to grab one unnoticed. The doctor saw that the patient was satisfied with the explanation, got up from his chair, Oksana did the same, and again she was escorted by a nurse to her room.

Twice a day, a gloomy nurse with a face that didn't have any expression as if it was frozen forever, brought pill and watched as Oksana swallowed it. She would ask Oksana to open her mouth and stick her tongue out. She looked very carefully in her mouth to be sure that Oksana didn't hide it under the tongue. Sometimes, when she didn't feel nauseous and was awake, she thought, "It would be nice to have a book to read," but it was only for very short periods, and then she was sleeping again.

Week after week, it was the same routine. When she was awake, she thought, "I need to find a way to get out of here. I will ask to see another doctor." The nurse brought her next meal, and Oksana said, "I need to see a doctor, I don't feel good."

The next day she was taken to the same office and same pin-head invited her to sit down.

Oksana noticed right away that one push pin in the cork board was not holding a paper.

"I want to see another doctor. I want to know what the diagnoses you are telling me to actually means. I know that I'm pregnant, and my doctor told me that it's normal for a pregnant woman to feel nauseous and that is why I can't eat. You have no right to keep a healthy pregnant woman in your facility. I want to know who put me here," Oksana raised her voice, "I demand to know!"

She made her speech short and got up to her feet. Suddenly, she fell onto the wall. The doctor rushed to hold her up, but as he was walking around his desk, for a moment, not looking at her, Oksana, place her hand on the cork board, grabbed the silver push-pin with her fingers and balanced herself back to her feet.

"You see what you doing to yourself by not eating."

"I'm okay, just a little bit dizzy."

The nurse walked in, and she was escorted back to her room.

At night, before the pill took effect, she turned onto her right side facing the wall, and on the side of a mattress next to the pillow, she started to scratch the fabric with the sharp tip of the push-pin. Trying to make strokes in the same place she began to feel drowsy, and put the push-pin under her pillow, keeping in mind, "Tomorrow, I need to put the push-pin in my pajamas pocket."

The next two nights, she continued to scrap the fabric until she was able to put her finger in a hole. The mattresses fabric was very stiff, and she wasn't able to tear it to make the hole bigger, "Now I can hide the pills in the mattress."

When the evening pill was brought to her, she managed to hide it behind the last tooth at the back of her mouth, and she voluntarily stuck her tongue out. The silent nurse got used to Oksana's calm drug-induced behavior and didn't check her mouth very well.

So, now she was putting every pill in the hole of the mattress and was lying quietly in her bed pretending she was sleeping.

~

Nobody knew where Oksana was. She just didn't show up after lunch that day at her work and nobody has seen her since. Kiril contacted Vladimir and Andrey, but their sister just vanished. He called all the hospitals and emergency rooms, but not one ambulance attended such a patient, and no morgue had her body.

Kiril was devastated, "I lost my family when I fell in love with Oksana, and now I lost her too. Maybe she found out that I am married and ran away from me, but to where? She told me that she is pregnant, and maybe that scared her. But she was happy when she told me, and she saw that I was happy. What happened to her?" Kiril was lost guessing. Time passed, and Oksana didn't come back.

Without a family and love, he focused on his job. His high position in the company demanded a lot of his time, and he dedicated himself to his work like it was his own company. He was flying to Magadan many times and the relationship with Anton Sergeevich, who was managing the Magadan quarters, was in best of terms. They both worked at their full power and soon revenue doubled. The price for oil went up, and the company was flourishing.

CHAPTER 18

While Oksana was suffering being locked up against her will and struggling with her physical discomfort, Vera in her delicate condition felt much better than any pregnant woman could wish for. She was now four months pregnant and was full of enough energy to execute any assignment Dealers gave to her. Her $50,000 was gone a long time ago, and she needs money again because of her lover, Lev who wanted to produce a movie and she bought him a camera, but his project was still in developing stage.

She was glad when Peter called her, and she took the metro train to see him. This time, she had to deliver the small box, to Frankfurt to buy and drive to him another AUDI.

"This box looks small, but it is heavy compared to its size - don't open it," Peter warned her. She wasn't going to do it anyway. There was an agreement between Dealers and Vera that she wouldn't open the packages and wouldn't ask what she and her partner Andrey were delivering.

She got an instruction from Peter, "When you arrive in Frankfurt, rent a room in motel Wiesbaden. Go to buy the car and in the morning a man will come to get the package. You will say to him, "It's small." And he will answer, "It's heavy." Then you will give him the package. Leave it here for now and when you are ready to go, come and pick it up."

This assignment was easy compared to the delivery of a child and coming home she called Andrey.

During the last three months, they saw each other two, or three times a week to make love after dinners at restaurants and it was nice to have some adventure again.

They picked the day and went to the Tobacco Shop to get the package. It was the size of brick and heavy like a brick. She was laughing on the way to the car, "I'm carrying a brick this time."

The trip to Frankfurt was smooth without any problems. Not knowing what was in the package; they rented a room in motel Wiesbaden and left it there to go to buy an AUDI.

The next morning, a man knocked on their door, and when he walked in, Vera said, "It's small." The man answered, "It's heavy." The man took the package and didn't say any other words. He walked out and drove away.

There were no problems on the road, and they safely delivered AUDI to Peter. Vera got her regular $20,000, and she was financially set for a while.

~

Two weeks later, on TV, on every news program, all over the world, was the same news. The bold young man was lying in a hospital bed in Frankfurt, Germany. Doctors were puzzled trying to determine what kind of poisoning he consumed. There was no question whether or not that he got poisoned. The loss of hair over the entire body led to a suspicion that it was radiation. The experts involved identified the poison as Polonium 210.

The correspondent from TNN station in Moscow, reporting from Frankfurt, told us, "The man is Russian, former FSB Colonel Victor Varchenko, who before moving to Germany, worked at the new Government in Kremlin and personally knew the current president of Russia, Aleksey Lunin. Victor Varchenko's wife and seven-year-old son were among the victims who died in the ruins of bombed and collapsed apartment building in Moscow.

After losing his family, Victor didn't want to live in Russia anymore. He left Russia a year ago and lived in Frankfurt since he could speak German.

Living abroad, he was revealing the truth about corruption in the Russian Government, and he openly spoke and wrote the truth he knew.

Thinking of that, Varchenko was blaming FSB agents for blowing up the two apartment buildings where his family died. He pointed the finger on Chechen rebels in order to justify Lunin's subsequent war in Chechnya.

One possibility must be considered is that elements of FSB may be responsible and willing to use radiological terrorism as a tool of foreign affairs.

Nobody knows for sure who was responsible for this act. But it is the fact that Polonium-210 doesn't accrue naturally; it has to be created by irradiating bismuth in a nuclear reactor or particular accelerator, and only an industrialized country has access to radioisotopes.

The experts in radioactive materials found that from three types of radiation, it must be the Alpha type. It doesn't need heavy protection. It can be safe in a double paper envelope. A few salt crystals containing Polonium-210 is a lethal dose for an adult person. If a human digests it, inside the victim, Alpha particles are absorbed very rapidly, and the biological damage they cause is severe.

The experts explained to us that Polonium-210 is effective in the body for about 30 days. Because of its short life and rapid decay, a small quantity of Polonium-210 is intensely active. The lethal dose for a person is 0.89 micrograms and almost an invisible speck of matter.

Consuming this dose, a person will develop symptoms of regular food poisoning in 1-2 weeks, and in 20 days, death. The fact that he became ill so fast indicates that he was poisoned with many lethal doses.

"How did Polonium get into Germany, and who could killed Varchenko?"

"Oh, the killer was a bottom of the ladder man who didn't understand what he was doing."

"His friend, who we contacted, told us about War in Chechnya, which Victor Varchenko was against."

"Tell us more about this long and bloody war; the world wants to know the facts."

He told us, "Victor criticized the current President and the government for the poor handling of Chechnya's situation and the previous President for the first campaign in 1994-1996.

It started in 1991, when the mass demonstration led by the newly-formed Chechen National Congress, the Communist leadership of the Republic, was brought down, and when their leader, Jokhar Budaev, was elected president, claimed Chechen independence from Russia.

In I994, Russian troops invaded Chechnya after Budaev's government issued its own constitution, disregarding the Russian elections of 1993. The army was fighting for Grozny, the capital of Chechnya, in what came to be considered one of the worst military engagements of the 20th century; over 2,000 Russian shoulders were killed in the first several days. By spring, Russian forces secured about two-thirds of Chechen territory. However, resistance and sporadic fighting continued for another year.

In summer 1995, Chechen rebels seized hundreds of hostages at a hospital in Budenovsk, in southern Russia. The siege ended after a long and unsuccessful Russian commando operation in which over a hundred hostages were killed.

After Budaev was killed in a missile attack, he was targeted while using a satellite phone, and after several unsuccessful truces and attacks by Chechen rebels on Grozny, the negotiation with rebels took place, and the agreement was made to pull Russian troops from Chechnya.

Chechnya was given facto independence in January 1997, when Russia recognized Nakhadov's government following his victory in the Chechnya presidential election.

According to the general staff of Russian Armed Forces, 3,826 troops were killed, and 17,892 were wounded during the first campaign. Based on data from human rights organizations, anywhere from 60,000 to 100,000 civilians were killed during the conflict."

His friend took sip of water and continued, "Russia recognized Chechnya as an autonomic republic within Russia, and with Nakhadov's government claiming independence and calling the newly formed state the Chechen Republic of Ichkeria.

By 1998, amid kidnappings and overall growing lawlessness as organized criminal gangs and rival warlords increasingly got out of control, Nakhadov imposed the state of emergency. Chechnya's international position was worsening as well, after four engineers from Britain and New Zealand are kidnapped and later found decapitated.

Pressured by fundamentalist rebel groups, Nakhadov introduce Islamic Sharia's law in the first month of 1999.

The summer after rebel groups demanded a more Islamic government and Nakhadov's resignation; armed Chechen rebel troops invaded neighboring Dagestan in a campaign of an Islamic state. The clash with Russian troops began.

In Russia meanwhile, some 300 civilians were killed when a series of explosions rocked apartment blocks in the city of Moscow, Vladivostok and Buinarsk, as well as Dagestan. The new Russian elected president Aleksey Lunin lunched an antiterrorism campaign and redeployed Russian forces in Chechnya.

By the end of the year, an estimated 200,000 civilian refugees fled Chechnya for neighboring republics of Russia. After capture

138

and near-destruction of Grozny, Russian President declared Chechnya would be governed by Moscow. Control of military operations was transferred to the Federal Security Service (FSB). Federal forces were met with gorilla resistance from rebel forces, as well as from terrorist attacks and ambushes.

Formal military operations were considered ended in December 2001, after negotiations with Nakhadov's representative Akhmad Zakayev led to a peace settlement in Moscow.

But the terrorist attacks on Russian territory have increased since the start of a second campaign. In October 2002, Chechen rebels seized about 900 hostages in a theater during a performance of the Russian musical NordOst. A series of suicide bombings took place in Moscow in a summer of 2003, killing dozens of people. Since 1999 total losses in the federal forces 4, 572 were killed and 15,549 wounded. According to the newspaper Nezavisimaya Gazeta in 2003, there were up to 75,000 troops in Chechnya. Taking this into account, the casualties are likely to continue increasing. In 2004, the elected president of Chechnya was killed in an explosion just as he was giving The Victory Day speech in Grozny."

"Is this war ever going to end?"

"Many people will die not knowing."

When his Russian friend visited him in the hospital, Victor said to him, "They got me."

Detectives in charge of the investigation found out that before the day Victor got to the hospital, he spent two evenings with a young attractive Russian woman and had dinners in two restaurants, where he took her. He liked her a lot and was going to date her. Katrina, 25-years-old, just arrived to Frankfurt a month ago and rented a small apartment on the bank of the river. When Detectives went to her apartment to ask her questions, the apartment was empty. Who was this Katrina? Viktor couldn't say much about her because they spend only five hours together.

Where and how was he poisoned? If it was in a public place and other people could be exposed to radiation. The Frankfurt detectives and police was on their feet looking for the clues. Investigators checked both restaurants for radiation and didn't find any trace of it. Meanwhile the man was dying and before came to his end, he said who was behind this, "President Aleksey Lunin."

When Vera was watching the news, she thought about the agreement with the Dealers not to open the packages and not to ask what was in it.

"The last package was small and heavy, what if I am the one who delivered the Polonium to Frankfurt from Russia? It was suppose the small package could have contained liquid or powder, but it could have been very well protected in a brick. Would a brick protect me from radiation? My own life and my child's life were in danger, it's good that I'm not curies and didn't opened the package, all I needed was money.

So I'm the one who delivered the Polonium-210 to Frankfurt from Russia. In this case I'm the bottom man. I need to stop my business with Dealers for the better times." And like always, she swept the bad news away like the dirt from her dress and went to Lev's apartment to see how her producer is progressing.

That evening, she went to Andrey's Disco to shake off the negative thoughts, "After all, I am not a politician trying to solve the world's problems".

Andrey was glad to see her, and after a few drinks, he watched her dancing in the sparkles of light moving her body like a snake under the rhythm of the music, throwing her arms up and shaking her booty.

"She is driving me crazy, this woman, her short skirt and the legs, it's the best legs I have ever seen, and they are mine."

The music stopped for a moment and Vera went to the bar, where Andrey was behind the counter, they kissed through the counter and he poured some alcohol in her glass.

"When are we going to marry Andrey? These legs could run away from you and very fast." She stretched out her leg and provocatively ran her fingers up and down her bare skin and licked her lips.

"You are driving me crazy, I know I promised you, but we need to wait a little more."

"In five months, you will be a father, my dear; do you want to leave your child without a name?"

"We still have plenty of time, don't worry. Go dance; I'm enjoying watching you." She pulled Andrey to the dance floor and they both forgot about the rest of the world moving to the beat of loud music.

CHAPTER 19

The warmth of the June sun thawed the ground enough to dig the graves.

"It's time to bury your friends; they've waited long enough. I know that you would like to be there to pay your last respect to the victims, but your legs are not healed yet, and Mariya will help me." Michail nodded his head and thanked him with all his heart.

Ivan and Mariya walked into the forest leaving Sasha with Michail. They carried shovels, three crosses with the names written on them, went toward the hill where the plane crashed. A month ago, Ivan cleared the ground from small bushes, and the soil was prepared for digging. When the snow melted, the plane fell onto its belly, and the door was easy to reach. Earlier, he made a ladder from tree branches so they could climb into the plane.

"Look at this Vania! I didn't know that the inside of a plane is so beautiful. Yes, Michail had a good life before he got to our poor house."

"He is more fortuned then these poor people because they are dead, and Michail alive."

"I agreed with you. It's better to be poor and alive.

This was Mariya's first time inside an aircraft. She walked behind Ivan to help him get the men from the back of the plane and then the pilots in the cockpit.

The bodies were still frozen and in good condition because it was still cold at night and the sun during the day wasn't very warm yet.

"I can drag them by myself. It's easy going downward," Ivan said as he brought the body of a man from the fuselage down to the ground.

He did the same with the pilots, and they started to dig the graves. The soil on the top was manageable, but half a meter down it was still frozen and it took more effort to dig. They worked many hours and then the hole in the earth was finally wide enough to put all three bodies together in one grave. Before lowering them into the ground, they emptied their pockets to gather their personal documents that would someday be returned to their loved ones. Then they wrapped them in light blankets that were found inside the plane and put them to rest. They covered the graves with soil and put three crosses on their grave. "Rest in peace," they both said. They gave a moment of silence and then returned home.

"Now their souls are free, and they are with God."

"The ancients feared death. We, thanks to Christianity, fear only dying, but they died without fear because it happened so fast."

~

One afternoon, when all necessary chores in the house were done, Ivan said, "I think we can take the splints off your left arm." He took a pair of scissors to cut the fabric which was wrapped around Michail's arms that held the splints used as a cast to keep his bones in place until they healed. Michail was watching his doctor, nurse, and friend work on his arm and tears of gratitude filled his eyes. "I have to be as strong as my friend."

They both held their breath waiting to see if his arm healed. Ivan carefully cut the fabric piece by piece, freeing the arm. Michail moved his fingers and then raised the arm from the plank

143

and bent it at the elbow and wrist. It felt good to move his arm and hand after keeping it in one position for so long.

"You gave me my arm and my hand back," Michail smiled, turning and twisting his arm, "Vania, if not for you…"

"Don't mention it. Although, it's still going to be a long time before you fully recover." Ivan massaged Michail's hand and feet as he did all throughout his healing, "Learn to use one hand at a time, but very carefully not to damage the fragile bones, and next week, we will free your right arm, and you'll be able to use both hands. A little more patience and everything will come because patience is the key to getting better."

"Ivan, you are so wise; sometimes you speak like a prophet," Michail smiled.

"Thank you, my friend; my hand is almost like new. It looks like the bones grew nicely together and I don't feel any pain."

Ivan collected the pieces of fabric, and Michail reached out to touch Ivan's hand with his free hand, "Thank you, Vania."

Ivan spent a few minutes in the kitchen and walked into the room with Mariya, who was holding a tray with tea. Ivan put the table he made for Michail next to him so he could eat in bed, and Mariya placed the tray on it.

"Let's see if you can use your hand," and they watched Michail put a spoon of honey in his tea and held the cap with his fingers.

"Mariya, Mariya, Mariya," Michail sang her name, and they laughed. Sasha joined them, and Michail twirled Sasha's brown curls with his fingers.

"I've wanted to do that for a long time," he said, and they all laughed.

Later in the evening, Michail didn't want to impose on Ivan to tell more of his story, but Ivan came to the room by himself and continued the story, "We were trapped for almost two weeks on the train, and finally it stopped for the last time. But it was not the

144

end of the journey. At night, they transferred us to another train, and we spent three days in train cars made for transporting animals. Then we came to a stop. We couldn't even guess where we were. At night, the sliding door opened, and they escorted us to a truck. There were people speaking a foreign language who joined the four of our guards. We were put into a truck without windows and arrived at the final destination.

It was day time when they opened the doors on the back of the truck, and it took some time for our eyes to adjust the bright light. I saw a very old white building. The children walked slow which gave me a chance to look around, but it was not much to see. The small yard was surrounded by a wall made of bricks. I only saw one entrance with gates in the distance. There were no trees or even grass. The ground looked like dry clay.

We were escorted through a narrow corridor to a room, maybe twenty square meters in size. On the gray tiled floor were mattresses next to the walls around the room. Two small windows with bars on the outside were facing a brick wall.

Now I could see how the foreigners look. The foreigners all had thick, dark straight or curly hair, some of them with mustaches and the rest with trimmed beards. Their eyes were charcoal black or dark brown, and their skin was darker than ours. They looked like black crows, and they spoke in an arguing tone and pronounced words very fast.

Young people, like me in our group, never left Siberia from our childhood and these people were foreigners to us. I couldn't even guess who they were. It was evident to me that we are on the side of the south of the country.

We didn't eat for a few hours, and our stomachs started to let us know and for that reason, nothing else was on our minds.

The children were exhausted and weak from hunger and fell asleep on mattresses. We were all quiet, and suddenly Gregory said, "They are Chechens, and we are in the Caucasus

Mountains." Everybody gave a quick look at Gregory and dropped their eyes and heads to the floor.

"So we are in the Caucasus Mountains in the south of the European territory in Russia."

It was not comforting to know that we were far away from our homes. The door was unlocked, and a man with a thick mustache brought food in on a big metal tray. It had stacks of white bread that were thin like pancakes, greasy pieces of lamb with a bone placed on the top of cooked rice, a few apples, and a brown ceramic jar with water.

The food smelled so good. There is nothing else on your mind when you hungry.

We woke up the kids and ate the food sharing the jar with water to flush it down. After they had removed the empty tray, one by one, we were escorted to a toilet in a wooden shed behind the house. It had a terrible smell, and giant flies were noisily flying around. Then after satisfying our hunger and relieved ourselves, we all laid down on our mattresses in the hot room and got into a trance of not existing.

The morning light through the window woke me up. Then cooked buckwheat was brought to us on a tray, and it only had ten spoonfuls, so we made sure the children got some first.

We wanted to know more about this place. Gregory looked like an intelligent man to us, so I asked what he knows about Chechens.

It happened to be that Gregory was a professor of history and taught in one of Magadan's institutes. He was visiting our area to visit his parents and go hunting with his father.

'Well," he whispered in a very low voice so the people behind the wall couldn't hear him.

"Chechnya is a region located just north of the Caucasus Mountains on the south of European Russia. Chechnya was inhabited for thousand years by the people speaking in an isolated

146

language. Once conquered by the Ottoman Turks, the Chechens are predominantly Muslim. Sunni missionaries from Saudi Arabia reinforced the Sunni faith there in the 17th and 18th centuries.

The Russian Empire under Catherine the Great annexed Georgia, a predominantly Christian country that borders Chechnya in the south at the end of eighteen century thereby formally gaining control of Chechnya. Afterward, Chechens declared a holy war on Russia, which escalated during the following century culminating in the Caucasian War which ended in the middle of nineteen century. The resisting Chechen tribes were headed by Imam Shamil, a military and religious leader whose charisma was recounted by Leo Tolstoy's novel, Hadji Murat.

This kind of violence is not new to Islam. The Turks near the end of the Ottoman empire were notorious for burning the Christian churches with the worshipers inside to the ground. It was common practice throughout the Ottoman years to lock the gates of the towns on Fridays, and after prayer, they would slaughter all Christian in the town.

Chechnya was conquered by Russia and became a Soviet Republic, but Russian forces didn't stop there. In 1934 Stalin deported 400, 000 Chechens and Ingush to Kazakhstan.

"Are these Muslims getting revenge by kidnapping Christians?"

"You know, Sergey, there is too much confusion in the world when comparing religions. The Christian Historical Book says that the Son of the God saved a person from being stoned to Death. The Muslim Historical Books says that the profit of God has a person stoned to death.

When religion controlled the Western world, it committed many atrocities such as a Crusades and the genocide of the new world cultures."

147

"Are the Islamic societies at the same stage of cultural development that the Europeans were in ancient time, and are they using their religion to get what they want?" asked Sergey.

"The Crusades slaughtered thousands and thousands of Muslims, and now Christians are fighting with Muslims to protect themselves from fanatics, who are distorting the true Muslim religion. The war between religions continued through the ages until our days, and we are the victims of this war."

"We are not religious," Leda said, "but we are born to a Christian nation, and it teaches people to be good to each other."

"You know Leda, Christianity works while infidelity talks. We feed the hungry, clothe the naked, help the sick, and seek the lost, while infidelity abuses and babbles nonsense and profanity. I can give you all a lecture about religion; this is what I teach my students. The history of the Christian religion has developed supreme affinities for the best things: for the noblest culture, for purest morals, magnificent literature for most of the civilization, for most energetic national temperaments, for the most enterprising races, for the most virile and progressive minds. We are not conscience to religion, but the truth is not so much that man has a conscience, as that conscience has man."

"Tell us about the Muslim religion, I'm only seventeen and haven't lived long enough to know as much as you, Gregory," Lena asked in her girlish voice.

"Muslims are praying Allah, but listening and learning from the Prophet Muhammad. Just like Jesus Christ, he spoke to people. "Listen to me and take these words to those who could not be present here today," he said, and he taught people to do good things."

"So, the Prophet Muhammad taught good things?"

"Yes, he said, "Return the good entrusted to you to their rightful owners. Hurt no one so no one may hurt you. Remember

148

that you will indeed meet your Lord, and he will indeed reckon your deeds. Beware of Satan, for the safety of your religion."

"What did Muhammad say about women?" Leda asked.

Gregory answered, "Muhammad said, 'You have certain rights regarding your women, but they also have rights over you.' He instructed man to take women as their wives only under Allah's and with his permission. If they abide by the man's rights, then they have the right to be fed and closed in kindness. He also said to treat them well and be kind to them for they are your partners and committed helpers. And it is your right that they do not make friends with anyone to whom you do not approve."

"Why did they abduct us, do they think that they are superior like Nazis thought?" I asked.

The Prophet Muhammad said that all mankind is from Adam and Eve. An Arab has no superiority over a non-Arab nor does a non-Arab have any superiority over an Arab. Also, a white man has no superiority over a black man nor does a black man have any superiority over a white man. Also, every Muslim is a brother to every Muslim. Muhammad taught that nothing belongs to another person unless it was given freely and willingly.

"I think," Sergey said, "Religion has only brought mankind war, pain, hate, suffering, and ignorance. People are using religion to commit crimes."

"Man will argue for religion, fight for it and die for it; anything but live for it. It's true that in the name of God was done a lot of crime, but it doesn't justify the brutality of kidnapping innocent people like us because of a religion that teaches good and positive behavior toward humans," Gregory stopped there because he heard footsteps approaching the room.

We wanted to hear more, but the door opened, and a man with a thick mustache walked into the room and picked up a mattress with 5-year-old Svetlana sleeping on it and carried her out the door. We didn't see Svetlana anymore after that, and we

149

couldn't find out where they took her. Our lives were now in the hands of terrorists."

Ivan got up on his feet, "It's late, and Mariya must be sleeping, goodnight Misha."

Though it was late, Michail couldn't fall asleep right away being disturbed by Vania's story. Will justice prevail over the crime of hurting a grown man, or child? Where is the justice? Justice advances so lethargically that crime often escapes from its slowness. It's slow, and doubtful course causes many tears to be shed."

"But justice, as the truth, will always rise up," he thought before falling asleep.

~

It was a busy season for all family. The summer in Siberia is very short, and food for the household and the animals needed to be prepared and stored for a long winter. The medicine plants needed to be collected and dried; berries and mushrooms had to be preserved. Also, the necessary repairs in the house, and shed needed to be completed. There are countless jobs that need to be done in the two and a half months of warm weather. The average temperatures in July are from 5 to 16 degrees Celsius, when winter hits, it's minus 40.

"He has such a difficult life," Michail thought about Ivan, "and this hard life is after all his suffering. I don't know if I would be able to live like this. This is not living; it's just surviving."

When the winds come in the winter, the temperature drops to minus 60, and it became unbearable to live here. And the short summer is not much better with millions of mosquitoes; life is so hard for this family. If I didn't know that they came here voluntarily, I would think that they were sent into exile for some reason."

Finally, it was summer, and Ivan was fishing at the small Ohota River not far from the house. Fishing and hunting kept Ivan busy. Vania promised to free Michail's right arm the following week. He moved his bed next to the window so that Michail could open and close the window without any help and to enjoy the fresh air. It would have been delightful, but the view wasn't very clear because the window had a fabric screen to protect the inside from billions of mosquitoes. Even through the screen, Michail often saw Mariya and Ivan covered with bugs from head to toe while doing their chores outside, and Sasha running with a branch in his hand chasing something in the grass. Those moments made Michail think about his little daughter, Angelica, and how much he missed her.

Finally, he intently watched as Ivan cut the fabric that held the plank to his left hand. Michail pulled the pieces of fabric helping him. Now he could bend his both arms in all his joints; it worked perfectly. He felt such joy that he had freedom and independence of movement. "Those who don't know a feeling of pain, don't know the feeling of joy," he said to himself.

With two his free hands, he could take care of himself and relieve Vania from his duty as a nurse that was a big relief for him, thou he wasn't embarrassed lately when Vania attended him. He had become a brother; that's the way Ivan saw it and the way he felt about Ivan.

The summer came and went too fast, and once again, it was cold outside, so Michail could only open a small portion of the window to refresh his room. When the green leaves turned to gold and red, Vania spent evenings with him. He continued his story while working on his project. He brought many things from the plane and was constructing the wheelchair for Michail to move around.

"So the first victim, little Svetlana, was gone."

"Oh, I condemn anyone hurting children anywhere and in anyway, Vania".

"Who can't? It's unimaginable, but one-by-one, Rita-8 years old, Olia-8, and Kolia-9 were taken by the man with a mustache in another three days. Only Kostia-10, the oldest remained. He was sitting close to me all the time like I could protect him, but the next day, he was also taken. The kids just vanished, disappeared from our lives and the lives of their parents. Now just seven of us were left waiting for our fate. I never knew what happened to Sergey and Gregory, and Leda, Lena, Katia, and Mila, because I knew in my heart that I was next.

"The next morning, the man with mustache walked into the room and pointed to me with his finger. I got up from the mattress, looked at my friends for the last time, and said goodbye. I saw the red eyes from crying on the girl's faces and walked behind my kidnapper.

That was a sad and scary moment. I'll be now all alone, nobody to talk to and what they will do with me."

I was escorted to the front yard and got into the back seat of an old Volga car which lost all its color. With my kidnapper sitting next to me in the back seat, the car moved leaving a cloud of dust behind it.

It was very hot inside of the car. I still was wearing my heavy boots and the winter jacket I wore hunting in the forest, and sweat was running from my pores. By my estimation, it was at least thirty degrees Celsius. A cloud of dust surrounded the car, so I couldn't see where I was taken. It was a very old car, and we drove very slowly for a long time, maybe three or more hours on an empty road without any pavement through fields with grass and bushes here and there. The car stalled a few times and it was hard to start the engine. When the dust settled, I could see that we were approaching the foothill of the mountains and toward a stone wall.

The wall was made of large white with gray color stones and was about three meters high. When we got to the brown gates, made of a solid metal, my kidnapper opened it, and the car drove into the front yard and stopped in front of a two-story building painted in a sunny orange color. There were four very large windows with rounded tops on the first floor with a double window size space between them. Those windows had a beautifully designed screen painted in an orange color. In the middle of the house was a big door with a rounded top. On the second floor, each side had three narrow windows and one small rounded window over the door. The house was big and looked very festive.

I was glad that I was alive and that my prison didn't look so bad, but soon I understood that I overestimated my captors. A large man escorted me from the car. He had short black hair, and his face was covered with a cloth.

He walked me to the back of the house. He stopped at a hole dug in the ground. The hole was a little more than four square meters and covered with the cross bars and a metal screen that was level with the ground. Through the screen, I could see that was a mattress on the dirt floor and nothing else. He pulled up half of the screen that was divided in the middle and nodded his downward. He demanded in Russian, "Get in." I walked nine steps down a metal ladder. The guard closed the screen, locked it, and then he was gone. I found myself in a caged-grave left alone with the sky above me.

It was terribly silent and felt like it was on purpose. All I could hear was my heart beating."

My wrists got tight, and all body became tense and painfully agitated in protest. I screamed at the top of my lungs looking through the screen at the sky, "Let me go! Free me! Let me go!" Hearing the sound of my voice, I shuddered as if I had suddenly woke up from bed dream. My face distorted in torment, "Let me

153

go!" But nobody heard my scream from the deep grave. "What cruelty, I was locked in a bandit's den."

Suddenly, my body became very heavy and I dropped onto the mattress. How long I was sitting under a burning sun, I didn't know, but I understood that this was the final destination of my journey and that this was the end. I lost everything, and all I can do is put myself in the hands of the fate."

I could imagine the walls of prison, but I never thought that I will be kept in this grave looking hole. The sun was right over my head and it was so strong that I felt exhausted from the heat. I was thirsty, but when I climbed two steps on the ladder, I couldn't see anything accept the sky. I went down to the ground and sat on the mattress."

For a long time, I was sitting and thinking of my terrible journey and thought, "I'm only twenty two years old. How long will I be in this pit? Will I be able to survive? Can I escape? To find the answer, I need to live.

I still had my father's watch with me, so I looked to see what time it was, and it was eight in the evening. The screen was opened and a blanket with a pillow was thrown to me, after that a skinny bearded man handed me a basket with food.

I drank the water and couldn't quench my thirst. I ate a piece of half cooked greasy lamb and rice with my fingers because there was no spoon. At least the food was decent this time. "

When I finished eating my food, the guard took the basket and gave me a metal bucket with some water in it and I knew what it was for.

A gold and purple sunset lit my grave-like hole in the ground. When the evening drew near, I became more frightened, "Only God knows why I'm finding myself under this strange sky? What did I do to deserve this? I felt that my wings were broken and I can't fly any more. These savages don't have a moral conscience to put me underground alive. When will I be free? If I get free, will I be able to forgive this violence? There is forgiveness for all people on earth. There is infinite grace in the world, but will I forgive? I closed my eyes and pondered over my fate reflecting the moments of my life at home with Mariya. When I opened my eyes, there was gray clay wall in front of me, and I understood the seriousness of my situation."

"I put my head on a pillow and covered myself with my jacket. Hours later, I woke up to cover myself with the blanket because it was got chilly.

"I woke up in the morning. It must have been very early because the sun hadn't come out yet; the air was damp with dew, and I felt cold. I was startled with a loud bang when the screen above me slammed to the ground. The familiar guard handed me the basket with food. It was cooked rice and I believe goat milk in a small aluminum container. There was no spoon in the basket, and I ate with my fingers again.

When I finished my breakfast, the guard opened the screen and pointed on the waste bucket. I claimed up ladder carrying the bucket with me. When I got to the top, I saw two other men carrying the same looking buckets with their heads down.

"Go," the man demanded and didn't say anything else and pointed to the other men. I rushed with my bucket, looking at my feet on the gray ground with patches of grass. I followed them to the foothill which was a long distance, and then I saw a small river with fast running water and rapids.

"I thought to myself, "So, I am not alone here; there are two more captives." I noticed that their faces were not shaved and one man had dark hair on his head and on his face and the other man had light hair, the color of sand. We were accompanied by a large guard, the same man with a forest of black heir on his face, who I met yesterday. He stood very close to the water and didn't take his eyes off us even for a second.

The two fellows tossed the waste from their buckets into the river and rinsed it a few times with water. I was learning something every minute by following the other two men. The fast running water made me fantasize about what would happen if I jump in water. But I pushed this thought away because the guard who was making splashes in water with long tree brunch without leaves watched our every move. He would kill me in instant.

I hadn't bathed since I was abducted and my body was in agony for water. It was like God heard my prayers. The two other captives took off their clothes, stood up to their knees in the water and washed themselves. Then they washed their clothes, and after wringing the water out, they put the wet clothes back on. I was still was wearing the same pants and shirt, made of heavy fabric along with the heavy boots for hunting in the forest, and these clothes were too hot in this climate, but at least my clothes were durable, and I was glad to have them because the other two men's shirts and pants were torn in many places and it looked like they had been for a long time. I left my jacket made of heavy fabric like a tent under my pillow; it will be good for cold weather if it comes. I walked in my underwear into the water up to my knees and washed myself in cold water. It was the first pleasant thing I experienced since I was captured. I tried to keep up with the other men, washed my clothes and put them back on wet just as they did. The thought of escape flashed in my mind again, but I forced the impulse away because if the young men didn't run away, it meant that it was impossible.

The sun was hot and my clothes dried very quickly.

When we returned from the river, the two men were put to work. They rolled big stones from the stockpile we passed on our way to the river. They rolled large stones in front of them to the side of the wall and to the corner where construction of the wall stopped. I realized that I had been brought there to build this wall.

Go and work," the guard said in Russian. His intense black scary eyes burned a hole in my forehead. I turned around and went to the stockpile of stones and tried to pick one up and it was too heavy. "This wall must be built by the hands of giants," I thought, and rolled it as the other men did.

After working in a bent over position for a couple of hours under a very hot sun, I was exhausted and thirsty. Sweat was running from my forehead over my face; blinding and burning my eyes. I wiped it with my sleeve and continued to roll the stones.

My hands got cut in many places, and as soon the blood dried, I injured them again. My back was aching from bending all the time, but seeing, what the other two men were doing, I forced myself to continue rolling the stones.

I wanted to talk to them, but we were watched by the guard who told us to remain silent."

Around noon, the skinny man with thick eye brows and thick black hair on his head brought three baskets of food and put them next to the pile of stones. We ate greasy, bony lamb again with a flat piece of bread, and drank water. The rest of the day, we continued rolling stones, and then I was the first to be escorted to my grave-cage, so I didn't find out where the other two men slept.

The next morning, I felt a sharp pain in my back muscle from working the day before, but who would hear my complaint? I climbed out of my hole, hunched over, and was put back to work. We did the same job every day and it was like that until we finished with the pile of stones." "After a few days, I saw that the other men were put into the same type of underground cell as mine on opposite side of the field, but at a distance from each other. I figured that it was specifically done that way so we couldn't communicate with each other.

Is this my life now?" I thought. I was so exhausted from hard labor that every evening I collapsed on my mattress. I remembered Mariya was learning in her books about slavery. Whatever makes a man a slave, takes half of his worth away, and that is how I felt.

My hands were sore and bled from ripping my skin on sharp edges of stones, and nails tore into my flesh. My back was aching all the time from bending over all day long, day after day."

Alone in my cage, I thought, "I don't know if I'm capable to work like this all my life. This is real slavery. I compared the emptiness of my existence with my previous life, when my heart was full of love for Mariya and I could go and do whatever my heart desired. It's called freedom, and now I'm trapped in captivity. I couldn't suppress this thought and a storm raged inside me. These are the best years of my young life, and I'm wasting laboring it away in Chechnya for bandits with black forest on their faces. Even wild animals are not so cruel to their own species. Someday I'll be free; I know I will be, but for now, I need all patience I can muster in order to survive.

When the last stone was rolled to the wall, that morning the other two men walked one behind another to the low built structure with a small elongated window close to the roof. I walked behind them and brought the tools to work with the stones; picks like the mountain climbers use, splinter, and a large harmer. We put the tools in wheelbarrows with a one behind another, walked out of the gate, and headed toward the mountains. The guard was closely watching our every move.

When we got closer to the foothill, we turned to the right to walk around the hill, then pushed the wheelbarrows up a hill until we reached the site of the quarry. I watched what the other men did, left the wheelbarrow at the bottom, grabbed the tools and claimed to a spot where I thought I could start.

I followed the lead of the other two men working. I put a heavy split into a crack in one solid, big piece of stone and smashed it with the harmer. The rock cut on one-half but remained a solid piece. I placed the split in another location and hit it again with all my power many times. Both portions of the rock were loose. I used the pick, pulled one stone to the bottom and barely had time to step aside, as the rock started to roll downhill by its own weight. I did the same with the other portion and both pieces went to the bottom where the wheelbarrows were left. I watched the other two men do the same."

After we collected enough stones to fill the wheelbarrows at least three times, we strained to pull them because they were very heavy. Only two stones fit in a wheelbarrow, and we hauled them to the stockpile of stones.

Why don't we bring them directly to the wall?" I thought, but did what the others were doing. We brought the stones to the pile, returned to the quarry, and claimed back to the top of the hill to split more stones.

We worked into the late evening. I was exhausted to the point I didn't think I would wake up the next day, but I did, and everything started all over again.

We were not allowed to talk to each other, and I didn't know the names of the men. When I walked behind the chubby one, I saw that he had thin, dark hair on his head and at the top, there was visible baldness. His face was rounded with high cheek bones. I think he was about thirty years old and he was a little bit shorter than me. The leading man was taller than me and very young, maybe my age or even younger. He had sand color hair standing up like porcupine needles that were unevenly plucked. His face was narrow and he looked too skinny to me. They both were Caucasians.

I wondered, "How long have they been here? Did they build the front wall themselves?" But I didn't have an answer to that.

This slavery reminded me Gulag prison. I guess I should be grateful to them that they feed us a little better than 200 grams of bread a day. Only Stalin with his satanic religion in Georgia could

159

torture and throw people into mines that are not capable of working. I hope Muslims are not like Satan.

Can you believe, Misha, that people worship Satan? 98.5% of Georgians are Satanists."

I know it was introduced in Georgia in 3 B.C. and since that time it has been a dominant religion. Their Patriarch Ilya, during his reign, passed numerous laws which are known for their brutality and being inhuman. In Georgia, it is legal to torture animals, but illegal to kill them.

That is in Georgia, but I was in Chechnya. I don't know if they are any better than Georgians.

It was the end of the summer, and the days were still warm, but the nights became cooler. One day we worked in heavy rain. From early morning, the sky was overcast. The rain began to fall so lightly that I couldn't see it, and then suddenly, it was like the sky open right above me and poured over my face and hands. My clothes got soaking wet. The rain didn't stop and I was wet all day. Water squished out of my button-up boots with every my step. Close to the end of the day, the sky got brighter, but the rain still drizzled.

When we worked in the quarry, we didn't see each other often behind the rocks. I saw the men when the guard called us to stop working. They were also wet and had a sad look when they saw our guard was wearing a waterproof coat with a hood and rubber boots.

When I returned to my grave-cage, my mattress was soaking wet. At the front of my mattress was a puddle of gray muddy water. The clay floor was slippery and didn't absorb water. I lifted the mattress, and turned it upside down, but the bottom was as wet as the top. Under my mattress was a sheet of plywood that was shorter than the mattress, and a big portion of the mattress was muddy and soaked with water. The pillow and blanket were also thoroughly wet. After I had squeezed the water out of them,

160

adding more water to the puddle on the floor, I put the mattress on its side leaning against the wall and slept on the wooden platform covering myself with my wet jacket. It still was raining. I didn't fall into a deep sleep because I kept seeing Mariya. The rain stopped and the night was like black soot without single star. Seeing her in my mind seemed so real. The mirror of memory reflected her. The image was so clear that I truly saw her with my own eyes.

In the early morning, I felt as cold as ice, my teeth were chattering uncontrollably and I felt that I had a fever, but I forced myself to get up and went to work. My limbs were so heavy, like weights were attached to them, but I pushed myself and did my best not to show my weak condition. I just don't know how I managed to get through that day, because I was so weak; I thought that at any time I would collapse.

When we were working, the skinny man was sneezing all the time. He must have been catching a cold as I was, but we both continued working. The next day, I didn't feel fever and felt a little bit stronger, but I was coughing after that for a long time.

We were forced to work in any harsh weather: rain, cold, snow, and wind. We were slaves. We obey, or die; that's the only choice we had.

Our guard was sitting all the time watching us. From time to time, he would lay on his side like Roman Emperor, supporting his head with his hand, chomping on a grass stem and spiting it out."

I was following the chubby guy, and the guard walked behind me when we were rolling the wheelbarrows. I wanted to turn around because I felt as his black eyes drilling into the back of my head, but I never did. I knew that this wild animal would beat me to death for that."

161

When the stockpile of stones reached the same height as the first one was, we rolled them to the wall for many days, and then went back to the quarry.

That day we finished in quarry much early and were escorted back. I thought something was unusual that day.

I never saw who lived in the big house because we were mostly at the back of the house where we worked and lived. From time to time, I saw some people walking on the property, but I didn't know if they were workers or if they lived there. I saw couple of kids, but only from distance.

One day, we were walked to the back of the house and the skinny guy opened one side of a metal door, the typical entrance to a basement, and we walked down stairs. There were two levels in the basement. We stepped onto the top level and I could see the bottom of the basement. The top level was hanging over the lower level like a balcony. The small windows gave dim light to the gloomy place. When I looked in front of me, I saw prison cells with metal bars on the doors. There were five of them in the row. The skinny guy went to the last open door and disappeared behind it. The chubby man passed one cell and disappeared inside another. The fifth door was for me. I open the door, and I walked inside. Then the guard closed the doors, secured the metal bars and locked the cells.

Will we be left alone or will the guard watch us?" Either way, I decided to keep quiet and see what the other guys will do. I laid down on my mattress and didn't hear any words from them.

We heard the noise of a car's engine, and later, people were talking inside and outside the house. I heard words, but they spoke in their native language. All I could understand were names like Mansur, Saif, Adele, and heard the laugh of children. It lasted until about midnight, and then it was dead silent in our jail. In the morning, the food was brought to us later than usual. We heard cars leave the property and after that, we went to work.

Michail was listening to Ivan and imagined the scenes Ivan described in detail. "Adele's brother's name is also Mansur. That name is popular in Chechnya," Michail thought but didn't interrupt Ivan.

"Summer was over. It was still warm during the day, but the nights became very cold, and I slept all night in a curled position to keep warm."

"One morning, we were walking to the structure to pick up the tools and wheelbarrows. I saw a young woman with a big basket. She was carrying it in front of her from the river side. Whatever was in the basket must have been very heavy because she was holding her shoulders back to balance the weight in the basket. I was walking behind the chubby man and I saw him turn his head toward the woman and continue to look at her while she was passing us.

Suddenly, I heard the guard screaming in his native language and running towards the chubby man. Then he hit him with his fist so hard that poor man flew a meter from where he stood and dropped onto the hard ground. He was laying and not moving. The guard picked him up by his collar and continued yelling at him with anger in his face. I thought that he would hit him again, and I almost felt his pain. That proved that he was watching our slightest move.

Since I didn't know where the left side of the wall was that we were building ended, I couldn't estimate how long it would take for us to bring all stones to this side, but if it doubles the size of the front, it will take forever just to bring the stones, and after that, the wall still needs to be built. I completely lost track of the days.

Day after day, we did the same routine. Calluses covered my hands, and I injured them often scratching them on sharp rocks.

"Once I was working in the quarry and just broke the stone. My left leg was stretched when my right was bent. In that

163

position, I was hitting the splint with the harmer. When I hit it the last time, the rock started to fall on my stretched leg. I jerked the leg, but it was caught between the stones and a falling rock hit it. I screamed from the pain. The rock must have broken my leg. I think I heard a crunch, or at least it felt like it. The guard jumped from his place and ran a few steps. When he saw that I continued working, he went back to his place. It seemed like only the Fibula was broken because I could still put some weight on the leg. The pain was so bad that I thought I would lose conscience. After a while, I couldn't step on my foot.

When the time came to put the stones in the wheelbarrows, I told the guard that my leg's broken. He hit me on my cheek. Thankfully, not that hard because if he hit me harder, I wouldn't have been able to stand on my feet, and that would be the end, he would have killed me.

It was time to finish working for the day and the guard shoved me with his hand to get into the chubby man's wheelbarrow, and said one word to him, gesturing with his hand, "go."

"I was blaming myself for not to be careful and wondered what will I do tomorrow; the bone won't grow back overnight.

I didn't have breakfast in the morning and wasn't asked to go to work. I was glad and even grateful that I wasn't forced to work. I was lying on my mattress in my grave-like hole, feeling hungry because it was past noon and I still didn't have any food. I was fighting my hunger all day long, and when evening came, there was still no food. I was lying on the mattress at night cold and hungry. I had plenty of time to think about my fate, and Mariya was in my mind, like mother, she would nurse me with food when I wasn't feeling good. I fell asleep with her in my mind.

"I woke up the next morning hoping that I would get something to eat, but the day passed, and there was no food, and nobody came to my jail cell to check on me. My empty stomach

164

was ravaging my insides. All my thoughts were reduced to a mere morsel of food. I was so hungry that I felt a terrible pain in my stomach, but even more, I was thirsty and was swallowing my saliva to keep my mouth moist.

That is how they are going to kill me," I thought, "They going to starve me to death.

I spent the sleepless night cold and doubled up in pain. Inside me, I felt the weight of all stones from which the wall was build. The nights were extremely cold, and I didn't have my heavy jacket to keep warm. I was still cold when the new day started.

Ivan was talking with his head down staring at the floor at that point. He looked at Michail who was swinging his head from side to side in disbelieve of what he was hearing.

"Without water," Ivan continued, "and food, I felt very week. I wasn't living anymore, I just existed. I was motionless lying on my back and wished I could fall asleep and not wake up again. But when I did wake up, there was no food and nobody came to my hole. From time to time, I didn't feel the pain in my stomach, but the hunger feeling didn't go away."

Three days of terrible torture for me. Feeling very week without food and water, and chilled to my bones, I didn't move. My empty stomach that contracted in spasms made me suffer. Three days passed and I didn't hear any noise, didn't see anyone, and was losing hope that I would live. On the fourth day, I was so weak that I couldn't raise my hands. I stopped asking myself how long could I hold on. The hunger tore at my stomach and suppressed my will and courage to resist. Soon I will die. The feeling of hopeless overtook to me. I was laying on my mattress, not able to move, looked at the sky and felt almost at peace and became sleepy. My last thoughts were. "How long person can survive without food and water?" I didn't have the answer because I just didn't know. When I die, will I go to paradise or an inferno? But I didn't know that either. With this thought, I passed out.

When the sun reached its zenith on the fourth day, I was lying with my eyes closed. I knew that I was still alive. Suddenly, I heard the screen opening. Not able to move, I opened my eyes, and all I could see were black flies circling my face.

Then I felt a bucket on my chest. I gathered up all my power and reached with my hand to get a piece of bread from the basket. I bit a small piece and swallowed it without chewing. I devoured the rest afraid that it would disappear. Little by little, I felt my strength coming back. It was water in the bucket, and I couldn't satisfy my thirst. Careful not to spill a drop, I stopped, thinking that I would need to ration the water and that maybe this was my last supper. I ate the greasy lamb, sucking one every bone, and stuffed my mouth with rice. When I finished my meal, I felt stronger. I gathered the bones and put them under my pillow in case I became hungry again.

They brought food and water twice a day from that point on; I still collected the bones just in case the food stopped coming again. They were white and dry, but I kept them regardless.

Ten days passed and my leg didn't give me any pain. Finally, I examined it with my fingers, and a happy thought went through my mind. "Maybe my bone is not broken, maybe it just cracked." First, I stood on my knees and then on my good leg. My head was spinning; I was very weak from being dehydrated and hungry for so long that I almost fell onto my mattress. Placing my hand on the wall, I gradually switched the weight to the damaged leg and didn't feel much pain.

"Oh," I sighed, "it's not broken. I wouldn't be able to stand on my leg if the bone was broken. Thank you, Lord, I will live. Mariya, I will live."

They didn't come get me to work for two weeks but fed me twice a day. Little by little, I got my strength back. Oh, Misha, that was my vacation." "All the wounds on my hands healed while I was resting.

After two weeks, they gave me a crutch, and I faked having a broken leg when I went to work in the quarry."

Soon after my accident, I was transferred to the basement where it was a little bit warmer at night. The winter came with snow, and it was very cold. Sometimes the temperature dropped to minus 20 degrees Celsius, and we worked and slept in the harsh conditions all winter."

To work outside, they gave us jackets with a cotton layer between two fabrics and gloves. It was too cold to sleep at night. It was like this day after day and nothing changed."

A year had passed. We did the same job and ate the same food every day. I suffered from cold and exhaustion but kept going.

Every person has some property of his own," I thought. "Nobody has a right to it but himself." Sometimes I wanted to scream, to call for help, but we were in the mountains, and nobody would hear me. All it would do is make it even worse for myself and the other men. I knew that they would beat me to death, or kill me in an instant because human life for these savages was nothing and I was a slave to them.

There was still no end to the wall on left side. "It will stretch to the river," I thought, and it did.

When we finished bringing the stones, we started to construct the wall. It was an even more difficult job to carry stones that weighed maybe 20 kilograms while climbing a ladder without any support. We mixed the crushed stones and clay together with water and put the mix between the stones. Without talking to each other, we managed to alternate the operation between the three of us. It was hard not to talk to each other or anybody. I didn't even hear my own voice for a long time. Only sometimes, I would talk to Mariya in a quiet voice when I was alone in my jail cell.

The winter passed, and the spring came, and then another summer. The wall was almost complete, and I thought, "What is waiting for me next?" "We continued working in the quarry, shaping the limestone's into large rectangular bricks. "It must be for construct another building because there was enough space to build another big house without affecting the large yard.

I didn't know how many years passed since I was brought there. I lost track of time, but the pile of the stones we cut and carried was huge. We lined them up against the wall on the right side, and it was almost the length and height of the wall.

Time didn't matter for me anymore; I knew that someday I wouldn't wake up, and that will be better for me because this wasn't living. I felt myself becoming a grown man, but I didn't know exactly how old I was. I took my watch with me every day, and I knew what time was, but I lost track of the years. I thought that the sandy head man looked like he was about thirty now, and the chubby one was almost entirely bald.

It was hot summer day when we were cracking the rocks in the quarry; suddenly, I heard the guard yelling something in his native tongue, and he was running toward us to the right of me. Then I saw him pull the skinny man by his sleeve from the behind the rock yelling loudly and hit him in his head. I didn't know what was taking place because he was far away from me and working behind a big rock.

The guard dragged him down below and continued to hit him. The man was holding his hands up trying to protect his head and fell to the ground. The guard smashed the sandy head man with his boot, giving it all the power he had, and continued smashing his bleeding head again and again. That moment indignation overcame me, if I hadn't been so far from them, I would have thrown myself on him and beat him with all the strength is had in me.

"He will kill him," that thought made me want to vomit. And he did."

After beating the defenseless slave the death, he walked away breathing heavily and sat on the grass leaning against a stone. The sandy head man was lifeless. When we finished working, the guard told us to drag the body to the age of a cliff, and he pushed the body over the edge. We heard muted thud sound from below and knew that the sandy head man was gone.

"Oh," Michail sighed, and covered his mouth with his hand and closed his eyes, "He killed him."

"Yes, he killed him. I saw it with my own eyes, which substantially affected me. That was murder. It was second bloody murder I witnessed of people who I knew. They were killed in front of my own eyes. I could smell the blood and remember the scent of Sasha's blood on the train."

On the next day, just two of us remained, and we had a different guard. We hadn't seen him before. He had the same complexion as me, an average size man with a triangle shaped nose, thick black hair, and his face was unshaven. My face was covered with hair but wasn't very long. I had a piece of glass which I picked up from the ground a long time ago and was trimming every hair individually which kept me busy at night before falling asleep."

The new guard was much younger and different. He didn't sit all the time as the other guard. Sometimes he went for a walk but never lost sight of us. One time, the guard walked on some distance, and I moved closer to the chubby man. Not looking at him, I quietly said, "Ivan," and replied, "Anatoly."

A couple of weeks passed. It was a hot summer day, and we were working on the big gates. The river was only a few meters from us, and the white water rapids made a lot of noise."

"Our guard saw that we are working on the wall and doing our job, and he walked to the storage building, which was located

169

at the center of the long side of the wall. It was a long distance away. I was watching him, and when he disappeared inside, I counted to ten and didn't see him. Without giving any thought, I said to Anatoly, 'Follow me and run to the river.' Anatoly didn't hesitate. We both jumped into the cold, fast-moving and we were quickly carried away.

We were swiftly floating down a turbulent stream. I could see waterfalls in the mountains behind the fortress looking stone wall of my jail, and it disappeared behind the hill when the river made a sharp curve.

My heart was pumping in my chest from the anxiety of possibly getting caught. Questions shot through my mind like lightning bolts, "Am I on my way to freedom? Will we escape? How far we are now?" I looked back from time to time when I had the chance and didn't see anyone. By then we were far away and even if the guard followed us by jumping into the river, he wouldn't catch us. We were being hit by large stones in the water and slowed down by sinking into deep pockets behind them. With barely enough time to catch our breath, we were launched back into the fast water only to be hit by another big stone. Our bodies were being pulverized like a piece of raw meat from crashing into one large stone after another. Suddenly, I heard a loud noise and saw a straight glittering line between water and sky. "The waterfall, we are going to the waterfall. How far will we fall?" There was no time to swim to the shore. We went over the falls and dropped from the height of a three-story building and then sank deep under the water. I didn't think that I could hold my breath long enough to reach the surface, but I did, and we were carried further downstream. Ahead of us was a cascade of small waterfalls. I looked around and didn't see Anatoly at first, and then I saw him behind me, "Oh, I am glad I didn't lose my friend." We got tossed over a couple of more falls, but they were not as high or deep as the first one.

I was tired after swimming in rapids for so long and being crushed by boulders, beaten, and almost drowned, but the thought of getting caught and returning to the grave-cell made me continue to fight. We stayed in the water for many hours swimming downstream and by the sun's position; I estimated that it was about seven o'clock in the evening. By that time the rapids were gone and the river become calm and wider.

The landscape on the shoreline changed to a flat land covered with bushes and trees. "We can hide in the bushes for a night," I thought, and was going to recommend it to Anatoly, but suddenly, I saw a house a little bit farther ahead.

"Tolia," I called him and waved my hand instructing him to swim to the shore. We got out of the water, crawled behind a bush, and laid on the grass to catch the breath."

Still under in shock of what just happened I couldn't find the words to speak since I didn't have a chance to talk to anybody for many years. Anatoly must have felt the same."

"Freedom, I'm free, it happened," I was telling to myself and couldn't believe it was true. Every moment, of every day spent in confinement, was flashing in my mind; I still there in my mind. This freedom wasn't real for me yet. We didn't talk for a while and just remained on the grass waiting for it to get dark. I felt incredible inside me like I just was born again and didn't know how to walk yet. What to do? Where to go? How to we even begin and what is waiting for me? I wasn't scared anymore; I felt excited."

Our shelter was a big bush and through the leaves, I saw the moon creeping out of the clouds and coloring the sky around with blue light. It was very quiet. The trees around us looked like giants in a magic kingdom, and only the rustling of leaves in the breeze disturbed the silence. For the first time in my life, I discovered the nature around me. For so many years, all I saw were stones and gray looking ground. I could still see the clay walls of my cell where I knew every centimeter of every spot. That moment, I swore to myself that I would never be a slave again. I will fight for my freedom or die trying. It's easy to say, 'or die,' but when you are looking into eyes of death, you don't want to die. Why didn't I try to escape before? Because I didn't want to die and that was my fight for life."

"Tolia," I addressed my brother in misfortune, "I almost lost all hope living every day for years in slavery, but inside me, I never could submit myself to violence. It's against my nature, but protesting was living deep inside me all these years. Sometimes, I thought what if we changed places, could I do the same to the others know I wouldn't be able to hurt people? Are they people or some unknown species?"

"They are heartless monsters, wild savages, Vania. They are not people.

It's so nice to talk to someone who understood and to such a kind human being. Until that moment, I was surrounded by enemies. All those years I talk to myself and Mariya without a sound. I noticed that even my speech was slow like I was learning to speak."

"We lived so many years next to each other and never had a chance to exchange by a single word. I didn't know anything about that man. Now we could say hello to each other, shake hands, and learn a little bit of who we are. It was my first experience of freedom to talk and to touch another person, and it felt good."

We talked a little more about our captivity and how the thieves stole the best years of our youth.

Tolia said, "It would have been easier to bear our jail time if we could have talked to each other, but they even deprived us of this natural need. It was cruel of them to violate the freedom of other human beings. They bought us from slave traders to build their fortress. But, what about the killing of a human being? They

172

killed Nicolay in front of us, for what? What did he do to be killed?"

"I don't know why."

"Me neither, that's pure cruelty; that's scary evil."

We could have talked more about the thieves who stole our lives, but it was late evening, and it was time to start our new life.

Our clothes were still wet, and I felt cold, so we headed toward the house. We walked around the house and peeked in the windows.

"Looks like a woman with a child is alone in the house," Tolia whispered. I agreed with him.

"Should we knock?" Anatoly looked at me indecisively.

"Yes," and we knocked on the door.

Surprisingly, the woman opened the door for us, and I rushed to say, "Please, don't be scared, we are honest people. There was an accident with our boat, and we've been swimming for a long time. As you can see, we are wet and hungry. We will work for you in exchange for some food."

We didn't evoke any suspicious by the way we looked because she said, "Come in." After the hell-jail-underground grave, I was so happy to walk inside of the house. It was not a big place, but it felt so nice to be inside a cozy room like it used to be at home. The young woman left to another room and came back her arms full of men's clothes and we were still standing in the same spot at the door.

"Come in and have a seat. My husband died last spring. These were his clothes; you can have them."

While we were getting out of our wet clothes and putting on the clean, dry clothes, the woman went to the kitchen and called us to the table. I sat at a real table on a real chair and felt my eyes get swollen from approaching tears. I suppressed the lump in my throat to hide what I felt. Then the smell of a chicken soup tickled my nostrils. We were delighted and thankful to eat chicken soup with plenty of chicken meat and different kind of bread, vegetable salad, and a sweet drink made with berries.

"Ah, Misha, it was heavenly delicious after so many years having the same food every day that they fed us. She was silently watching us eat, and after we had finished, she said, "I live alone with my little son right now, but next spring, I'm going to Makhachkala to live with my relatives."

"Are there many people are living around?"

"There are no villages close by, but we are near the city of Hasavjurd."

"You said that you are going to Makhachkala, is it on the Caspian Sea?"

"Yes, it's right on the coast."

"How will you get there?"

"There is a road from Hasavjurd to Makhachkala; it's about eighty kilometers."

I smiled at her.

"My name is Nicolay, and this is my cousin Victor," I lied about our names.

"I'm Nina."

"Nina, we are very grateful for your hospitality. What can we do for you?"

"You rest well tonight and tomorrow I'll ask you to help me with the firewood. It needs to be split and stored for the winter. I need just enough to live through one winter.

"We will be happy to do it for you."

"I will make the beds for you in that room," she pointed to an open door.

Nina left to another room, and I noticed the calendar on the wall. For the first time since I was abducted, I found out what year it was, and it shocked and scared me. I was a prisoner for eleven years."

"Oh," Michail gasped, "eleven years? Oh, you poor man, Vania."

"I said goodnight to Tolia, and for the first time in eleven years, I took my cloth off and lay down on clean sheets in real bed. It was soft, and it felt like I was floating on a cloud. "I never will be a prisoner again," I swore to myself before falling asleep. I slept through the night, but kept alert just in case we were chased, but nothing happened.

In the morning I asked Nina, "Can I use one of your husband's shaving blades?"

She gave it to me.

"You can keep it. My husband doesn't need it anymore."

After my face was clean shaven, I saw a man's face with strong features in the mirror. I could see that years were added to my face, but to my surprise, I was pleased with the changes. I looked like a mature, grown man, and I thought. "I'm thirty-three years old, and I don't look bad, not bad it all."

After breakfast, we worked all day splitting wood and at the end of the day the job was done. Nina was so impressed with our efficiency and speed, that when next morning we were leaving her, she was regretting losing us, and as a token of appreciation, she gave us some money and enough food to last us three days.

Tolia and I walked to the road and headed to Hasavjurd and from there, we headed to Makhachkala. On the way, we talked about our abduction, and Anatoly told me that he and the sandy head man (Nicolay), as we called him, were in that place two years before I came. They were the ones who dug the holes in the ground where we were kept, and they built the wall in front of the house. He said that he was kidnapped at night from his village next to the city of Magnitogorsk. We talked about the cruelty and brutality of people who kept us in slavery, and in conditions incomprehensible to a human being.

175

This pain we experienced through our suffering in captivity was more than physical pain and deeper than pain most human could endure. They robbed us of years of our lives and were hurting our souls.

We spent two days on the road and slept night under bushes at night. All I wanted was to go home, but my home was far away, and I didn't have money for the trip. So when we got to Makhachkala, Anatoly and I decided to go our own ways. I went to the fishing boats. I explained my experience with fishing was hired to join a crew. Since I didn't have a home to go, I asked if I could sleep on the boat for a while. I'm the only the one who slept and ate on the small boat, and the expenses were deducted from my pay. I so got used to the hardship and poor living conditions where I was at the last eleven years that life on the boat was a luxury to me. Most important to me was that I was mostly at sea and out of sight from the people who could be searching for me. I was free at last.

Oh, what a difference; I was working for myself and was paid for my labor. There were no sharp eyes following me anymore that watched my every move. It was like the gray clouds over me dissolved, and my world was lit up with a new light of freedom and hope; my life was in my hands, and it was an incredible feeling.

When I received my first pay, I started to put some money aside for the trip to go home. After working with the crew for three months, I decided it was time for me to start moving to the North East. I said goodbye to my friends and took a boat from Makhachkala to Astrakhan on the Volga River.

In Astrakhan, I got hired to work on a much smaller fishing boat, about five meters long, the kind of boat that most Caspian fishermen use.

Below Astrakhan, the Volga River, the sea's largest single water source leads to a thousand smaller streams as it flows

176

through a vast marshy, sparsely inhabited delta. White-tailed eagles, ducks, herons and hundreds of other species depend on these wetlands. The marsh serves as a filter cleaning the river. The last streams of the delta give way to the open Caspian where the water is shallow, clean, and fresh to taste. Large blocks of whistling swans float on its wind-ruffled surface.

I inhaled the clean Caspian Sea air while looking at the sky and open water, and an incredible feeling of happiness engulfed me. "I don't need to go to cage underground; I am a free man."

Our boat was about one kilometer from shore, and the net was set into the water. In the mid-morning, we pulled up oysters and a variety of sturgeon. Two of us brought the fish from the boat to the dock and placed it on the granite floor of a large structure. This fish looked like a cross between a catfish and a stegosaurus; it had whiskers and rows of sharp, bony protrusions along its back where other fish would have fins. I watched as two men in white robes, boots, and surgical gloves washed, weighed, and measured the fish. One was 1.6 meters long and weight 18 kilograms.

One man carefully sliced open the fish's belly and revealed a roe (a mass of eggs contained in the ovaries of a female fish) with thousands of gleaming small black eggs. The man scooped out the roe and moved it in a sink, placing it on top of a nylon sleeve, gently massaged the massive roe and its supporting tissue. Then the eggs fell onto a finer screen.

Then it was washed with icy cold water and placed in a stainless steel bowl in small, colder room and it put on a scale. It was 3.4 kilograms of roe. Then salt was measured for this amount of roe and gently kneaded into the roe of eggs. The man in white robe did it with his fingers for a couple of minutes, and when he stopped, he told me that the roe had become caviar. Then the man tenderly transferred it into tins and secured the lids with granite disks and placed them into a refrigerator until the next day when they would be picked up by trucks for delivery to Europe and Asia.

After working for eight months in Astrakhan and saving money, I thought it was time to move farther North, and when I looked for the money in my thin mattress to take with me, it wasn't there. My heart dropped in my chest. Thirteen months of hope and hard work were swept away in an instant. I was sat for a long time thinking how to react to such criminal act and came with the decision to get my last pay and leave the boat without saying anything because my co-workers changed many times and it was useless to look for the money.

By boat, I went to Volgograd. I took a construction job that was building a hospital. I did different kinds of jobs, but mostly in constructing the walls of the building. It was convenient for me to have this job because for people like me they provided a place to live in a dormitory. I slept in a room with nine other men. This time, I kept my money with me in secret pockets. I sewed a pocket on the inside of my work jacket. I stayed in Volgograd for seven months, and once again by boat, went up north to next big city on Volga, Saratov. I was impressed with Volga and how it was between two cities where the water is slow moving.

I stayed in Saratov for two months working at construction jobs and moved again by boat to Samara for one month and finally to Kazan for two months. In the last three cities, I did a variety of hard labor jobs to collect enough money to buy train tickets, first to Yekaterinburg where I finally purchased a ticket on Trans-Siberian Railway.

After two years since I escaped my prison, I was heading home. I had nothing with me except a canvas bag containing enough food for two weeks of travel on the train, and enough money for the ticket on a boat from Vladivostok to Okhotsk.

I choose the top shelf in the train to I put a mattress with the white sheets that I purchase for the trip. I ate my food and drank hot tea, which I was able to make by using the boiler at the end of the carriage. It was June and from the train window, I saw masses of green forest running backward and I could see all the carriages of the train when it curved to the left or the right. I had plenty of time to remember the hard life I had for the last thirteen years.

The rhythmic clunking of wheels made me remember when I was forcibly put into a cargo carriage to an unknown place and an unknown future. I didn't know at the time that I'd be sold to slavery. How can people could be so cruel toward their brothers? We are all relatives on this earth, aren't we? I suffered a lot.

But now, I was going home. I thought about Mariya. "Will I find her available after she buried me a long time ago? If she got married, that would be the hardest thing to accept because she is the one who kept me alive all these years."

There was only one day remaining of my trip on the train, and I was agitated by the expectation of the unknown. I tried to imagine Mariya's face, but all I could see her curly brown hair tied into a ponytail.

Finally, I stepped onto the platform at the Vladivostok railroad station and the same day I was on the boat to Okhotsk. All those years, I kept my father's watch, the only possession I had from my former life. I was wearing it on my wrist since I was free, but after being in the water with me, it stopped working. It was my only treasure, and I kept it.

Okhotsk, I read the sign on the port station and my mind translated it into, Mariya.

She was attending an institute at that time to be a teacher.

"At this hour she must be teaching in school." So I immediately went to the first school on my way, but nobody knew who she was. I went to another school, and one teacher said that she knew her and told me where the school was where I could find her. It was already two o'clock in the afternoon and the first shift in school was finishing.

I ran to the third school and the moment I was facing the entrance door, I saw a woman walking down five steps, holding a school case in her one hand and her other hand was pressing a stack of papers to her chest.

"It can't be a mistake, Mariya," I cried. I stopped, and she froze in place, my bag fell on the ground, and suddenly she dropped everything from her hands and ran toward me screaming,

"Vania, Vania," and her head fell onto my chest. I wrapped my hands around her, and we both cried loudly like children, choking from our tears.

"Vania, I never gave up hope that you would be back and that you couldn't leave me without saying goodbye. I waited for you all these years. I swore to myself that I would never mourn because all these years I knew you are still alive. I was waiting for you," her voice trembled and tears poured from her eyes.

"That is all I need to know, my Mariya; that is all I need to know." Incredible happiness engulfed me and swallowed me like an ocean wave. I couldn't loosen my arms. We stood like that hugging each other for a long time; then we collected our things while holding each other. We slowly walked home to gather the fragments of our previous life and to build a new one together. She couldn't wait to know where I was all those years.

"Vania, where did you come from?"

"I came from slavery."

Mariya didn't take my words literally because she couldn't imagine where I was for thirteen years. She knew that she would know the entire story later, but for now, she said, "No one is a slave whose has free will."

"This is true, Mariya. I always knew that I'd be free."

"This is not me; it is Tyrius Maximus," said Mariya with a laugh. She still didn't understand that it was the truth."

~

Michail's face was wet with tears, and a knot of bitterness stuck in his throat.

"Vania, your story touched me so deep that I need time to recover from your wounds. How, after so much bitterness, you remain such a positive and loving person?"

Ivan only smiled instead giving an answer and left the room to return with the wheelchair.

"Oh, Vania, hard labor and hard life didn't take away your nobility." Michail himself answered his own question.

"The fall season is very short here, and soon it will be snowing again so as soon I finish with the chores of the season, we will free your legs, just wait a little bit more, Misha."

When Vania left the room, Michail was drying his eyes and thinking about Vania's horrible life in slavery which lasted eleven years and his struggle to survive in captivity. He thought about his loneliness and the pain of losing his love, about hard work and humiliation. He thought about his long journey home and how fortunate he was to have Mariya back.

"She was only the one," he said, "who kept him alive." If there is anything better than to be loved, it is to love someone; I know it. The pain of lost love like darkness overshadows a man, and if he can find the way to his lost love, he knows that he lives.

"Thanks to Vania and Mariya, I'm recovering, and soon I'll see the ladies of my life. How are they feeling with the loss of me, their husband and father?" He fell asleep with the names of Laura, Angelica, and Oksana in his mind.

CHAPTER 20

Once Oksana made a hole in the mattress and hid the pills in it; she felt much more alert and focused. "I feel better now, and the nausea is calming down. How long have I been here? It must be more than two months. My doctor said after three months I will feel well and will enjoy the pregnancy. I need to call Kiril; he will get me out of here."

"I need to make a call, please," Oksana asked a nurse.

"Sorry, but you not allowed to make phone calls here."

"Just one call, please," Oksana pleaded.

The nurse walked away without answering.

"I want to see a doctor," Oksana raised her voice and demanded.

Another nurse entered the room and handed her a pill. She said, "The doctor will see you now."

She walked to the doctor's office, and Pin-Head invited her to sit down. Oksana didn't have a chance to ask the doctor about a phone call before he said, "Oksana, it is the policy of the hospital that we terminate your pregnancy."

"Are you out of your mind?" She screamed.

"I'm not, but your state of mind indicates that you're not in a position to have a child. The faster we do it, the better it will be for you."

"Over my dead body will you touch my child."

Oksana screamed, and she jumped from her chair ready to run away.

Two huge orderlies in white robes walked into the room and restrained her by holding her arms behind her back, and dragged her to the corridor. Oksana was kicking and screaming, but they wrapped her in a white jacket and tied the long sleeves around her waist. The nurse put a cotton swab with chloroform her nose, and she lost consciousness.

Hours later, when Oksana opened her eyes and noticed the wet, bloody mess under her blanket, she was horrified to find that they took away her child. They just ripped it out of her body. She screamed at the top of her lungs. She threw the blanket on the floor and jumped from her bed and saw her nightgown wet with fresh blood.

"Murderers, what have you done?" She was screaming and screaming. But her scream only attracted more violence.

The nurse walked into the room with one huge man, who dragged her back to her bed and forcefully held her while the nurse and inserted a needle into a vein in her arm.

When Oksana woke up in the late evening, her body hurt from the wound from removing the baby. She felt wet and cold spot next to her body and when she looked under the blanket and saw the red sheet soaked with her blood.

A desperate scream shot out of her throat. With her eyes closed, she tossed her head from side to side, and with her mouth wide open, she wept in despair. "How could they do this to me? Who gave them the right?

Oksana's grieve was even greater because she couldn't share it with Kiril or anybody while locked in isolation.

When there were no more tears remaining to shed, Oksana laid quietly with her thoughts. She imagined her crying child which she never will see.

"My child can't talk for himself because he is dead." She imagined the baby's face - wanting to reach out and take him in her arms, but instead, there was only gray emptiness. The fog around her was choking her and the baby's face slowly disappeared into the mist. Her hands were empty; her heart was empty, and her life was destroyed. She called out, "Baby, my baby," and there was nothing except a terrible feeling of loss and loneliness. "He is gone, and I never will see him; he is gone before he was born; I never will know him."

Icy lips of a young woman were whispering: "I was anticipating my life with so much happiness, but when they took my joy away, my delightful forethoughts vanished into nothing." For a moment, she thought she heard her baby's cry. "With you, my baby, I lost everything."

And words of Shakespeare came to her mind. "Moderate lamentation is the right of dead; excessive grief the enemy of the living." She thought, "What is there to live for? I don't have a friend in this world only enemies and killers. They can't kill you because you already live in my mind. I will find you my baby, and you will have your mommy."

She put her finger in the hole of the mattress and one by one started to pull out the pills she stashed for the last month. She swallowed the first pill, then another, and then the next until she couldn't find any more. Suddenly, sleepiness took over her body. She felt her head became heavy.

"I will see you soon, my baby," she said and then she fall asleep. When her spirit was leaving her body, she heard an Angel speak, "Earth has no sorrow that heaven cannot heal."

CHAPTER 21

Ivan came to the room one morning, and said, "The time has come to free your legs, Misha," Mariya and Sasha joined the big event. Ivan cut the bandages that held the wooden splints in place and carefully pulled them out.

"Bend the leg and let's see if it's in one piece."

Michail tried to move his leg. It felt very heavy to him. Slowly, he bent it at the knee and moved the foot in different directions.

"It works," he laughed.

"Now bend another one."

Michail did the same with both legs, and they both worked perfectly. He laughed in sheer happiness. Everyone else laughed joyously with him, and Sasha was the loudest.

"Now try to stand on your feet."

Ivan held him under his arm and helped lift him. Michail put his feet on the floor and gradually got up. Everybody was holding their breath as he stood on his own feet.

"Maybe they are not strong yet, but they are holding you."

Michail alternated the weight of his body, and his legs held him up.

Mariya pushed the wheelchair closer to Michail. Ivan held his arm and walked him two steps to the chair and helped him to sit on it.

"This will help you to move around until you can stand and walk on your own."

Then Michail asked Ivan, "Come here." Ivan got closer, and Michail hugged Ivan with his both hands, looking in his eyes, and said, "Thank you, Vania," kissing him on his forehead, trying to hold in his emotions.

Mariya and Sasha hugged Michail, and Michail hugged little Sasha back with both hands and kissed him on his brown curls.

Michail turned his wheelchair around, and for the first time in more than a year, rolled out of his room. For the first time, he sat with the family at the dining table. Now, it seemed all things for Michail, were for the first time.

"Take it easy Michail, let it be gradual, and don't put too much stress on your new legs. When I pulled you from the plane, I wasn't sure that you would live and with all your broken bones. I didn't think that you would ever are able to walk again, but you've miraculously recovered and I'm very pleased."

"It wasn't a miracle Vania; it was you and Mariya's kindness, and hard work that brought me back to life. I promise thatI will never forget what you have done for me."

"You would do it for me, Michail, wouldn't you?"

"Of course I would."

"You see, it's just normal human behavior, that all it is."

The first snowflakes of winter were dancing outside the windows, and soon all ground would be white. Michail started standing on his feet more often, and Ivan made a pair of crutches for him to help as he learned to walk.

The days become shorter and the long evenings made them continue the conversation.

"Why did you choose this remote area to live, Vania?"

Having my experience with the kidnapping, I didn't trust anyone and couldn't live the same life as we did before. I wanted to protect Mariya and my child from any harm, and that is why I chose to move to the mountains far away from civilization. I hid in mountains for eleven years, and nobody found me. It was hard at the beginning to start from scratch, but it was worth it."

"Did you build the house and shed all by yourself?"

"Mariya and I built it together. When we first moved here, we had a horse, so we could bring tools and material for building the house, like glass for the windows, hinges, nails, and many other things.

I went back to the city many times to bring everything for the beds and kitchen. Then our horse died. She was an old horse, and we didn't have transportation after that. But by that time we had everything we needed. Mariya help me until she couldn't help any longer when her belly was so big with the child she slowed down. And then our son was born. I delivered him myself. What a joy it was to see a human being coming life and into my hands. Before that moment, I only saw death. When he was born, there was no question of what name to give him. Sasha, I promised Sasha, who died in my hands, that he will never leave me, and I will always be with him, and he lives now in our Sasha."

"What about his education, Vania?" Michail asked stroking Sasha's hair as he stood next to the wheelchair.

"For now, Mariya is tutoring him, but in the future, he has to go to live in the big city to get a higher education, but he's still too little to worry about it now."

"Sasha, when you grow up, who do you want to be?" Michail asked.

"When I grow up, I want to be a captain of a big ship, Uncle Misha."

"That is a very good profession, Sasha, and I believe you will have your ship one day."

Michail started focusing on his family that he left behind, "My beautiful girls and my boys. I wonder how are they, what a surprise will be for them to see their father again. I wish I could talk with them, but Vania, after his horrid experience, chose to live far away from civilization. I don't blame him because it's so peaceful here, and nobody can harm anybody."

~

Remembering every word of Ivan's story Michail also thought about the cruelty of other people, who violates human rights, freedom and he shared his thoughts with Ivan.

"It's a fact that not all Muslims are terrorists, but it certain, and exceptionally painful, that almost all terrorists are Muslims. History reveals that Muslims kept children hostage in Beslan and North Ossetia. The other hostage-takers and subsequent murderers of the Nepalese chefs and workers in Iraq were also Muslims. Those involved in rape and murder in Darfur, Sudan, are Muslims, with other Muslims chosen to be their victims. Osama bin Laden was a Muslim. The majority of those, who manned the suicide bombings against buses, vehicles, school, houses, and buildings, all over the world, were Muslims. The World Trade Center in America was destroyed by Muslims. The Chechens, who abducted thousands of Russian men, women, and children for numerous years, including you, Vania and the people, who shared your awful fate, were Muslims."

These are the people, who have smeared Islam and stained its image. It's become a shameful fact that terrorism has become an Islamic enterprise; an almost exclusive monopoly, implemented by Muslim men and women. Muslims right now are at the center of 14 global wars. What they did in America on September 11, 2001, that killed 3000 people at once is unthinkable. All this happened, Vania, and you didn't hear about any of it living here where there is no communication with the world, but the crime never stopped."

"It's better that I don't know about these crimes. I have enough pain to last me the rest of my life, but I know from the history in old times that more people of all nations have been massacred in the name of religion. Christians killed millions during the Crusades. Torturing and killing in the name of any religion is pure evil."

"I know, but now new radical groups are infesting the world and they are the ones committing these monstrosities. Will the world ever be free of the barbaric crimes committed in the name of Allah? Even we Russians, who are the first paymasters and creators of the PLO, and the weaponry source of choice for many Arab nations, cannot escape this fate, because, ultimately, we are all infidels, and the crimes will continue until people realize that they will all be judged by one God."

They spoke more about cruelty and unjust with the hope that it will eventually be in the past.

CHAPTER 22

In Yekaterinburg, the first trucks were ready to roll. Three men were hired for each truck. Mansur stayed in Yekaterinburg when the first truck left to the forest to hunt around small villages.

In a couple of days, it was reported to Mansur, that the first operation was a success, and the trucks were on the way to Chechnya. At the end of the month, all ten vehicles were operating. More trucks were working in the cities of Budenovsk, Kizlyar and other cities on the roads to Chechnya. Thousands of Chechens fled their destroyed homes and scattered around Russian and other Republics looking for a job or committing crimes. Only a few people stayed to rebuild Chechnya. The Republic needed working hands and material, especially stones and bricks. All the remaining young and healthy men were collecting stones in the mountains.

More profit will come from young, beautiful and shapely women. They will be shipped to America. There is an escort business in New York, where a man can order a particular woman. She will spend time with him and escort him to the functions that wives are not invited.

~

Mansur started learning his father's business from an early age. "Was it love for Allah, or was it a thirst for money?" he thought. "This is our fight and revenge for what they did to us."

190

Major fighting had died down in Chechnya since the second war in 1999, and the separatists were driven from power, but rebel attacks plague the mostly Muslim region. Officially, the war in Grozny was over now. However, the city is still in turmoil.

450 Rebels are still fighting in Chechnya. Since the counterterrorist operation was lunched, between 3,000 and 5,000 people are missing after being abducted. A roadside bomb struck a Russian military armored personnel carrier outside the Chechnya capital in Grozny, and many were dead or wounded.

Russia occupied Chechnya and killed, plundered, and raped our sisters in Chechnya, and then the brothers in Chechnya started a jihad against the oppressor Lunin. The world leader launched a campaign against our brothers and sisters and are suffering from the terrorism of Russians. Who is the real terrorist? Has Muslim blood become so cheap that nobody cares?

"They are fighting with us; we will fight with them," Mansur thought, justifying his actions. The business was operating well, and Mansur went back to his home. From there he called his sister, "Adele, you should come to see the house I'm building, only a few final touches left inside before it's finished. It's four times bigger than the old house. The entrance is from the river's gates. Our father is very pleased with the result. Now you and your children can spend summers here again. Your husband's money helped a lot in my business."

Mansur could now relax on his property and finish building his dream house. His business operation was in full swing. More vehicles were purchased, and the money poured into his and Ali Akmadov's pockets, and 25% was coming from Vladimir's pocket.

"Are you happy with the return? Mansur asked Vladimir when he called his sister to invite her to see the new house."

"I see that the diamond business is working very well and very glad that I made the investment," Vladimir replied.

CHAPTER 23

Andrey was watching Vera's belly growing and decided it's time to marry her. "But before I do, I better make a call to Vladimir and tell him about the news. He dialed the number.

"Vladimir, guess what?"

"What are you up to, my brother?"

"I want to ask you to be a Godfather to my child."

"What child?"

"In a month, Vera is going to give birth to our child."

"I didn't know that your girlfriend is pregnant, why didn't you tell me before?"

"Why should I, you don't tell me about details in your life."

"So, are you going to marry this Vera?

"You asked me to tell you, so I'm informing you that Vera and I are going to get married, and we have a child on the way."

"Ah so, then, we have to celebrate the event, my brother."

Vladimir thought to himself, "Damn it, I knew that my brother would do something stupid; he never was smart and needs to be watched all the time." Vladimir was sitting in his office, "I didn't only have this to ponder about with Andrey and his child. Who is this Vera? She must be the same as Andrey without any brains. I need to check it out."

He didn't waste time to find out about Vera by sending detective Tihonov to investigate her.

"Am I paying you good enough, detective?"

"Yes, you are paying me good money, I'm satisfied."

"I believe you can soon retire and fly to your permanent vacation, but before you do, I need you to do one more job. I'll visit you tomorrow afternoon."

"I'll be here, waiting for you."

Like always, Vladimir executed his plans right away. The next morning he was sitting in detective's office to talk face to face.

"This time I'm inquiring about my brother, and his pregnant girlfriend, Vera. Find out who is she, what relationship she has with Andrey. Find out everything about her and be careful."

"Don't worry, so far you've been satisfied with my work. I'm always careful and creative as you've requested."

The detective and his agents found out a lot. She was in her last month of pregnancy and it was easy to spot her. She often left her apartment with a young man resting her hand on his arm, but it was not Andrey. As they found out, it was her neighbor Lev Kruglov, who lived with his sister on the same floor across from Vera's apartment. His agent obtained many photographs of her with Lev, and the detective showed them to Vladimir.

"My brother is a total idiot. He is going to marry Vera and have a strange baby. Hundreds of millions of dollars will be shared and wasted on Vera, another piece of trash, because the baby is not Andrey's, but Vera's boyfriend Lev and my dummy brother is thinking that it is his child. I thought that she is without brains, but she has more brains than my brother. What a smart cookie this Vera and my brother is a dummy. My family is a bunch of idiots, starting with my father when he married his Swan. Then my stupid sister, and now one more insufficient. I will show you marriage idiot."

Vladimir didn't waste any time to call Peter at the Tobacco Shop.

"I need a 'wet specialist'. I'll pay you $10,000 in cash."

"No problem, but first put the $10,000 in my account."

193

"Five now and five after."

"Agreed."

Vera was often short of money because she couldn't work for Dealers anymore and she lived on money Andrey was giving her. She also shared the money with Lev, who was making movie shooting his pregnant Vera in different stages of her pregnancy in her home and outside.

That day, she came to Disco Club to remind Andrey about their marriage and get more money from him.

"Vera I don't think we will make a big deal of it. We will just simply get married, and when the child is born, and we will celebrate both events same time."

"That would be all right as long as we get married right away. I want our child to have his father's name."

She left, and Lev met her around the corner to walk her home.

That visit was also photographed and reported to Vladimir. When Vladimir saw pregnant Vera with Lev, Vladimir knew it was time for action. "The stupid one that only a grave can kill," everybody knows this expression in the Russian language, and it is true for Vladimir.

No one was required to pay an admission fee to enter the club because there was a bar and anyone could come and have a drink to watch the dancing crowd. However, to use the dancing floor, people were required to pay.

The 'specialist' visited the club a few times before, and it was easy to find were Andrey's office was. When nobody was watching him, he opened the door on the left of the office and found a spacious storage room. The room was full of furniture and other things like big light fixtures and holiday decorations on the shelves, and it was very easy for a person to hide in this room.

He came to the club, in the evening before the club was closed and hid in the dark room behind the furniture. The door to the storage room was next to Andrey's office, and both doors were facing the bar and dancing floor. From there he could see what was going on in the big hall through a small opening in the door.

Andrey usually was the last one to leave the club. When the last worker locked the entrance door behind him, the 'specialist' knew that they were alone. He slowly put gloves on his hands and took out his gun. Quietly, he left his hiding place and stood behind the office door, being aware of every sound in the office. He knew that the room is not big, and the desk was facing the door.

Andrey was finishing his paperwork and was going to leave soon. He got up from his chair and at that moment the 'specialist' rushed into the office and pointed the gun at Andrey.

"Who are you, how did you get here? Don't hurt me. I'll give you all money I have, just don't hurt me."

The 'specialist' didn't bother to answer; he held the gun pointing it at Andrey, walked to the back of his chair and made him sit down. With one hand, he held the gun to Andrey's head, and with another hand, he opened the drawer and pulled out Andrey's gun. "That is usually where guns are hidden."

Andrey was resisting by trying to push the chair back, but the 'specialist' didn't prolong the agony, after all, he was a 'specialist.' He pushed Andrey on his back and held him down, so Andrey's head was pressed into the deck. Andrey tried to pull his head back up and tried to grab the gun, but 'specialist' was in a better position and did what he was paid to do.

"Get off me," Andrey shouted. He fought the attacker by twisting his body and pushing with his legs, but the criminal was much stronger than him. Pressing Andrey harder to the desk with one hand, using his other hand, he managed to put the gun in Andrey's hand and held it pointing to the side of his forehead and pressed the trigger. There was a loud bang. Andrey's head dropped onto the desk and blood slowly ran out of his skull. Nobody heard the gunshot behind closed doors.

Then the 'specialist' positioned Andrey's hand with the gun in it to make it appear that he committed suicide. He fixed the papers on the deck and returned to the storage room.

He handled it very professionally, and it took him only two minutes to kill a person he didn't know. He didn't care in the slightest way because it was his job and he was paid to do it. The killer spent the whole night in that storage room peacefully sleeping on the floor until morning.

The next day, when the club was full of people, the 'specialist' left the storage room without being noticed.

Around noon, police notified Vladimir that his brother Andrey committed suicide in his Disco clubs office.

"Oh, no, not my brother. How did it happen? My brother wasn't suicidal," Vladimir exclaimed as he played his role perfectly.

"There will be an investigation, Vladimir Michailovich, but for now, all evidence indicates that your brother killed himself. We will look into seeing if somebody was threatening him or demanded money."

"Did you find a suicide note or anything that might point to what made him take his life?"

"No, he didn't leave any notes, the safe in his office is untouched and office in general in order."

"What's happening in our family, when will it stop? I'm losing them one by one."

"I understand your frustration, too many deaths in your family happened in such a short time. I offer you my condolences Vladimir Michailovich."

When Oksana died, her body was cremated, and the ceremony of burial was private. Only the two brothers attended her funeral. Andrey still was alive at that time. Her tombstone was placed next to her mother and fathers.

Now, Andrey also was dead and his coffin was in the funeral house. The Disco club workers were shedding tears. A young, beautiful woman in the last month of her pregnancy, dressed in black was standing on her knees with her head and arms on the coffin cover. She cried while saying the last goodbye to her dead boyfriend.

"I'm being punished for cheating and now lost Andrey and his money, and soon I will have a child with a penniless wannabe movie producer."

She cried, and cried, and everybody sympathized with her except Vladimir. He knew the truth about the child, and if she wants to pretend that that child is Andrey's, he has photographs of her and her boyfriend, Lev. It's too late to argue because Andrey is not here anymore.

Vera didn't argue, and on the next day, she got a check in the mail for $5,000 from Vladimir Michailovich for her tears.

Andrey was buried next to his mother, father, and sister. Only Vladimir and his loyal detective, Tihonov, were present at the burial. When they were silently standing and watching Andrey's coffin lowered into the ground, the detective remembered the words of a philosopher, "Ambition and greediness often puts men upon doing the meanest offenses, so climbing is performed in the same posture as creeping. The filthy rich man is not better than the creeping creature at his feet."

On his way home from the cemetery, Vladimir thought, "Now I know how my father felt when he was a multi-billionaire, and we were small people around him. He was a giant, and we all looked at him with the hope that one day we will rise to his high level. But there was too many of us, and we would never be at his height. Finally, I know what my father felt, and it feels good to be rich. It will be printed in newspapers that I'm Vladimir Michailovich Rennin the only one still alive from the family which fortune didn't protect from death.

197

CHAPTER 24

"My business is booming," Mansur thought. "But after I pay 25% to Vladimir and half of 75% to my partner, Ali Akmadov, I have only 37.5%, when I'm the one who does the job, and I am the one who is taking the risk.

It's not just, and it shouldn't work like this. Vladimir is a greedy man. Isn't he ashamed to take 25% of my money after he became so wealthy? He got all inheritance to himself, and still not enough."

The angry thoughts were crowding together in his head, and he was searching for a solution. The more he thought about it, the more he hated the greedy Vladimir.

"You are a shameless bastard. I'm not going to give you any more of my money; I'll send you where you belong.

"If you weren't my sister's husband, you would work like every infidel in the quarry. You fulfilled your role, and now I can do it without you."

Mansur's mind was clarifying the picture.

"Adele is the wife of a new Billionaire, Vladimir, who is the son of a dead Billionaire. His father, Laura, Oksana and Andrey are also dead, so all the money now belongs to Vladimir. In something happens to Vladimir, everything is transferred to Adele, his wife, and her children. Billions of dollars and it growing; is that a fortune, or what?" Mansur was calculating.

"I believe that all those deaths are not an accident. Vladimir thought of a way to get rid of them, and now after he inherited all the family fortune, he is getting a big portion of my small business. He is a clever guy, but I'm smarter than him. I don't need to rush. I will suppress my thoughts for now. I will take a little vacation and go to Chechnya to my new house."

"Adele," he called to his sister, "Come with me to Chechnya and leave the children at school in Moscow. Our aunt will take good care of them like always, and besides, your husband is too busy for you right now. Our father doesn't feel well, and he wants to see you too."

"Is the Airport in Grozny working fine?"

"Yes, from there we will fly by helicopter to our new house."

Vladimir was a very busy man, and Adele did whatever she pleased. She just told Vladimir that she is going to visit her father because he is lonely and doesn't feel well.

After all the stress Vladimir had with the burials, he was glad to be left alone.

The helicopter landed on the marked circle outside of the stone wall behind the river, and a golf cart drove them with their luggage through curved bridge built over the fast running river and rolled through the iron gates which opened for them to enter.

A big orange colored house struck the attention of Adele. She saw the construction of the house before when she was visiting her father with the children, but for the first time saw it completed.

"It's a beautiful and huge the house, Mansur. I like the arches with the columns up to the second floor; it looks like a monument. What did you do with the old house? I hope you didn't destroy it."

"It's still there, behind the new one."

"The garden is so beautiful, Mansur."

The small, yellow gravel pressed on the roads trimmed with short green bushes. A lot of gigantic trees in different shapes with clay jars decorated the yard.

Adele walked behind the new house and saw the old house where she was born and where her father still lives.

"It looks so small compared to the new one."

"Before you see father in his old house, let's go inside the new one, I want to show you what I built."

He opened the door, and Adele ran inside. The floor was made of brown and white checker patterned marble; four brown columns connected by three arches supported the balcony of the second floor.

The tall, but narrow windows rounded with pointed tops in which the glass was divided into many sections creating a Middle Eastern motif, and the ceiling at the entrance was open to the roof with modeling of a small design through all the ceiling. The walls were covered by ornaments with inserts of panels with blue and white tiles.

"This is a wonderful house, Mansur. It's gorgeous and reminds me of a mosque; only a minaret is absent," She giggled. "I like the open floor and walls with a Middle Eastern traditional design."

There were two staircases on the sides of the entrance with iron railings that led to the second floor. Adele, in one breath, ran to the top.

"Where is my room, Mansur?"

"Your rooms with the children's rooms are on your left."

"The red curtains are beautiful, and my bed is so pretty too." Adele jumped on her bed and spread her arms lying on her back. Then she examined the other antique furniture carved from wood with intricate decoration sofas with many bright colored pillows. The very heavy ornamented, hand carved round tables with several framed photographs of many generations of their family, silver pitchers and many small items like encrusted boxes, decorative plates, and antique vases.

"Mansur, you thought of everything to the smallest details; even the bright color fabric on stools is an excellent choice. You have wonderful taste. The rugs on the parquet floor are just magnificent."

Satisfied with her brother's choices, she went to see the children's rooms.

"The right side of the house is even bigger, as you will see. Someday, I will have a wife and kids, so I built it for them, but for now, I'll be here alone."

"I'm so glad that your business with diamonds is doing well so that you could build this huge expensive house, but you are so busy Mansur with work and building the house that you will never find the time to find a wife for yourself."

"That is my business to worry about, Adele."

"And father, will he stay in the old house?"

"He got used to the old place and doesn't want to move. The kitchen and all staff are living in the old house. Now, there will be enough room for everyone."

Then they walked to see their father, who was now seventy years old and his health wasn't good anymore. He was sitting next to the window on the second floor and looked at the solid iron gates in front of the house, and farther to the valley and mountains behind the stone wall.

"I remember Papa, when you build the stone wall, I think I was eleven that time, and it was an empty field around our house, and see how beautiful the new house looks."

"It's all Mansur's doing."

"Mansur is smart; he looks after me. He is real Muslim, and I'm proud of him."

Adele and Mansur left father and walked in the garden. There was no trace of the old grounds. A green carpet of grass covered all ground, and gravel covered the walkways that led to benches around the garden.

They walked between green bushes and through the big gate made of curved iron trimmed with the same stones as the wall and went all the way to the river. They sat on the large stones lining the shoreline of fast running water and Adele thought about how her children will enjoy playing here, and Mansur thought how to get richer and make his father even more proud of him.

Adele went to the house and brought the camera with her to take pictures of the new house so she could show it to Vladimir and the children at home. And they photographed themselves in the garden next to the bushes growing against the wall.

"Adele, you enjoy the fresh air, and I'll go to my office in the house to work."

From his office, Mansur called to find out if the delivery was done, the merchandises were sold, and the money was in his account. The next party was expected tomorrow. "Good, bring more," he thought.

The old ones would say that appetite grows while you are eating.

The idea once entered his mind and grew bigger with every minute. His obsession and desire to be rich motivate him to execute his plan and thought that Adele's children will be raised in the Muslim religion. He thought, "The less number of infidels in the world, and especially in our family, the better." He stayed another week with his father and sister and left for Moscow to execute his plan.

Since the war in Chechnya began, thousands of young men were ready for any job as long as they could make their living. It doesn't matter to them if it is building or killing. Death in their minds is not the end of life. Their entire philosophy is the value of mortality after death.

"It is better that Adele will be far away and not involved or suspected of anything. The best way to get rid of him is to hire a suicide bomber. Somewhere on the road, or even more simple, in a restaurant, I better leave it to the executor."

And it didn't take long for Mansur to find one. The older brother encouraged his 19-years-old brother to blow himself in order to kill the infidel. His brother said that Allah would give him twenty virgin wives after his death. So they named the bomber, 'the 19'.

Mansur's people were watching every step Vladimir made outside of his business building and his home. A week later, Mansur got the phone call.

"Mansur, the Subject, as Vladimir was labeled, is at a restaurant in Metropole with a male party. His table is next to the window, and I can see him from Pokrovka Street. He is wearing a navy blue suit, white shirt, and a yellow with white stripes tie."

"Good, bring 'the 19'."

In a few minutes, 'the 19', dressed in a business suit with buttoned jacket, walked into the restaurant and took the table close to Vladimir's. He was pretending that he was reading the menu while examining the Subject with yellow and white stripes tie.

After he was sure that he is the right one, he slid his hand inside his jacket and quickly jumped from his chair and rushed to Vladimir's table. A massive explosion like a ball of fire shook the building. People who were in the center of explosion just disintegrated in the blast.

The explosion was so big that people with their tables and chairs were blown far away and hit the walls. There was a huge fire in the hall. The broken glass from the upper floors was falling down, and debris was flying in the air spreading in every direction.

The blast hit the pedestrians outside, and bodies were everywhere. From the other side of the street, people were running and screaming in a panic, covering their heads with their hands, afraid that whole building would collapse.

A white cloud of smoke still was blocking the view when the fire engine arrived and put out the fire.

The broken glass from the windows and the flying debris injured many pedestrians on the road. Bodies of dead people were scattered all around. The air filled with the screams and moans of injured people. Ambulances were attending the injured and picked up the dead. Police surrounded the large area around the explosion site, keeping the curious out and started the investigation, but there was nothing to investigate. It was evident that the explosion was not accidental such as a gas leak. It was bomb intentionally detonated to kill people.

The news didn't reach Vladren, the Architectural Firm until the next morning. They learned about the explosion on the evening news in their homes and that their boss and the party, who had dinner with him in the restaurant, were missing. They suspected that Vladimir Michailovich died in the blast because his secretary arranged the dinner for her boss at that restaurant.

An employee said, "He got what he deserved. What about Adele? Was she there too?" Mansur called his sister to tell her that her husband died in an accidental explosion, which took place at a restaurant two days ago.

"What did you say, Vladimir is dead?"

Adele dropped the phone on the floor and screamed in a loud voice, but nobody could hear her except the people who worked for them in the house.

"She will get over it very soon. Especially when she learns how rich she is now," Mansur thought and hung up the phone.

When the shock passed, Adele went to see father and told him about the accident. "Inshallah" (God's willing), as Muslims will say. "Allah must have done justice," father thought, "Allah is always just." But he used other words to comfort his daughter,

"We are all in the hands of Allah, my dear. I believe that my illness is the punishment that I didn't pray enough to Allah." It sounded right for both of them in their native Chechen language.

The next day, Adele flew to Moscow, and Mansur came to her apartment to comfort his sister and the children. Adele was devastated by the accident. She even didn't have the body of her husband to cry over.

"We are all in the hands of Allah."

"That's the same thing father told me,"

Some time passed before she could talk to people. She contacted the Vladren Firm, which was now hers and asked them to continue the business as usual until she figured out what to do with the firm. She hadn't realized yet that the oil fortune now belongs to her.

The radio, television, and newspapers were full of news about Rennin's family tragedy. It was enough news for the whole week, but only the news didn't reach the little house in Siberia in the range of Suntar Hajata.

CHAPTER 25

The winter was in full swing again. The snow covered the big empty field in front of the house. Michail used his wheelchair to move around the house and gradually started to use his new crutches, one short step after another. He was becoming more mobile, but it was too early to go out on the snow. He did small jobs such as helping dry the dishes with a towel when Mariya washed them after the meals and helped Sasha with his studying. Earlier, Ivan brought all books inside that were on the plane. Michail and Sasha often read a book together, alternating reading aloud.

Little by little, Michail's legs became stronger, and one day when the weather was calm, after Ivan cleared the snow, Michail was able to walk out for the first time after almost two years. He bent over and picked up a handful of snow, made a snowball and threw it far away. Sasha, Ivan, and Mariya joined him, and laughter was filling the air. They rolled big snowballs and built a snowman together. After that, they had a nice meal and celebrated their simple life.

The family met the New Year of 2006 with happiness because Misha was able to walk as and was healthy.

Finally, the snow started to melt from the warmth of the sun.

The spring was slowly arriving to warm the cold land. Buds were blooming on black branches. The air was full of the forest's sweet aroma. Michail felt reborn waking up in this new land. In his mind, he often traveled to a far away time in Moscow. He focused on every member of his family and was full of expectations.

The time was approaching to thank the gracious people that helped him and move on.

"One day Vania, I have to leave you, I have a family far away, and they don't know that I'm alive."

"Misha, we knew that this day would come, and we accept it, though it will be empty here without you."

"Vania, I'll never permanently leave you. I'll always be with you, and Mariya, and Sasha. I promise I'll be back. You gave me my life back, and that was the most precious gift I ever received in my life." Michail got so emotional that Ivan stood up from his chair, and they hugged like two brothers.

Late May, the sun melted the last of the snow and the time came to ask Vania for one more favor. After dinner, Michail said, "Vania, two long years have passed and because of your and Mariya's gracious help, I'm standing on my feet, and I'm capable of walking a long distance. Can you walk me to the closest place where I can use a telephone?"

Ivan was expecting this request, and simply asked, "When would you like to go?"

"I would like to see what is still on the plane and say a final goodbye to my unfortunate friends, and after that, we can go."

"Then tomorrow we will go to the plane and the next day Mariya will prepare food for our trip. We will pack supplies because we need to sleep in the forest."

"How many kilometers to Okhotsk - Isn't that where we are going?"

"It's about hundred kilometers, but we will walk only a half of it. When we reach the Ohota River, we will board a boat that will take us to Okhotsk.

"I know I'm asking so much, but..."

"Don't worry about it, Misha, you are my brother, and I want to help you."

Next day they all went to the plane. The air was chilly, but the snow that hid the plane had melted. Michail saw what remained of his plane.

"It is injured as I was," Michail said with sadness in his voice, touching the plane.

"Here is the grave of your friends." Ivan walked Michail toward the wooden crosses that marked the spot.

They stood in silence for a few seconds to pay respect to the victims of bad weather.

"They were good people, why did they have to die?"

"Nobody knows their fate."

The small ladder Ivan built to remove the bodies was still there and they climbed inside. Everything was familiar to Michail but seems as though it was from a different life that now is only a vague memory. They got back on the ground, and once again, stood for a few minutes paying their respect to those that didn't survive the crash. Michail loudly pronounced their names they said a final farewell. They returned to the house to prepare for tomorrow.

In the morning, the food was ready for them. Michail packed his personal things and items he retrieved from the plane that belonged to the other three men to give them to their families. He hugged Mariya with a brother's love, and then he put his hands on the shoulders of 10-year-old Sasha, and said with a smile, "The day will come and you will have your own ship, Capitan." Then he hugged him as father would. "Don't cry, I'll see you soon, Sasha, very soon, I promise."

Sasha and Mariya stood outside the house and waved to them until they vanished behind the trees.

They walked all day along the stream which became a small river with small rapids and continued to walk the river's edge until they reached a small cabin. They used pocket knives to cut off branches from pine trees and lie down on them. They wrapped themselves in blankets and put more pine branches on top of them to keep warm and slept through the night.

"I wonder Vania, who built this shelter, was it you?" Vania only smiled instead of answering. In the morning, they made a fire and boiled water from the river then ate some of the food Mariya prepared for them.

Michail was following Ivan and they pulled a small boat out from under the brush that was carved from a tree trunk and dragged it to the water. With two sticks shaped like paddles, they started their descent down the river. After traveling a few kilometers, the calm river turned into rapids. It was hard to keep the vessel in an upright position, but it wasn't long before the river got wider and returned to calm water. In six hours, they were in Okhotsk.

They hid the boat although it was useless now, because Ivan couldn't go back by boat against the rivers flow. They walked to the post office where public telephones are located. Ivan sat on a bench while Michail went to a booth to make phone call.

"Rennin Corporation, may I help you?"

"Hello, is this Svetlana?" Michail recognized the voice of young receptionist.

"Yes, who am I talking to, please?"

"Svetlana, I'm happy to find you still working there and glad to hear your voice. Please don't panic - this is Michail Alexandrovich Rennin calling."

He heard the sound of the phone dropping.

"You are alive, Michail Alexandrovich," Her voice shook.

"Please don't drop your phone again. Yes, I'm alive and well. I was in a plane crash, but I survived, and a family saved my life. I was recovering for two years at a house in a deep forest. Svetlana,

I need to talk to an official person who is in charge of helicopters. I need it immediately to get to Okhotsk."

"Michail Alexandrovich, I'm transferring you to the executive director, Anton Sergeevich Titov, you must remember him."

After the shock had worn off from finding out that Michail was alive, Anton Sergeevich said that two helicopters would be on its way in a minute.

Michail and Ivan went to the assigned area where helicopters could land, set on a bench and here Michail decided that the time came to tell Ivan the truth about himself.

"Vania, I couldn't tell you about myself before now because it wasn't right time, but you need to know that I'm not just a geologist and engineer, I'm very wealthy man. I'm rich beyond your imagination. The oil field in Magadan where I was flying two years ago belongs to me."

"Ooh, no."

"It's all true, Vania. I'm very rich man."

Vania didn't express his excitement because it was hard to believe that Misha is a rich man, he was just Misha a minute ago, who fell from the sky, and suddenly he is a rich man.

"I don't know what to say, Misha," Ivan said, "I think I will now have to address you as Michail Alexandrovich."

"I'll always be Misha for you, Vania."

Ivan still was staring at Michail with surprise in his eyes.

"What you just learned about me doesn't make me a different person."

"Being rich made you accustomed to good things and what we offered you was so little."

"Don't think this way, Vania. You gave me what you had. If a man gives the last of what he has, he has given everything."

"You are good man, Misha, and I'm glad I met you in my life."

"It's true, Vania that money is a bottomless sea in which honor, conscience and the truth may be drowned, but there is a vast difference in one's respect for the man who has made it himself, and the man who just has money. I didn't inherit it, it took a sharp mind and a considerable amount of effort, and may be luck, but I did it myself. There is no difference between the two of us in that respect. It doesn't matter what I possess and what you do not. Material items are trivial. It's the soul that matters. That is what the most valuable thing in the world. In that aspect, you are richer than many people on the earth and your kind soul is the treasure."

Their conversation was interrupted by the noise of the approaching helicopter.

Ivan felt a sudden sadness saying goodbye to his closest friend for the last two years. It's always hard to say goodbye, but at the same time, he felt satisfaction in his heart that he had an opportunity to do something good in his life.

They spend the last three hours sitting on a bench together and in a few minutes, Michail will be gone.

The helicopter slowly landed on the field.

"Let me hug you, Misha, one for the road," Ivan raised on his feet.

"I better go back before it gets dark; Mariya and Sasha are waiting for me."

"You don't need to rush, Vania, this helicopter will take you to Mariya and Sasha."

"But you need it for yourself."

Another helicopter was heard quickly approaching the landing field.

"There, you see, that one is for me."

"Oh, I believe now that you are a very wealthy man, Misha."

They hugged as brothers and Misha walked Ivan to the helicopter.

"Kiss them both for me, will you? I'll be back, Vania. I'll be back, my brother." Michail shouted in Ivan's ear, "Just wait for me. I'll be back."

"Goodbye, Misha. Go to your family. They have been waiting for you for a long time," Ivan shouts.

Vania flew to Mariya, and Michail took his flight to Magadan.

~

The news about Michail Alexandrovich spread with the speed of lightning. At the headquarters, all the office workers were waiting for the helicopter to arrive. When Michail stepped out of the helicopter and stood on the ground, he was met by a big crowd, greeting him with applause. Everybody ran to greet their boss who miraculously appeared after being dead for almost two years. But he was very much alive and well.

The workers loved and respected Michail Alexandrovich and after the tragic news about his death, they decided to preserve his office as it was when he was alive. They walked him to his office. The kind gestures of his workers made him even closer to them than he was before the accident.

He sat at his desk and addressed to the people standing at the door, "I'll be as kind to you as you have been to me, I promise."

The simple words were met with a loud roar from the ecstatic employees.

When everybody left his office, he thought, "Vania should be home by now," and soon after, it was reported to him that Ivan was safely arriving at his home.

"Mama, what is that noise outside?" Mariya looked out the window.

"Oh my goodness, it's a helicopter."

"How did they find us and who are they?" Her heart pounded in her chest. "Vania is not here, what do they want?"

The helicopter slowly descended to the empty field in front of the house. Sasha began to run to the door, but Mariya stopped him. Then she saw Vania, walking from the helicopter toward the house. Her jaw dropped. "Men don't always fall from the sky; sometimes they walk." Sasha bent down to be cautious of the roaring propeller blades and ran to his father. Vania turned to the pilot and gave him a salute. The helicopter lifted off the ground and flew away.

"Papa, how did you get in a helicopter?" Sasha shouted in excitement, skipping all the way to the house.

They walked in, and Mariya looked at Ivan with a question in her eyes.

"Mariya, you can't believe, what Michail is turned to be."

"Vania, what are you talking about?"

"He is a rich man."

"He gave you the helicopter to bring you home?" Sasha said with surprise and excitement, "He must be very rich."

"I've seen how rich people live and the big houses they have, but to have a helicopter of his own, it still hard to believe."

"It's his own? Wow!" Sasha was astonished.

"Yes, and not just one, he has two, Mariya. Can you believe it?"

"Where did he get money to buy helicopters?"

"He owns oil fields in Magadan."

"Oil fields, but to own fields, you need a lot of money to buy them."

"You forgot that he is a geologist and an engineer, he is a very well-educated man, and he calls me his brother," Ivan said and looked at Mariya and Sasha with a smile and tears in his eyes. "Looks like, we've had the privilege to know a very a rich man personally."

"A rich man fell from the sky," Sasha said laughing.

"Sasha, don't talk like that about Michail. He is rich, but I respect him as a very good person."

After the excitement had cooled down, life in the mountains went back to the routine of working days. There's much to do in the short summer.

~

Michail sat quietly at his desk. The changes in the past few days occupy his mind. The house in the mountains, the family he just left, the crashed plane, the graves of his friends, the greeting his employees; it was all crowded his mind. Little by little, his mind started to focus on business. He called the executive director, Anton Sergeevich Titov, and asked him to join him in his office to bring him to update.

When Anton Sergeevich walked in, he thought, "I don't know where to begin. I have two things in my mind."

"Anton, first, I want to ask you how the company managed without me and then please contact my family. They didn't hear from me for two years, and this will be the exciting news for them."

For a few hours, they discussed business and Michail was pleased with the company situation. It was prosperous, and the profit tripled from two years ago. Oil prices are higher, and the profit margin is bigger. Also, there was new drilling, and the wells are producing an enormous amount of oil.

"I couldn't be happier to find my company in such good condition, Anton. Thank you for taking care of business, and I thank you for treating the employees the right way."

The conversation about business came to the end, and Michail was wondering why Anton was not leaving his office. He rose from his chair and sat back down a few times.

"Is there anything else do you want to talk about, Anton?"

"Michail Alexandrovich, I don't know how to say it, but did you hear anything about your family?"

"No, I haven't had a chance yet to contact them. I was going to after we finished with business. I don't have a cellular phone yet, so would you be so kind to ask Svetlana to connect me with my son, Vladimir. He must be at home right now because it's late evening in Moscow."

"I better start with Vladimir, he is a man and can easy handle the news about me, then Laura," Michail thought.

Anton nervously covered his mouth with his fingers, stared directly into his boss's eyes, and said in low voice, "He is no longer alive Michail. I'm sorry to bring this bad news to you, but there was an explosion at a restaurant in Moscow two weeks ago, and your son Vladimir died in that explosion. It was an act of terrorism as the officials are saying. I'll bring you the newspapers." Anton saw the blood is leaving Michail face. He stopped to let the words settle.

"There was a story printed every day about it in the last two weeks."

"It happened two weeks ago?" Michail was gasping the air, "Oh God, I was two weeks late to save him. Oh, God, Oh God," Michail groaned in disbelieve.

Anton stood in front of his boss and saw how his face changed. Pale and lifeless, he silently sat at his desk with his head down and eyes closed. Anton walked out of the room and returned with a stack of newspapers, put them on the desk in front of his boss and walked out.

"No one wants to be in the position to tell a father that there is death in the family. It's better that he read it himself and find out the truth from newspapers."

For a long time, Michail was sat motionless and wasn't able to open his eyes. When he finally opened them, in front of him, the newspaper headline was screaming in large black letters.

"The Billionaire Vladimir Michailovich Rennin finds his death in an explosion at a restaurant in Metropole yesterday evening."

It was like a thousand needles pierced his heart at once. First, there was extreme pain, and then it became paralyzed.

"OH, God? It can't be true."

Michail couldn't read any further. He dropped his head into his hands and held it tight, swinging his head from side to side. Groans came out of his chest.

"My smartest son, he was my first child, and now he is dead. Why did I survive to outlive my son? Why did it happen, why?"

Then, he read the article about the explosion that took place two weeks ago. His mind scattered with thoughts, "He was successful and rich, and some people couldn't accept it. Rich people always have enemies. In two years, he made a billion dollars with his Architectural Firm. There must be a mistake in the newspaper; it has to be an exaggeration.

Feverishly, he read the article again, and his face was crying without tears. He was sitting, not moving, in silence for a long time. Images of his son flashed in his mind, jumping in years when Vladimir was a child, a teenage boy, and a handsome man in his business suit, and couldn't visualize him dead. "Oh, God! Vladimir, how did you become a victim? What happened to you? I was so looking forward to having my family back. Oh, My God, why?"

If somebody said it to him, he wouldn't believe it, but the newspaper wouldn't lie. The bold type like burning hot metal was hurting his heart.

He couldn't see this bold letters anymore and pushed the newspaper to aside and he gasped for the air when new headline screamed at him.

"28-years-old Andrey Rennin committed suicide."

"What, Andrey, my son Andrey is dead too? Oh, no. Not my Andrusha." "Noooo it can't be," he shouts.

"It can't be true, my second son, it can't be real, my both sons dead?"

Michail couldn't believe that he lost a second son in a matter of minutes.

"Andrey committed suicide? My little son, why did you do it? What was wrong? Oh, Andrey, Andrey, how did this happen? Why did you take your own life?" Michail was devastated, "I wasn't there for you either."

All Michail could do was sit and sob in astonishment.

Then, he forced himself to read the following.

"28-years-old son, of vanished oil magnate, Michail Alexandrovich Rennin who presumably dies in a plane crash two years ago, was found dead in his office at the Disco Club he owned with a bullet in his brain."

"Bullet in his brain?" Michail heard his own voice.

"It was thoroughly investigation and the experts came to the conclusion that Andrey Rennin committed suicide. The motive is unknown."

Michail dropped his hands to his knees and cried, rocking himself in back and forth motions with his eyes closed not able to absorb the words he just read.

"Andrey, my second son, is dead; both of my sons are dead. I don't have sons anymore. Oh, My God!"

His mouth opened with a silent cry, and he buried his face in his hands. He got up onto his feet, walked to the window and dropped himself back in his chair.

217

"Both of my sons are dead. No, no, it's not possible that I lost two children in one moment."

For a long time, he sat on his chair in front of a stack of newspapers on his desk not able to move.

"Why are there more newspapers on my desk?" he asked himself?

Then he put the newspaper to the side and read another headline in bold letters:

"Young and gorgeous Laura Rennin…"

"Oh, no, ooh no," he cried out loudly.

"…the widow of Billionaire Rennin died in automobile crash."

"Oh no, not Laura," he cried in despair. His face froze in with a crying expression, "Not Laura, not my Laura."

Michail was paralyzed for a moment, not able to take in his mind the words he just read.

His head dropped onto the newspaper, and a loud scream broke the silence of the room. White circles were moving and overlapping each other in the darkness of his closed eyes. He swung his head back, and his body shook as he cried.

Anton was standing behind the door and heard his cry. He never saw a man that could cry that hard. He was going to walk in and comfort the distressed man but decided to let him cry his heart out because tears take the bitterness away.

Michail was trying to recall his wife's image in his mind and couldn't see her.

"Laura, my swan, my beautiful swan." Instead of her image, he saw white bubbles in his tightly closed eyes. He sat swallowing his tears for a long time.

"I rather be dead myself than to lose my children and my wife. Where is Angelica?" With shaking hands, he grabbed

218

another newspaper and brought it closer to his eyes to see better through his gushing tears.

"Where is my Angelica?" he cried.

He pushed the newspaper to the side and found another headline.

"Suicide is in psychiatric clinic #1."

"Oksana Michailovna Rennin...'Aah, Aah,' he cried dropping his head back, covering his face with his hand and with closed eyes, swung back and forth in his chair. "Oksana, my daughter she is dead too?" His body was shaking from crying. He felt ill and wanted to vomit.

He couldn't continue reading anymore.

"What happened to my family? They are all dead. Why are they are all dead? Why? It would have been better if I died in the crash than to lose all of them," he was talking to himself as he sobbed.

When he finally opened his swollen eyes, he continued to read, "….the daughter of the oil magnate Michail Alexandrovich Rennin, who vanished two years ago in a plane crash, committed suicide in a psychiatric clinic."

A sharp pain went through his heart when he read the word 'psychiatric clinic'. "Was it my fault?"

He couldn't read any further. He covered his face with his hand to hold in a horrified scream, and his body began to tremble uncontrollably.

"What happened to my family," he cried. "Why they are all dead? He continued repeating the same questions. "It can't be. This is a mistake. It can't be that all my family is dead." He picked up the newspaper with his trembling hands and continued reading:

"A nurse found her in bed this morning. She was not breathing. She was pronounced dead by the hospital's doctor. The

219

autopsy showed that the patient took a large amount of medication in one dose."

Michail's body bent in half, and his head dropped down on the desk. The heart in his chest was tearing apart and a bitter knot stuck in his throat. Silence and emptiness surrounded him. He couldn't think or absorb all he just read. It was too much for any human to take.

It was dark outside of the windows. He sat for hours not moving. He felt as if a mountain fell on him, pressing on him, and crushing him with its heavy weight. Finally, he got up and lied down on the leather sofa, buried his face in a pillow, and cried like never before in his life.

He didn't hear the door open when Anton walked into the room and found him lying on a sofa.

Anton heard him screaming and crying, but didn't interfere. He thought, "It's better for him to learn on his own about the tragedies that took place in his family in last two years."

Michail didn't sleep all night. He couldn't take the pain inside, understand what has happened or believe it. It's a nightmare, but he wasn't sleeping. At dawn when the first light started to break the dark sky, he fell into a deep darkness of not existing.

After two hours, he opened his eyes. The devastating news of last night about tragedies in his life overwhelmed him. "It's wasn't a dream; it is all true," he said in his mind.

"Is it worse to be dead or to lose a family, everything you love and cherish, or to be in slavery, as Ivan was for eleven years?" He couldn't find an answer.

Yesterday, he was going to fly to Moscow to see his family, but there is no family to fly to now. "I lost them. I lost them all at once. And all it started when my plane crashed during the storm in Siberia. If I wouldn't have flown that day, maybe nothing would have happened, maybe all my children would be alive, but it's too late now, it's too late. Is it worse it to live after I lost everybody I loved?"

The door slowly opened, and Anton Sergeevich poked his head in the doorway. Not hearing an invitation to enter, he walked to the office with the cup in his hand.

"Coffee, Michail, I brought you a cup of coffee."

Michail put his feet down on the floor and sat on the sofa.

"Thank you, Anton." He moved his heavy hand in a gesture of inviting him to sit down. Anton noticed Michail's red swollen eyes.

"Do you know, Anton, anything about my little daughter, Angelica? I can't read any more of the newspapers. What do you know about her? Tell me now."

"There was nothing printed in newspapers about your little daughter, Angelica." Anton shrugged his shoulders. "There has been nothing on the TV news about her, she must be alive, but we don't know anything about her. We live so far from Moscow, but if you go there, maybe you can find her very fast."

Michail took the cup in his heavy hand and sipped his coffee. Then he said with rushed voice, "I need to fly to Moscow; please prepare the jet for me, Anton."

"It's ready for you Michail. Shall I fly with you?"

"Yes, if you don't mind."

"We will fly after breakfast, which is waiting for you in the cafeteria, or would you prefer to have it in your office?"

"I'll go to the cafeteria, thank you."

Svetlana jumped from her chair to say hello and saw the swollen eyes of her boss.

On his way to the cafeteria, a couple of people greeted him with a 'good morning' Michail, and respectfully passed him without any questions. They all knew that he read the newspapers, which were saved for the sake of history. Anton joined him for breakfast, and then a car took them to the airport.

They landed in Yakutsk for refueling and then made a stop in Yekaterinburg before taking off for Moscow. They didn't talk much on the plane. Michail had a lot to think about, and Anton respectfully didn't interfere with his thoughts. The jet safely landed in Moscow.

There was no home to go, so Anton told the chauffeur of the limousine to drive to the new hotel "Europa" on Arbat Street, where he booked a suite on the top floor for Michail to stay for now. Michail requested that Anton stays with him in the suite. Once there, he began searching for the old Butler who worked for Michail before the accident and made the other arrangements to help his boss get back into Moscow.

The news about Rennin being miraculously alive was the main story in all newspapers, radio, and television. Michail didn't want to hear or see the news anymore. His mind was focused on his daughter.

Michail couldn't face the people in Rennin's corporation. He wanted to be left alone for now. His priority was to find his little daughter. "God, please let her be alive, don't take her from me too," he was praying.

He called the detective agency and asked Detective Kazanov, who worked for him before, to visit him in his suite. Kazanov already knew the good news and expressed his happiness to hear from Michail.

"What can I do for you?"

"I need to find my daughter. I don't know anything about her for the last two years - find her for me."

"Give me a couple of days Michail; I'll put my best detectives on it right away, and you will hear what we find out about her very soon."

The press was still covering the news about the miraculous return of Billionaire Rennin. The news spread throughout Moscow with the speed of sound. The newspapers were speculating about his survival in the forest of Siberia, but they could only speculate, because only Michail and Ivan, with his family, knew the truth.

At the end of the second day, there was a phone call from Detective Kazanov.

"Michail, we found your daughter. She is alive and well."

Michail couldn't hold his scream of excitement, "Alive!" All his body started to shake, and he could barely say, "Where is she?"

"She is at Detsky Dom, the orphanage on the Volhonka Street."

"Orphanage, of course, nobody in the family is alive to take care of her. Thank you."

"Anton," Michail yelled, Limousine!"

They jumped into the limousine, and he told to chauffeur to drive to Volhonka Street. They stopped in front of Detsky Dom. Michail jumped out of the vehicle, not waiting for the chauffeur to open the door for him, and took a deep breath.

He walked ahead of Anton and opened heavy door. He found himself in the big hall and heavy set woman walked to greet him.

"Are you Michail Alexandrovich Rennin?" And she walked ahead to her office, suggesting with her hand to sit down.

"Is my daughter, Angelica Rennin, with you here?" His heart was pounding, anxious to see her.

"Yes, she is," as she pulled out a folder with the girl's papers and put it in front of Michail.

"What is this, where is my daughter?"

"It's our policy to have this document signed and to verify the individual before we release a child. We need to compare your blood type with the that of the child."

"Anton, call headquarters to find my personal physician and ask him to bring the records with my blood type immediately. I'm not going to leave this place without my daughter."

It took an hour to receive the paperwork that verified the blood type of Michail Alexandrovich. The heavy set woman compared the types of the blood, and they didn't match.

"What are you saying? Angelica is my daughter."

"The blood work shows that she is not your child, and we can't release her to you."

"Maybe this child has the same name but is not my daughter?" He thought in panic. "But what are the odds that another child would have the same name and be the same age? It's her in the photograph; it's Angelica. She is my daughter, I know, she is. How can I be mistaken?"

He questioned, "Whose signature is on my document, which doctor signed it?"

"Look, it's your doctor's signature. Doctor Reznik, very clear in black letters on white paper," the heavyset woman said in an insulting tone of voice, "This man is telling me that I'm not able to read correctly."

"That is not my doctor. I never saw a doctor Reznik in my life. I'll prove it to you that she is my daughter," Michail rushed his words as he jumped from his chair and ran to his car.

"Whoever did this to me will pay dearly for it."

Anton followed his boss getting in the limousine and couldn't believe the misfortune of this man. Even billions of dollars could not protect a person from tragedy. "Oh, God, this is impossible after all that happened to this poor man, now he has more troubles."

On the way to the hotel, Michail called detective Kazanov.

"Find out why our blood doesn't match."

"The document with my blood is signed by a Doctor Reznik. Who is this doctor? I never was his patient."

In only took a few minutes for the detective to call back, and said, "The doctor worked for the Psychiatric Clinic #1, but he is not there any longer.

"Find this Reznik for me."

The next day, he got the call, "Michail, this is Detective Kazanov. We located Doctor Reznik. He just returned from vacation on Crimean Peninsula. He is the one who admitted Oksana in Psychiatric Clinic #1. We are watching his moves. What would you like us to do next?"

Michail replied, "He has to explain why his signature is on my blood work document when he is not my doctor. Take him in and interrogate him. Find out how he had access to my doctor's file? Also, I need to know, who gave the order to bring my daughter, Oksana, to his clinic and who gave him the order to keep her at that facility."

Detective Kazanov pressured him during interrogation until Doctor Reznik confessed that he was paid by Detective Tihonov, who worked for Vladimir, to make a false blood work document of his dead father, and was asked by Detective Tihonov to diagnose Oksana with mental illness.

"Vladimir is a monster. What possessed him to do such terrible things? Arrest Doctor Reznik and Detective Tihonov immediately; they are criminals and don't belong in society, but first of all, I need to bring my daughter home."

"It's all money," Michail came to the conclusion, "I understand now, why Vladimir did it. I can't believe that my son could rob my daughter, his little sister of her money, but I'll deal with it later, right now, I must get back to the Detsky Dom."

While Detective Kazanov was looking for Doctor Reznik, the same time he sent his agent to find the original document with Michail's blood work.

They found the certificate in the hospital where he was born, and the official report was presented to Detective Kazanov, which proved that the document with the signature of Doctor Reznik was false. After that, Michail signed the required papers and the heavyset woman said, "Follow me, please."

225

Michail's heart was beating so hard that at and any minute it could jump out of his chest.

The voices of children filled the corridor on their way to the hall where he saw about thirty children under ten years old that were playing in a large hall with big windows that allowed the light of the sun to fill the room. His eyes scanned the room looking for a blond head of hair with large curls. And there she was. He couldn't mistake her. She was the one swan in the lake with the others, a copy of her mother.

Michail fell to his knees. The children stopped and became silent, staring in wonder at the strange man on his knees. Michail couldn't say a word. His lips were trembling, and his eyes were full of tears. He got the attention of his daughter and opened his arms. After a brief moment of uncertainty, she ran to him and hugged his neck with her arms. Her gold hair brushed his face, and he held her tight with his trembling body.

"She recognized me. She was waiting for me, my little Angel. She knew I would come," He said to himself with eyes full of tears.

Her head rested on his shoulder. Finally, he got up with Angelica in his arm and carried his 8-years-old daughter to the waiting limousine.

"It was worse," he answered the question he had in his mind about living after losing everyone he loved. "It's worse, my Angel."

On the way home, Angelica's head was resting in father's lap; she was holding him tight with both hands as he stroked her gold curls.

They arrived at the hotel, and Michail asked Anton to hire a private secretary to work for him.

In a few hours, Sergey Sergeevich, his new private secretary, and his assistant, started to build a new life for the father and daughter.

In three days, they moved to a new building which his son Vladimir built in the center of Moscow with a view of the Moscow River. It was a luxuriously furnished two-story penthouse suite which occupied the entire floor. On the floor under their suite, all staff and servants had their quarters.

The time came for Anton to leave his boss and go back to Magadan's family.

Sergey found the Nanny, who was looking after Angelica two years ago and they were reunited with delight. Angelica liked the new life with her father, but she missed the friends she made in the last two years at Detsky Dom, and it was arranged to bring her friends to her home to play with her. She had private teachers who were schooling her at home.

~

The pain of losing the older children didn't go away. Michail tried to find more details about the death of his oldest son, Vladimir, and the answer he kept getting was the same about a terrorist attack, possibly Chechens, without any further explanation. There were many more important people, who died in the same blast and it was hard to say, who the primary target was.

About his younger son, Andrey, he knew even less. Andrey wasn't as smart as his older brother. He lived a fast life; he must have made a mistake and paid for them with his life.

"But to commit suicide, maybe he got in a desperate situation for money, and I wasn't there to help him. Why didn't he ask Vladimir for help? Oh, Vladimir! Oh, Andrey!

If only I could bring him back, I would put him under my wing and protect him, but it's too late. He is gone, my little boy, my Andrusha, as your mama used to call you.

227

What happened to Oksana, she was one of the smartest children in the family? She was a lawyer and worked for me. How did she end up in the psychiatric institution? How did she get there? I need to find out about her death; something doesn't fit right."

He called his private investigator, Kazanov, and asked him to find out who Oksana was involved with before her illness.

It didn't take long to find out that she was dating Kiril Vasilevich Timoshenko, the Financial Vice President of the Rennin Corporation.

"Timoshenko, who I hired myself, dated Oksana? He is a married man with two children and Oksana didn't mind, or she didn't know? How did she get sick? There are so many questions I need to be answered."

Four days passed since Michail arrived in Moscow. He even didn't have a chance to step in the Rennin Corporation headquarters yet.

The next day, Michail arrived there and was greeted by the former president of the corporation, Kiril Vasilevich. He was former now because Michail came back alive. He returned to his position as Vice President of finances.

Before any talk about business, Michail asked Kiril a question that was on his mind, "I heard that you were dating my daughter before she got ill. Tell me what you know, how did she end up in a mentally sick institution?"

"Michail, you are wondering why I was dating your daughter when I was married, but my wife left me and went with our children to Yaroslavl and is staying with her father. I made a mistake not to tell Oksana about my marriage because she got pregnant. I didn't want to make her upset."

"Oksana was pregnant?"

"Yes, I was going to divorce my wife and marry Oksana before our child was born. You were no longer with us, and I even couldn't ask you for your daughter's hand. One day, she didn't return to work after lunch, and I was concerned as to where she was. I called Vladimir and spoke with Andrey, but they didn't know anything about her disappearance. After six weeks, we read in a newspaper that Oksana died from an overdose of medicine. She swallowed a lethal dose of medication at night and was pronounced dead in the morning. It happened in the psychiatric hospital, but why and how she got there, nobody knows.

I loved your daughter, Michail, and I lost her too."

There was much sincerity in his confession, and it sounded as it was the truth.

"I would like to be left alone," said Michail.

When he was alone, Michail called his personal secretary, Sergey and asked him to contact the doctor who was treating Oksana when she was in the hospital, "Tell him that I want to talk to him."

"My car, please," Michail said to the secretary on his way to the elevator. Two bodyguards followed him, keeping themselves at a distance not to be seen. Then they followed the limousine to the Psychiatric Clinic #1.

When he arrived, the door was immediately opened for him, and he was escorted to the doctor's office.

The primary doctor greeted Michail and expressed his condolences. Then he answered all questions Michail asked him.

"I took this position after the previous doctor quite his job. His name is doctor Reznik; Oksana was his patient. I learned about Oksana illness only after her death."

"So, she wasn't your patient?"

"No."

Even Michail knew that doctor Reznik was in police custody. However, he asked, "Where is doctor Reznik now?"

"I heard that he left the country, but nobody knows where he went."

"Tell me, doctor, in your understanding, when you read the history of my daughter's illness, was she that ill to commit suicide?"

"There's a very thin line between a normal condition and a mental illness. But if one doctor can see it clearly, another can see even more."

"She was pregnant, how could she kill herself, and her baby."

"The policy of the mental institution is to terminate the pregnancy before the embryo reached three months."

"So, they aborted her child?" Michail screamed at the doctor. Two huge men showed at the door, and the doctor gave them a sign that everything is under control.

Michail got up from the chair and walked out of the office with a chill in his blood, "If you are not sick and get behind these walls, you can get sick and can be locked in here until your death. Maybe someday I will know more about Oksana's death, but right now, I ran into a wall." His mind was jumping from one thing to another, and it was too much to absorb at once.

After he kissed his little Angel goodnight and went to his bed, he thought about his Laura, "Am I being punished for cutting a fresh flower at its bloom, being only 17, when I married her? I was 47 that time, and I didn't feel that old. But she loved me, and she wanted to marry me. How is it possible to let her go, this mesmerizing beauty. Today she would be 26, in her best years and still very young." Michail closed his eyes trying to see her next to him. "She was so natural, simple, powerful, electrifying, and an erotic Aphrodite. Her silky skin was flawless like white milk with a hint of pink. She awakened my deepest fantasies. Her mesmerizing dark blue eyes with a sparkle of turquoise drew me to her. She was a beauty with coral colored full and beautiful lips; she was my swan-princess. He didn't want to open his eyes and was trying to hold the image of her beauty in his mind, but the more he tried, the harder it was to keep the picture, and soon it dissolved in emptiness when he finally fell asleep.

Detective Kazanov found out what happened the day Laura died.

When Michail woke up in the morning, his first thought was, "She should have asked the driver to take her to her sick mother, but she was in a rush and drove herself. She must have been afraid that she wouldn't see her mother alive, and by driving too fast, she killed herself in an accident. She is with her mother because her mother died before her, and now I'm left alone with little Angelica. Oh, what would I do if I would have lost my Angel too, then it would have been better to be dead. It would have been better if Ivan never rescued me. Angelica is all I have now. Tomorrow, we are going to the graves of our family to put the flowers on the graves of Oksana, Vladimir, Andrey and their Mother. But where is Laura's grave? Nobody mentioned her burial."

Later, he found that Laura's buried at the Danilovskoe Cemetery. Her grave has a simple gray granite stone with her name on it.

"Here is your mama buried my Angel. She is sleeping in her bed here."

"Why did she have to die, Papa?"

"She is alive for us; she will always live in you. Put your flowers on her grave; she used to love flowers - because she was one of them herself."

Angelica put her flowers next to her father's bouquet; he looked at the name Laura Rennin on the gray stone and promised to her, "I'll bring you to be with the rest of the family, and I will build the Mausoleum for you and all Rennins."

They left Danilovskoe and went to the Vagankovskoe Cemetery. They found one row where black granite gravestones the same size were placed. After his first wife, Lyudmila was a

231

space where a stone with his name had been recently removed from an empty grave since he was alive. Michail has a black granite stone put there with Oksana's name even though her body wasn't there. She was cremated to hide the evidence of an aborted child. Next to it were Andrey's stone, and the last one Vladimir's.

He looked at the cold black stones with sorrow in his heart; "I will never see them again." The images of them flashed in his mind. He remembered when their mother was alive, and they were just little children. They loved them all equally. It was such a joy to have them, to raise them, to play with them, and now they are all dead and never will never laugh again.

He remembered the last time he saw all his four children together at the celebration of his birthday. They all were healthy, happy young people and Laura was the light of his soul.

In contrast with that happy time, the pain of sorrow was so sharp, that he thought, "There is no greater grief than remembering days of joy when misery is at hand." To cool himself down, he thought; "Time will pass, and they will live only in our memory. Time is a great comfort to grief, but to live through this period is extremely difficult. He held his tears inside to not show them to Angelica, because it will injure her, and the dead won't know that he is crying.

"Good or bad, they were my children," he thought, walking away with his only one child remaining.

All the way home, his mind didn't let him relax.

"Vladimir is the one who killed Oksana, and he killed her for money because, in my Will, I left 20% for each child and Laura. Vladimir was talking about an expansion of his business. What about Andrey, I don't believe that Andrey killed himself. Is he also was on his way? No, he couldn't do it. Somebody else did it."

Once they got home from the cemetery, Michail called Detective Kazanov to find out with whom Andrey was friendly with the last days before his death. He got the call from Kazanov two days later, "Her name is Vera. They were dating for the last two years. They often traveled together in his car to Frankfurt, Germany, where they purchased cars and drove them to Russia. She has a five month old son and lives on Millionnaya Street."

Michail demanded, "Find out whose child she has and all the contacts she had with Andrey."

The investigation brought them to the Tobacco Shop. Peter and his brother were under the microscope of Detective Kazanov. The business with the cars was uncovered, and they confessed that Vera and Andrey were working with them.

Vera was brought to the police station for questioning and the detective called Michail, "Vera is saying that it is Andrey's child and that he promised to marry her, but instead, he committed suicide."

Michail thought, "Something is not right here. If Andrey knew that he would have a child, why did he suddenly killed himself? And, if it's Andrey's child, why is Vera not after money for the child? This is very unusual behavior. Vera knows that Andrey was rich. I need to find out the truth about the child."

The detective informed Michail, "I have two brothers from Tobacco Shop in custody. We will find the truth. The so-called 'Dealers' are talking."

Peter and his brother were facing a long term in jail, so to reduce the sentence, they confessed that Vladimir asked them to find him the 'wet man.'

When all the evidence of Andrey's death pointed to Vladimir, Michail dropped his head into his hands and thought. "Vladimir killed not only his sister but also his brother. If it is true that he killed his sister and brother, how could he this monstrous act against his own blood? I can't believe that my first born child could do such a thing. "

The bitter feeling of disappointment in his firstborn poisoned him little by little since he learned the truth.

233

"I didn't know my son at all. Was he born a murderer, and from his childhood wore a mask of honesty and sincerity hiding the uncontrollable greediness that possessed him to became a killer after he learned about my death? How manipulative was he to make his younger brother kill himself. For the money, he murdered his sister. My son was a monster and for these crimes he paid the ultimate price of losing his own life. How to do I live with this grief? Now all of them don't feel anything; they even don't know that they are dead. All the pain, like an avalanche with its massive weight, suddenly crashed on my heart. I never will find the answer to why I was punished."

All his emotions were tied into one painful knot: the sorrow, the sadness, the bitterness, the love and disappointment of all that happened-the death. The loss of everyone he loved grew into a lump in his throat that was chocking him; the blood colored tears in his eyes were on the edge of rolling out.

~

He was preoccupied with his thoughts, sitting alone in his empty home, when the telephone rang. He shuddered like suddenly waking up from a deep dream.

"Michail Alexandrovich," as she respectfully called him, "This is Adele. I just learned that you came back to life. I'm so glad and relieved that you are alive. Too much happened in the family. I'm here in Moscow. Can I see you now? I can't bury my grief alone."

"Yes, of course, my dear, come and we will talk."

In a short time, she opened the door and ran toward her father-in-law with open arms.

"Vladimir is dead; somebody killed him. I know someone killed him." She laid her head on Michail's chest, "We need to find who killed him." He hugged her and stroked her long black hair,

234

"We will find the killer, and he will be punished for killing your husband and my son."

Michail thought, "She doesn't know anything about her husband, and it's for best that she finds out. She is a victim of the crime as well."

They set on the sofa next to each other, and Michail saw little faces peeking through the partially open door.

"You brought children with you, Adele. Let me see them." "Come to Grandpa," Michail invited them to the room.

"You are so big Ahmed, and handsome like your mother. How old are you now?"

"I'm 9, and Fatima is 7," He answered for his sister.

Michail kissed them on their heads and said, "Go to play with Angelica, she will be a good company for you while we are talking."

The Children ran out of the room, and Adele said, "Why did he have to die in that accident, why him, now I don't have a husband." She dried her tears as Michail stroked her hair.

"Since Vladimir is dead, I think I will go to live in Chechnya." She reached into her handbag and took out pictures of their house near Grozny and showed them to Michail.

"This is the new house that Mansur built. It's very beautiful and a very big house. It looks like a Middle Eastern Palace. I like it very much. Our father likes the old house better, and he lives there. Now that Vladimir is gone, and the war in Chechnya is over, I think I will move there with the children. Mansur gave us the left side of the house, and it has very spacious rooms. The climate there is better, and the winter is not that cold as in Moscow. In the winter, the temperature sometimes drops to -20 degrees Celsius, but winter is short, and the summer is long and comfortable from 26 to 30 degrees; I think it would be good to raise the children in our Chechens' tradition."

"It's your children, my dear, and you will make the right decision."

"I will leave you the pictures; I have many more of them. It's terrible, what happened in our family and now we all have to live with emptiness in our hearts. I better go now, goodbye Michail," and they hugged before parting. Michail knew that it was a farewell.

CHAPTER 26

Detective Kazanov suspected that it wasn't the end of the crime story, and there were more secrets to discover. Under more pressure, Peter and his brother confessed that they had been asked to give them the "wet man" that killed young women. With this discovery and after checking more details to be sure, he called Michail.

Detective Kazanov said, "I have information about the death of your wife, Laura. It wasn't an accident when she died. She was murdered."

"Murdered?" Michail couldn't believe what he heard. "But who would kill her and why? I wasn't there to protect her." This discovery severely hurt him."

In Michail's head, a picture flashed of the violent attack on the road and Laura, his Laura with her gold hair was the victim. The pain inside was unbearable after he learned that Laura was killed. The detective's voice interrupted his thoughts.

"Peter and his brother confessed that Andrey asked them to give him the "wet man" to kill young women, and they worked together with detective Tihonov."

One pain after another was dropping on bleeding father's heart.

"I believe that the two brothers were working together because it was a plan to take the inheritance of the fourth child," the detective concluded.

"Andrey couldn't kill Laura, he was too weak for that, so it was Vladimir, who dragged his brother into the crime. He used him and killed him after that.

"Just how greedy did my son have to to be to kill? After he knew what was in my Will and what fortune he would have, wasn't it enough?" Michail cried, "Andrey was too vulnerable, it was easy to convince him, and under pressure, he would give away Vladimir. So, Vladimir killed Andrey to keep him silent. Vladimir took a mother from an innocent child, and he robbed me of my wife," Michail took a deep breath.

"Ah, my son, he thought of himself as a great man, but he came up with his own idea of greatness. He must have had a very low standard of it in his mind. He wanted to take the throne. But thrones are uneasy, and crowns are always stuffed with thorns."

Detective Kazanov kept silent and just listened.

"Vladimir committed a monstrous act of killing his family and for that, he paid with his life. But who killed him?"

Detective Kazanov was guessing. "Maybe somebody else in the family?"

"Call me when you find out more about all my family."

"I will."

Michail's mind was scattered with thoughts, "I won't stop until I find why you are dead, Vladimir. I believe it wasn't an accident, and you were the last one in the chain of killing. Everything that happened to our family makes me think that you were murdered for what you have done or for your money. Who could kill for money? Only one person could get the money after his death, and it is his wife, Adele. Could she kill her husband, the father of her children? No, I don't think so, but then who killed you?"

Suddenly a thought came to his mind, "The detective hinted that maybe somebody else in the family was involved.... Mansur, Adele's brother! Of course, who can be else?"

238

Michail called to Detective Kazanov to inquire about Mansur Abu-Khan.

Obtaining information would be difficult because Mansur wasn't in Moscow. But he found that Mansur had a bank account in Grozny.

"Take some people with you and fly to Grozny. The city is destroyed, but I believe that the bank is still functioning."

"We will start right away, and we will find him," Michail. "I think I will divide people into two groups. One group will watch the airport, and the other will watch the bank."

"Be invisible and wait because one day he will come to the bank."

"We will fly tomorrow."

A week later, Mansur arrived in Grozny from Yekaterinburg. The detectives were watching for him to make a move.

From the plane, Mansur got in a helicopter and took off.

The detectives followed the helicopter by road in cars. It was about 40 kilometers from Grozny when the helicopter landed.

There was a stone wall surrounded a huge piece of property. A brightly colored big house could be seen on the other side of the wall, and a smaller house was behind it.

It was impossible to get inside the walls, so three detectives led by Detective Kazanov hid in the mountains and watched for any activity with binoculars.

They saw two small children running and playing in the yard. A young woman with long black hair was talking to them as she pushed an old man in a wheelchair through the garden. People were walking from the house to the river where they were rinsed clothes, and then they returned to the house. They saw Mansur a few times in the yard. Nothing unusual happened inside the walls for two days, but on the third day, the suspect left the property and flew by helicopter back toward Grozny.

"Let's move," detective Kazanov gave the command to his crew. They ran to the road, got in their vehicles, and followed the helicopter at a safe distance as not to be seen.

The helicopter landed on an empty field next to the road where a vehicle was parked.

"There he is, in a blue jacket, getting into a Jeep,"

The Jeep met a caravan of trucks which was coming from the north, and they headed toward Grozny. There were five trucks in the caravan that looked like military vehicles. The vehicles drove to the outskirt of the city and stopped in front of a factory building that was destroyed by the war.

The detective and his crew positioned themselves so they were not seen.

The door in the building opened, and two men dressed in gray color clothes approached the first vehicle.

Through binoculars, they could see six blindfolded people jumping down from the door on the back of the truck with their hands tied behind their backs, and they were walked to the door of the building. Then more blinded people were escorted to the door from the other four trucks. They all disappeared behind the door. Two men in gray clothes walked inside and secured the door with the metal bar and a padlock.

Detective Kazanov was watching as the Jeep and the trucks were leaving.

"These people were kidnapped, and Mansur Abu-Khan is behind it," detective Kazanov made the statement.

Using his cellular phone, detective Kazanov called Michail from his hiding place and told him about Mansur's business.

"Arrest him. Arrest him immediately;"

"We are moving!"

"I have no doubt that Mansur is committing the same crime as was done to Ivan. He has to be stopped and punished. He must pay for his crime." "History is being repeated, but this time, justice

240

will be done for Ivan and the other victims." Michail was outraged.

The Russian troops were still present in Chechnya in the case of an emergency situation. Control of the military operation was transferred to the Federal Security Service (FSB). Detective Kazanov contacted FSB. At nightfall, their squad surrounded the building where the hostages were being held.

"There are two Chechens are guarding the building outside. We don't know how many of them inside the building," detective said to swat commander.

The swat commander gave the order, "Let's take them." The soldiers opened the fire. Two of the guards were killed by the first shots.

The squad surrounded the building and shoot the lock off the door.

The soldiers rushed in, and shots were heard from inside the building. One soldier outside was wounded. The shot came from one of the windows with broken glass on the second floor. He continued shooting a barrage of bullets with a machine gun, but he was killed quickly by soldiers. The detective and his people could hear more shots inside the building, but it stopped in a matter of minutes.

When FSB opened the doors on the second floor, they found 31 young men and 13 young women, all hostages. Twenty-seven of them, all men, were just brought in. They were locked in a big room without windows in the middle of the building.

The hostages were taken to safe facilities, and because most of the hostages were from the same area of Yekaterinburg in Ural Maintains, they returned to their homes.

Mansur disappeared, but not for long. The FSB agents froze all three of Mansur's bank accounts in Grozny, Yekaterinburg, and Moscow. The money was in millions of American Dollars. The house behind the wall remained under the watch of the FSB.

"Michail Alexandrovich," Adele was screaming in the telephone. "We are surrounded by soldiers, what is going on? Are they going to kill us Mansur left this morning, and I don't know where he is. I'm so freighted for my children and my father."

"Don't be afraid, Adele, it is not your fault, but your brother committed the most ferocious act against humanity, and he will be punished for that."

"My brother, Mansur, but what did he do?"

"You will know soon."

Then he called to detective Kazanov and asked that they not to touch the family.

Mansur had been hiding in Grozny for a couple of months, and it was assumed that he somehow got away.

Maybe because he knew that he couldn't escape, or his conscious was talking to him, but one morning, he walked in the FSB station and gave up himself.

"I'm Mansur-Abu-Khan," he said. The officer on duty couldn't believe the luck.

"What made you give up voluntarily, Mansur-Abu-Khan?

"I came to confess my crime to spare my life."

"I didn't know that criminals of this magnitude have a conciseness," the officer thought as he gave the command to take him to a room.

The other two officers on duty showed him the way.

"Walk this way." They walked through a corridor and Mansur was locked in an empty room.

It was the weekend, and most of the staff was on leave. So the interrogation was postponed for two days.

Detective Kazanov was still in town and was called to join the interrogator on Monday.

Kazanov was standing behind the two-way mirror and could see Mansur. He was sitting dressed in white shirt, silently holding his hands on the table, and was waiting.

Something doesn't look right, the detective thought. "He looks different up close than from distance through binoculars and a photograph." He pulled the photo from his folder and looked closer at both of them to compare.

"Are you sure that it is Mansur-Abu-Khan?" he asked the officer in charge of investigation standing next to him, "Look at this photograph and him."

They both looked and agreed that it is not him. This man was skinnier and smaller and looked younger, though the face had a close resemblance.

They both walked to the room where Mansur was waiting.

"Who are you and where is Mansur?"

"I'm Mansur." The officer hit him in the face and screamed at him, "Where is Mansur?"

The man touched his burning cheek, looked at the officer, and said again "I'm Mansur." The officer yelled at him and hit him even harder. The detective threw the photographs onto the table.

"Do you know what is waiting for you? Oh, no jail for life. You will be hanged, but before that, you will be tortured until you confess and tell us the location where Mansur-Abu-Khan is hiding. How much did Mansur pay you for your life?" The officer raised his fist to hit him again.

"He promised to take care of my family."

"To take care of your family, and he promised heaven for you behind the clouds? The officer bent over and screamed in his ear, "Where is he?"

"He left the city and I don't know where he went."

"Take him away," the interrogator said to the officer as he walked out of the room.

"He could be anywhere, but he knows that he won't be left alone. He is cleaning up behind himself; that's what criminals usually do. So if he is not in Grozny, he is in Yekaterinburg."

Detective Kazanov, along with the FSB agents, flew to Yekaterinburg to arrest one of the biggest criminals in the country.

All local police were cooperating with the agents of FSB.

There are not many Chechens in Yekaterinburg, and their faces stand out among white skin people with mostly light eyes. So every suspected person was stopped in the streets and public places, but because Russian people that walk the city usually don't carry their passports or any identity proof with them it was harder to identify the person. So only those who were driving a car could be checked.

The FSB officer in charge of operation gave the order. "All vehicles that look like military trucks without windows should be stopped and inspected." Soldiers were patrolling the roads outside of the city as well as inside.

"He will try to leave the city and possibly will go to Moscow. It's easy to blend with the crowd there because there are more people from the south living near or visiting the capital."

"You are right detective Tihonov, but first, we need to look for him here."

"If Mansur is in Grozny, he could use a helicopter and easily disappear, but before he can, he has to use a car to get to a heliport."

Places to hide become smaller and smaller for Mansur.

"We need to go; you will drive, Ali." Mansur got into the trunk of a very old car and Ali covered him with an old rug and put two big sacks with potatoes on top to block him. He drove through the city and reached the outskirt on the narrow road surrounded by trees.

"We made it," Ali shouted so Mansur could hear him. Then he sees that the road ahead is blocked. "Damn it; they are everywhere." He pushed the gas pedal thinking he could go around the blocking vehicles, but when he got closer, he knew that it was over.

Soldiers surrounded the car. One soldier demanded, "Step out of the vehicle." Ali grabbed a gun from under his thigh and fired at the soldier. The soldier fell to the ground. Ali jumped out of the car and ran toward the trees, but didn't make it far. The other two soldiers fired their weapons at him, and Ali was on the ground.

Soldiers opened the trunk and behind the sacks of potatoes was Mansur-Abu-Khan.

The soldiers took him out and handcuffed him with his hands behind his back. One soldier used a radio in his patrol car to let FSB know that suspect is in the custody. Another soldier was assisting the fallen soldier, but his life wasn't in danger because he had a bullet proof jacket.

The FSB arrived shortly afterward, and Mansur was escorted to the station.

He was interrogated and confessed. He made a statement that Vladimir gave him money to buy the trucks, and he paid him 25% of the profit when he killed his brother, sister and his father's wife to have all their money.

"Who was the person who blew himself up to kill Vladimir Rennin and the others?"

"There are many of them; they weren't afraid to die."

Mansur Abu-Khan was convicted of crimes against humanity and was condemned to die.

Since that time, the search for disappearing people continued, but for as many that were found and returned to their homes, many others were disappearing.

After all the secrets of the family were revealed, and everything was over, Michail thought about the atrocity and sacrilege that was committed against humans. "The physical violation is indecorous evil, but to violate the soul is the biggest crime of the living."

Then he thought about what Napoleon said, "'In war, the moral power to physical is three parts out of four. And we are not even at war."

Soon Michail learned from Detective Kazanov that Mansur is in the custody and condemned to die.

In Russia, they don't wait for long to see if he has rights to hang on for his life. His crime was evident. The execution was done, and his name was soon forgotten.

Michail knew that justice was done.

One thought never left Michail's mind. That child Vera has, is he Andrey's son? Is it my grandchild?"

He called Detective Tihonov to find out about the boy.

He already had the answer. Andrey is not the father of Vera's child. The boy's name is Kruglov Andrey Lvovich and his father's name Lev Kruglov.

"We sometimes learn from the sight of evil than from an example of good; and it is well to accustom ourselves to profit by the evil which is so common, while that which is good is so rare. Who said it?" He thought, "It's the Greeks, who thought us to be civil."

The tragedy which happened in his family affected Michail's health. He gave the authority to Kiril Vasilevich to take charge of the business as he was an honest businessman who brought the company to the high level it was now.

"Now is the time to build the Mausoleum for my family, and for the last time, to bring them together, in death, as they couldn't do it in life," thought Michail.

The construction began on Vagankovskoe Cemetery.

In three months, they walked into the Mausoleum made of sparkling black granite from Karelia, surrounded by lilac bushes and trees. The wide entrance door had two halves.

On the front of the left half, which was an imitation of a door, was a full-size statue of the Swan-Princess made of milky-white marble with a tint of pink. It was an image of the Swan-Princess from the picture by Vrubel. With one hand she was holding the veil hanging from the crown, and the other hand was hidden behind the swan wing. The face of Swan-Princess was the face of Laura.

Inside, on the left wall, there were three white marble plaques with the names written in gold of his first wife who died at the age of 44, his daughter Oksana who died at age 26, and Laura who also died at age 26. Her body was brought from Danilovskoe Cemetery and placed in the Mausoleum.

On the right wall were plaques with the names of Andrey, who died at age 28 and Vladimir who died at age 30, and there was empty plaque with no name, on it. When the construction of Mausoleum was completed, and Michail stood in front of it for the first, he walked on the steps which led to the door and got on his knees in front of the mesmerizing beauty of the Swan-Princess statue, his Laura.

He put flowers at her feet, and said, "You always will be with me, because you left me your image. Angelica is a carbon-copy of you, my Love."

He looked at Laura's' statue and thought, "With the loss of my family, that chapter of my life is closed, and it is time to move to another chapter. I didn't have the time to watch after my family and to protect them from mistakes and disasters because I was too busy making money to build a fortune. I am one of the wealthiest people in Russia, and it will be enough money for many generations ahead, and the time has come to live my life. There are still people, who I owe my life, and now I will pay them back for their kindness."

Michail made all necessary arrangements for Kiril Vasilevich Timoshenko to take full charge of the business. His obligation was to report the financial situation to him, and the same arrangement was made with Anton Sergeevich Titov in Magadan.

Kiril Vasilevich wife, Tania, returned to him with their children, and it was critical for Kiril Vasilevich to recover from the loss of his love.

All this happened within seven months of Michail's return from Siberia, and it was winter in Moscow.

"Let's go, my Angel, I'll take you to your Mama's memorial."

They walked hand in hand to the Mausoleum as snowflakes danced around them. It was very peaceful and quiet there. Through the leafless bushes, Michail could see four guards at all four corners some distance from them; they were standing facing out.

"What a beautiful Angel-Princess, Papa," Angelica exclaimed seeing the white sculpture. "It's you Mama my Angel, she was the Swan-Princess, and you are the Angel."

Angelica raised her eyes and above the door she read the words of the inscription, "There is no grief like the grief which doesn't speak."

Five granite steps were clear of snow, and Angelica wiped the falling snowflakes from the steps with her gloved hand. They opened the door of Mausoleum with their key and walked into a warm room lit by bright light. As they stepped into the room, soft music started to play. Soothing, tranquil, flowing like water, like a free soul, crying and talking about life present, or those lost in the past, boundless like infinity, bringing peace to your soul, it was the music from Swan Lake by Tchaikovsky. Around on black granite walls were glittering flecks, like stars in a black velvet sky. There was bench made of white marble at the center of the room. Next to each plaque was newly placed fresh flowers.

Angelica read all plaques. They sat silently for a few minutes on the bench as each remembered the life they knew before, and then locked the door and walked away without looking back.

CHAPTER 27

Angelica was only 8-years-old, and for now, Michail was protecting her from knowing the dark secrets of their family. It was enough for her to lose her mother.

With nobody to talk to most of the time, Michail was often alone with his thoughts.

"Her happiness is the most important thing for me now. I couldn't protect my innocent ones, and now my only obligation is to protect my last child. She, like me, is the victim of violence and unjust. From now on, she will see and experience only the good side of life. I was too busy working hard for that myself and almost paid the ultimate prize for it. From now on, we will live a good life and give happiness to others."

In a dreamy state, he was sitting in a chair with eyes closed and his thoughts. In his mind's eyes, he was walking on the road straight and smooth with trees and flowers around. On one side of the road was one bush with red roses representing his first wife and then was more bushes with different flowers, it was his children. On the other side of the road was another bush with bright roses which gave an aroma and he could smell their delightful fragrance. That was his last love, Laura. He continued to walk on the smooth road, and suddenly there was a crack, wide and deep, so deep that he couldn't see the bottom of it. He could see only the darkness; the road ended, and he stopped. He barely could see the other side of the crack and he thought that over there is a new road and that it is his new path.

Nothing else was holding Michail in Moscow. For two long years, he was looking forward to seeing his family and to celebrate the reunion. But what he found on his return was death, humiliation, and grief. His city became cold and like a grave itself.

He got up from his chair and stood in front of a window and looking as snow covered the roofs and roads, and his shoulders jerked from shivering, he felt cold.

"I need to go far away from here to happy a place and bring my daughter to a better life. She is still very young and won't remember the bad things. I will do everything to make her happy."

The time came, and he called his daughter. He took her in his arms and holding her on his lap, said, "We are going on a trip, my Angel. Instead of flying by jet in the winter, we will take a train, the Trans-Siberian Railway to the end of Siberia. I want you to meet the kindest people in the world."

"Who are these people, Papa?"

"We will have plenty of time to talk about them, call your Nana, I need her to do preparations for the trip and tell her she is coming with us."

Michail called his private secretary.

"Sergey Sergeevich, take care of the household at home, you don't need to travel with us, but Nana, Butler, two bodyguards, doctor and kitchen staff will go with us by train to Vladivostok. Arrange jet from Vladivostok to Magadan and two helicopters from Magadan to Okhotsk. From there I'll make more arrangements myself."

"Everything will be done, Michail."

~

Angelica heard the sound of wills, making rhythmical noise.

"Did you sleep a little bit, My Angel?"

250

"Yes, but I was listening," Angelica said, pulling herself into a sitting position. "Will Sasha be my friend, Papa?"

"Sasha is two years older than you, he is 10-years-old, and he is a very good boy, very handsome and smart. He will be a very good friend to you."

Michail was trying to focus on the positive things. A big tragedy took place in his life, but the radio he turned on was announcing one bad thing after another:

"On Tuesday, December 3rd, Russian President Aleksey Lunin ordered special Kremlin inquiry into the three tragedies that hit Russia since the weekend. A plane crash, mine disaster and retirement home fire have claimed nearly 200 lives." It happened at three separate locations across the country in a matter of days.

"Russia should seek to develop new weapons in cooperation with foreign partners, the president Aleksey Lunin told to commission responsible for defense sector cooperation on Thursday, December 5th.

"More tragedies, more weapons and more killings-no more in my life," he thought turning the radio off and looked at Angelica. "You too my little one was a victim of violence, but it will be no more. We will fly far away from Russia and we will leave our past behind."

"Papa, tell me more stories about Mama and why you call her a Swan." He told her the story about how they meet at Tretyakov Gallery looking at the same picture. "She was so beautiful, your mama, and you look just like her, same eyes, same gold hair, same puffy little lips," he said stroking his daughter's large shiny gold curls and listening as she sang the melody without words.

"She has a beautiful voice, and she can sing," he thought, "just like her mama."

The train was making many stops in many big and small cities.

"Yekaterinburg," Angelica slowly read big letters on the station building.

"What is Yekaterinburg, Papa?"

Michail smiled to himself. Children are always asking a lot of questions that are required to be answered. So he started.

"Yekaterinburg was built at the beginning of eighteen century. This city will be soon be 300 years old. Once there was a German princess who married a Russian Tsar. Her name was Catherine the Great. She is the one who founded this city, and it was named after her.

"It's cold here and far from Moscow. Why did she choose to build a city here?"

"Its position had been chosen for its strategic proximity to the great mining operations in the Ural Mountains and Siberia. This city is also known to the world as a historical place. It was here, in a house that once stood on Liebknecht Street, that the last Tsar of Russia, Nicholas II, and his family were executed one summer morning.

"Was a Mausoleum also was built for them?"

"No, their grave is marked by a cross with their names, but in St. Petersburg in the museum, there is a special room which is dedicated the memory of assassinated royal family. It was a cruel act of the new government to kill them."

"Why people always kill the other people?"

"Oh, there are many aspects for that, but it is mostly the desire to have power over others. Sometimes humans seem worse than animals."

"Why?"

"Because animals kill to survive - people kill because they want to dominate or just being greedy, and this is evil. You will learn about it later in your school. Also, Yekaterinburg was the hometown of Russian President Boris Yeltsin, who just recently died."

"Everybody dies."

"Not anymore, my Angel, you won't hear about it anymore. I will protect you. Your Papa is strong." He shows how physically fit he is by flexing his arms and clenching his fists.

"Angelica laughed and hugged her father.

The train moved further, stopping for a short time in many small cities. The next major city was Krasnoyarsk. Of course, Angelica wanted to know about this city as well.

"This city is the oldest town in Siberia. It was founded in early 17 century and grew rapidly when gold was discovered in the region, and eventually become a major river port and industrial center. This city is built on Yenisei River, and as we will cross the river, we will plunge into the Taiga, the great forest that extends over most of Russia. Taiga is the largest remaining forest in the world."

Angelica was attentively listening.

"It's time to take a break and to have something to eat." Michail and Angelica were invited to the restaurant, and they shared the food the chef cooked with their employees. After that, they returned to their section, and both took a nap. When they woke up, the train had departed from Irkutsk.

From Irkutsk to the city of Ulan-Ude, on the left side of the train, they could see the open and flat surface of the water.

"This is the Lake Baikal, Angelica. It's not frozen yet; it will freeze on the end of next month, January. This is the deepest lake on the whole planet. It's 1,700 meters deep."

"Tell me, Papa, more about this lake and the funny name Ulan-Ude."

"Well, this is the oldest lake in the world about 30-million-years-old."

"30-million, is that old?" Father was watching his adorable Angel as she expressed her wonder and slapped her chicks with her small hands.

"Yes, that old. It's only about 70 kilometers wide, but 636 kilometers long. It contains almost one-quarter of the all fresh water on the earth."

"How did the water get there?"

"The lake is located between maintains and many rivers feeding the lake all the time."

The train stopped for a short time in Tanhoj, and their cook bought fresh fish from locals. For dinner, father and daughter were invited to the restaurant to have a soup called Ukha prepared with different kinds of fresh fish and vegetables.

The next day, they enjoyed fish baked in aluminum foil and after dinner, Angelica wanted to know about the city with its funny name, Ulan-Ude.

"It's also an old city that was founded in 17 century, and it is the center of Buddhist culture. It would be interesting to visit the Tibetan Buddhist monasteries nearby Ivolginsk Datsan. It is the center of Buddhism in Russia, but this is not where we are going."

"Two-thirds of the way is behind us and in a few days we will be in Vladivostok."

"Tell me about Vladivostok, Papa."

"Of course my Angel," he smiled at her. It was still a long way to go, and father continued, "This city was also founded a long time ago. It's located less than 100 kilometers from the Chinese border and just across the Sea of Japan from the main island Honshu.

Since its foundation in 19 century up to the middle of 20 century, Vladivostok was indeed a cosmopolitan city. In the early 20 century, Russians were outnumbered by Chinese, and during the years following the revolution; there were a large amount of Japanese and US population. Then for 33 years, the Soviet authorities closed the city as strategically important port to the Soviets, but now it's open for anybody to visit the city.

254

"Soon you will know about Siberia more than you know about Moscow, and it's good to know your country."

Angelica yawned and fell asleep. When she woke up, she was in Vladivostok.

"This is the end of our trip on the train; from here we are going to fly to Magadan, where your papa and other people are working. We will visit my job for a short time and then we'll fly to another city, Okhotsk."

"And then," Angelica continued.

"And then you will meet the kindest people in the world."

The jet was waiting for them and in a few hours, they reached the destination.

They arrived in Magadan in the morning and visited the headquarters. The staff and workers prepared a big party for them. The main hall in the big three-story-building was decorated with colorful balloons and greeting signs welcoming father and daughter. Little Angelica was given the honor to start cutting the cake and she did it with the help of her father because the cake was bigger than Angelica herself.

On the second morning, the jet was ready to fly them to Okhotsk.

They didn't waste time in Okhotsk and got in one of the helicopters which were waiting for them. The second helicopter with the two bodyguards on the board followed them. It was the same pilot who flew Ivan home.

The propeller picked up snow from the field in front of the house and disappeared for a minute in a snow cloud.

While Michail was getting to the ground and lifting Angelica out of the helicopter, the door of the house opened, and Ivan was standing in the doorway with astonishment in his eyes.

"Misha," he cried running to hug his friend.

Mariya and Sasha ran to join him. The four of them were dancing on the snow not able to break apart. Then they turned to

255

face the little girl standing next to the helicopter, dressed like Eskimos in a white fur coat with the hood covering all her face. She ran to papa's open arms, and Misha said, "This is my daughter, Angelica and this is Sasha; you wanted to meet. He walked Angelica to Sasha, joined their hands together, and the children ran to the house.

In the house was everything as Michail left. He walked to his small room, and the wheelchair was standing next to his bed. He covered his mouth with his hand and struggled to hold in the tears. "So much still to tell to my daughter," he thought.

The second helicopter landed, and the men walked to the house.

Ivan looked at Michail with the question in his eyes. "Who are these people?"

"Vania, I promised you that I would be back, and I came to take you and your family with me to a life where there will be no harm to you, no danger and no hardship. These two men will help you to take the precious things with you to the helicopter." Ivan was standing not able to absorb all of what he just heard.

"Where are you taking us, Misha?"

"I'm taking you to a faraway place that is paradise, where nobody will touch you, or your family. Do you trust me, Vania?"

"I trust you Misha with all my heart. But how can I leave the animals? They will die here without us."

"Don't worry Vania, I thought of everything. Tomorrow morning they will be transported to Okhotsk and will be given to the people who need them."

Mariya didn't ask any questions; she ran from place to place to collect her most precious items, like old photo albums, Sasha's school books, and clothes for Ivan, Sasha and herself. She gathered some food and put it in a basket. Ivan and the children went to the shed and gave some food to the animals.

256

Michail walked to his small room. The room looked smaller to him today than when he lived there. For two long years, it was his world. The surroundings were fresh in his memory as he came back home. For the last time, he lied down on his bed covered with the blanket Mariya sewed by herself and closed his eyes. Two years flashed in front of his eyes in a single minute. "I lost one family and found another; you never know where your life will bring you and what will make you wish to live and see the future." He got up, and everybody was already in the room waiting for him.

When everything was done, by the Old Russian tradition, they sat on the stools and benches around the room for a half a minute.

Two men took the all precious items that were gathered to the second helicopter.

Mariya and Ivan, the last ones to leave, walked out of the door and left it unlocked. They walked a few meters and turned around for the last time to see the house they build with their hands; a small house, but it was their home, a happy home. Then they held hands and walked to the helicopter. The children and Misha were waiting for them. They took their seats; the moving propeller picked up the snow blocking the view and in seconds were airborne.

From the air Ivan and Mariya looked on the house, for the last time saying goodbye and put their fate in the hands of men, who they trusted.

There were sparkles of excitement in Sasha's eyes. He was flying in a real helicopter; he had only seen pictures of one when his father came back from Okhotsk.

In Okhotsk, they got into a jet similar to the one which crashed next to their house and soon landed in Magadan.

From Magadan, two bigger planes got up in the air and headed west. That was an incredible treat for the entire family; neither of them flew in a plane before.

"Is it all yours, Misha?" Ivan asked Michail sitting next to him on the plane.

"Yes, it's all mine, Vania, and much more, much more, just wait a little bit."

The memory from his life was mixing in Ivan's head. "The grave-cage in Chechnya and wretchedness of existence, the cold and snow of Siberia, the hardship of working and living in the mountains, but I got used to it. Did I do the right thing to leave my home? Maybe I can't live with people anymore?" All these questions were clouding his head.

"We are flying first to Moscow, Vania. We will stay a few days to see the city. It's beautiful city, our capital, Moscow. We'll go to Red Square and the Kremlin. It will be very interesting for Sasha to see the big city. From there we will fly to the islands in paradise."

Ivan didn't ask any more questions. In his mind he said. "I respect the secret which Michail is keeping from me, where he is taking us. Life is a mysterious thing; you never know where it will lead you. I see that Michail had a better life than I had, all my treasure is my family, and this was enough for me to have."

At the same time, Michail thought, "Sooner or later, I have to tell Ivan. After all, I don't have any family left like him. As hard as it is, I have to tell him about my tragedy. It is a long way to Moscow, and we will spend many hours on the plane."

He collected himself and started.

"I have to tell you, Vania; something happened in the two years while I was recovering from injuries from the plane crash." Ivan looked at Michail and was concerned.

"It's painful for me to say, but it happened, and you need to know about it."

Michail took a deep breath and continued, "My oldest son, Vladimir committed a gross crime to kill his sister, brother and my wife, and he did it for money." Michail was shocked by what he was hearing.

Ivan opened his mouth, but words didn't come out.

Michail stopped to take a breath and then continued, "Thinking that I'm dead, he wanted to have all money which I left in my 'Will' dividing it equally among my four children and wife."

Ivan was stunned by the words he heard and there was silence for a long time afterward; they both needed time to absorb the secret that had now been brought into the open. It was as hard for him to say anything, as it was for Michail to continue. Then Ivan broke the silence, "Is there any justice on this earth, Misha? How could it happen to you after you were almost killed? I thought that I was an unfortunate person, but what said is worse than I can ever imagine."

"I don't know about justice, Vania, because my wife and daughter were good and innocent people. Why they have to die?"

Michail took a deep breath and looked in Ivan's eyes, and said, "But, you know that the guilty ones will always be punished; there is no escape for them. They all pay the highest price for their crime; they all pay with their lives.

"Who are they?" Ivan was confused, is Michail talking in general, or is there more to it?

"My son, Vladimir, paid for his crime with his life."

"Vladimir, your son, is also dead?"

Yes, Vania, and the person, who killed him, was Mansur, Vladimir's wife's brother. Vladimir was married to a beautiful Chechen girl, with charcoal black eyes and long black hair."

Ivan raced his eyes to the ceiling of the plane and closed them, then dropped his head down. "Mansur," he thought, "I heard this name, when I was a prisoner in Chechnya, must be a popular name there."

"Mansur," Michail continued, "who was following his father's steps kidnapping people and selling them into slavery, just like you were kidnapped. He was convicted and executed a month ago. He and his associates are the ones who kidnapped men and women. But his business came to the end."

Ivan was listening in silence. "So, not only the people who kidnapped us many years ago but there are the other people, who is doing the same things now. History is repeating itself," Ivan thought as Michail continued, "It will be interesting for you to hear this. I learned about it from the people who found and arrested Mansur in the United States of America."

Michail continued, "A massive crime was uncovered. Arrests are usually made early mornings when the suspect is still sleepy and not ready to be resistant.

At 6 o'clock in the morning in New York, agents of the Federal Immigration Service, which not that long time ago, made a report to the FBI who arrested illegal immigrants from Egypt and two American women that were with him. At the same time, the office escort-service Elites which is located in Manhattan, the business district of New York, was searched.

The same day, the arrested were delivered to Manhattan Federal Court, where they started a criminal investigation. The arrested were charged with export-service in the delivery of expensive prostitutes in cities of the United States.

The leading criminal prosecutor named 43-eyars-old Egyptian citizen Abdela Pady Mansur Abbacy and his girlfriend, Elena Troshenko.

The order for the arrest of the accused was given to an immigration service agent who gave the judge an affidavit that described the charges.

260

The document said that escort-ladies made one or two day trips to different cities, where they work as prostitutes in rooms of hotels. Three women, all Russian, decided to tell the court when and where they traveled for sex-assignments.

The court found out that the escort-service had a minimum of 200 women working in shifts of 40 women per day.

They advertised their service on the Internet. The clients were promised to meet supermodels that were overwhelmingly beautiful, such as, Veronica, Katrina, Elena, and others. They guaranteed pleasure in hotels on the East and West coasts of the country in the price range from $500 to $1500 per hour. The records show that the escort-service paid about $70.000 to hotels in one year.

Half of money prostitutes were getting from clients was paid to the Russian girlfriend of Abdela, and she put them in banks accounts opened in names of non-existing companies.

That day, when the arrests were made, on Internet was a photograph of beautiful Katrina Yevtushenko, and it was said to hurry up to order her service because she will be in New York only until Sunday.

Ivan shook his head, and said, "The world is diseased. It's unbelievable."

"As prosecutor unveiled that the workers of Elites served 22 cities, including New York, Boston, Chicago and San Francisco. The bank accounts in connection with the company Elites were found to have deposits made of $6 million, but experts think that real profit of company much bigger, because the majority of clients paid cash."

"That is where Mila, Leda, Lena and Katia were sent to prostitute in America," Ivan thought. His memory recalled their faces. "Did they get back home? I hope so. But if they did, they are broken souls."

Their talk was interrupted by the pilot as they approached the airport in Yekaterinburg. As usually, the plane stopped in two cities for refueling

After Michail had shared with Ivan his tragedy, they both needed to have time to rethink, adjust and accept what they both new. They didn't talk about it anymore. It was enough for both of them to contemplate until they arrived in Moscow.

A black limousine brought them from the airport to the Rennin's residence.

The two-story apartment looked like a palace to Mariya and Ivan. They thought they were in a dream.

"I'm very rich, Michail said to me in Okhotsk, but I didn't know that he is this rich. This is where he was from when he fell on our small house, which Mariya and I build with our hands. I never saw anyone in my life, who lived like this."

They slept the night in an incredibly beautiful and soft bed. They ate delicious food with meats, nuts, and fruits, and drank the most delicious wine. "Just like kings," Ivan thought.

The next day, a limousine took them to the Red Square and the Kremlin. Ivan and Mariya, being born and living all their life in a small city in Siberia, have seen this Tsar's palaces only in picture books and never walked into any museums like this before, and if not for Michail, they never would have the chance to see it. "How good it is for Sasha to see it, the real history of his country," Mariya thought, walking next to her son.

From there, Michail took them to Tretyakov Gallery and walked to the hall where Vrubel's picture is displayed.

"This picture is named 'Swan-Princess by artist," I call it, "The Portrait of Laura."

I met her when she was standing in front of it. I fell in love with her that same moment," Michail sighed. "She is gone, but her image is following me everywhere. You will see it again soon in different places," he said leaving the room.

262

They traveled by limousine and walked on the streets of Moscow, and there was no end to their delight.

On the 3rd day, Mariya asked Ivan, "Everything is beautiful, Vania, but it's not ours and where will we live? We are not used to this kind of life. There are too many people here."

"Wait, Mariya, I trust Misha, he knows what we like, and he will make it comfortable for us."

Mariya's mind was at home in Siberia, when she heard Ivan's words, "Think of the possibilities for Sasha, what kind of life would there be for him to stay in our house, especially when we would be gone?"

"You are right, Vania, for Sasha, I'm going to the end of the world."

On the 4th day, Michail said, "I did what I needed to do to take care of my business in Moscow. He made the required documents for Ivan's family to travel abroad. "I think that it's enough of winter and the cold for us, now I'll take you to the real paradise."

"What can be better than this city?" Ivan asked.

"I thought that Moscow was a safe place to live and to have a family, but found that it has the same crime as anywhere else, at least it was for me. No, Vania, I'll take you to a safe place where nobody can hurt your family."

The next morning, the two jets were ready when their limousine and caravan of cars arrived at the Sheremetyevo Airport. The sky was gray, and snow was tossed up from the ground with every step of their winter boots. The temperature was freezing, but the hearts were warm with excitement. Sasha and Angelica ran up the stairs of jet and disappeared inside. Ivan and Mariya followed them quietly, completely surrendering their fates to Misha. The pilot's voice asked to fasten the belts; the jet rolled to the runway and in a few minutes they were airborne. Mariya was looking outside of her window.

"Vania, we are in heaven. The sun is bright, and the clouds are white just like the snow at home. We didn't see much sun in our life, and I feel that the sun makes me happy."

"I never thought that I'd leave our mountains, but there are other beautiful places on the earth and Misha will show them to us."

After six hours flying, the jet landed in Hawthorn Airport in London. The waiting cars picked them up and drove through London. They stopped at Trafalgar Square and walked around the city. Then they went to the National Gallery, the Museum of fine art, and did some shopping in fine stores. They drove to see Buckingham Palace where the Queen lives.

"This is the home of my family," Mariya thought and drew in her mind's eyes her little house in Siberia next to the Palace. "It would fit through these gates. It was small, but it was mine, and now I don't have a home at all." She kept her thoughts to herself.

They spent the night in a luxurious hotel in London. It had a marble floor, gold decorations, and vases with flowers. It was like Misha's place in Moscow. The suite where they stayed and all surrounding just overwhelmed Mariya.

"I was born in Okhotsk, lived in the mountains, and I never thought that I'd see not only Moscow but other cities and countries. She thought, "Michail is not just a man who fell from the sky, but an Angel from Heaven."

The next morning after breakfast, the cars took them to the airport, and in four hours, the jet landed on the Gran Canary Island.

When they stepped onto the ground, the warm breeze and smell of paradise overcame them. Mariya opened her arms as she wanted to embrace the air.

"What a heavenly place it is, Vania!" Mariya has never been in the south and the climate was new for her. You can read about it, but to feel it is an entirely different thing.

From the plane, they were transported to a helicopter that took them to their final destination.

"Look, Angelica, we are so close to the water, and it's blue." Sasha was thrilled with the new discoveries.

"It is turquoise-blue," Angelica said, "Like my Mama's eyes were."

"That's right, Angel, just like your eyes are.

Right now, we are flying over the Atlantic Ocean and its very beautiful water here on the south. Your home, Sasha was very close to the Pacific Ocean and much closer to the north."

"I love Oceans, and when I grow up, I want to be a boat Capitan." Sasha still had his dream.

From helicopter window, they saw an Island in the distance and a small white dot surrounded by emerald greenery.

"What is that, Vania?" Mariya exclaimed, "Is it the paradise place, where Misha is taking us?"

"Yes, it is."

When they approached the island closer, the small dot became huge building on a green land. The helicopter made a sharp turn and landed on the marked circle.

Michail, Ivan, Mariya and children stepped onto the ground. In front of them, in the distance was a huge magnificent, brilliant white palace with a sparkling dome in the center of it. In front of it were wide stairs made of white marble.

"This is your home now, Vania," Michail said.

Vania was overwhelmed by the grandeur of the building, and he didn't know what to say.

Michail moved ahead, and they followed him to the steps. On both sides of the wide staircase, fountains were shooting water to the blue sky, sparkling in the bright sun.

With every step, the structure became bigger and bigger until the magnificent, breathtaking Palace was right in front of them.

"Wow, it's as big as the Queens Palace," Sasha exclaimed.

"It's not that big, but has enough room for everyone," Michail said.

As they walked down the wide road covered with fine yellow gravel which led to the palace, on the left and right was a beautifully designed landscape. As the five of them slowly approached the structure, two rows of people, maybe 20 of them, in uniforms were standing like soldiers in silence.

"They are free people, Vania. They voluntarily took the job of taking care of the house and the people who live here. They can quit their job anytime and go home, and most of them live in their homes with their families not far away from here."

They passed the people and stopped at the entrance.

The massive gold doors were wide open, and they walked inside to the enormous entry room.

"What is this?" Mariya threw up her hands. "Oh, this can't be real." She was turning her head around and couldn't believe her eyes. The Huge interior was a dazzling sight. She was surrounded by overwhelming beauty.

There were pink and green marble columns in a wide circle that surrounded the hall. She looked at the polished marble floor under her that reflected their silhouettes. It was white with gold, beige and other earthy color designs of carpet made of inlay, just like in king's palaces.

Her eyes moved further and stopped at a huge round fountain in the center of the hall. At the center of the fountain, standing on a pedestal, was a large marble statue. A bouquet of water streams curved from the center like flower petals and fell into the basin of the fountain made of pale green marble. She moved closer, and everyone followed her. The statue was made of milky white marble with a tint of pink. Her gown reminded her of the feather of a bird.

"This is the Swan-Princess from the picture at the Museum, in Moscow," Sasha exclaimed. "Only here, she is alive," Angelica added, "because she is my mama."

"True?"

Sasha was right. She looked alive because a rainbow was in every drop of the water. It was sparkling, moving, and glittering like millions of diamonds.

Mariya couldn't take her eyes of the fountain. They walked around it, and they could see what Misha was telling them about the beauty of his wife.

Ivan, as well as everybody else, raised his eyes higher and looked at the ceiling above the fountain, and they saw the cupola of the dome which was made of crystal glass, beveled with a curve design to break the sunlight into seven colors of the rainbow. The ceiling was no less than four-stories high and the sun illuminated entire hall.

"Oh," Mariya gleefully exclaimed, "I never imagined that beauty like this existed. The sun itself is in this crystal ceiling."

Their attention was taken to the back of the hall. Across the hall, there was another door the size of large gates, made of transparent lacy black metal with a gilded, flowery design. Through the lacy design, they could see the open space of a park, which was bright emerald green against the black with gold gates. They turned around, and there was a second-story with a row of pink with green marble columns that were smaller in size supporting the third floor. On the second and third floors, were balconies with black and gold lace railings and white with decorative gold doors for the rooms.

They stood in silence, not able to talk. Michail was watching their reaction. Then they heard the music of Swan Lake by Tchaikovsky. Mariya put her hand on her chest, and said, "It's too much, and I can't take it anymore. She closed her eyes and hummed with the familiar music.

"Oh, Vania, hold me, or I will faint. Not only an Angel but the entire Heaven has fallen on us," said Mariya.

"I must leave you, for now, till dinner. Take a look around and try to adjust to your new home. A member of the household will show you your rooms," said Michail.

Michail walked away and a young woman in uniform, a little younger than Mariya, said in Russian, "Следуйте за мной, пожалуйста (follow me, please)," and walked ahead.

"This is our new home, is it where we will live now?" Mariya couldn't grasp what was happening, "It is like a fairy-tale, this place."

Ivan, Mariya, and the children followed the young woman and she brought them to one of the doors. She pressed the button, and they walked into an elevator. When the elevator door opened, they were in a spacious hall with a high ceiling. The room was lavishly decorated with mahogany furniture and silk upholstery that was fit for a museum, with gilded and burgundy trim molding and murals on the ceiling and walls, with magnificent marble sculptures, crystal chandeliers and colorful vases with fresh flowers.

"It can't be real," Mariya was telling herself, "It just can't be real."

The young woman in uniform said that she is going to take the children to their rooms, and they will see them later. They walked out and closed the door behind them.

Mariya and Ivan turned their heads to each other; their eyes met, both their jaws were hanging, and the mouths were open in astonishment. They just stood in silence and looked around in disbelieve.

Then like curious children they slowly walked around afraid to touch this museum thesaurus with their hands.

Their silence was interrupted by knocking on the door. Mariya said, "Come in, please." A woman in uniform walked in carrying clothes for both of them and placed them on a wide bench next to a door. She politely said, "You will find everything in your dressing rooms, this is for today after your bath," and then she walked out and closed the door behind her.

After she was gone, like curious children, they walked to one room which was a bedroom with a magnificent wide bed for the King and then to the marble tiled, spacious, beautifully decorated, bathroom with colorful marble walls, mirrors and the sink and the bathtub with gold faucets. Adjacent to the bathroom was a closet with mirrors full of men's clothes.

Across from the King's bedroom was another bedroom, one made for a Queen with feminine decorations.

"Oh, Vania, it's breathtaking beauty. But, are they sleeping separately here?" Mariya asked and touched the cream color silk embroidered with flowers bed spread and looking at the crystal chandelier on the ceiling.

"For how long will this be our home, Vania?" But Vania didn't hear her questions; he was on the balcony and looked outside on the garden beneath.

"Mariya," he called out to her, but she was too far from him to hear his voice.

She was looking for him and found him on the balcony, big enough to call it a terrace. He was standing next to the lacy curved black metal railing. All around were vases filled with tropical plants and flowers, deckchairs with colorful cushions.

From the second floor, they could see the center of the magnificent park with walkways on both sides, trimmed with green borders of bushes and curved flower beds with different colors of flowers.

Along the walkways were white statue replicas of ancient Greek and Roman figures. Many fountains were placed

269

throughout the garden. In the distance, surrounding the estate was a plush, green forest. Further in the distance, they saw blue water of the ocean.

They were both overtaken by the beauty.

On the other side of the huge open hall were the children's rooms. Angelica was here before, but it was a long time ago and she didn't remember much.

Like all children do, they jumped and ran around in excitement. They were called to take a bath and then dressed in fresh, comfortable clothes. Nana, who came with them to live on the island, attended to Angelica. She combed the mane of her large gold curls and pinned them to the back of her head with a sparkling hairpin. Sasha was introduced to his Butler, a Spanish-speaking, smiling young man, named Alfaro. They quickly found a way to communicate very.

Michail thought ahead to hire the Spanish person so that the children could learn a new language from an early age.

Angelica, with her Nana, had their rooms and Sasha with his new Butler next to them. Their rooms included exercise equipment and toys for their age.

"What is your name?" Mariya asked when the young woman in uniform came again knocking at the door.

"My name is Sofia, and my husband is Oleg. We will help you to adjust to this lifestyle. Michail Alexandrovich invited us to live on this magnificent Island, and he gave us a job. We are extremely happy here.

When you need us, you can press the button on the wall, and one of us come to you. When we work, we have a room next to yours, but we have a house outside of this property as well. Very soon you will get used to living here - it's paradise on this island. For dinner tonight, you will find a dress in your dressing room and clothes for Ivan in his dressing room. She pressed the button, and Oleg showed up at the door.

"Sofia, you can call my husband Ivan Antonovich, but call me Mariya, I like it better."

"Okay Mariya, call us Oleg and Sofia, we like this also."

"Mariya, one more thing I need to tell you. You have your own kitchen here if you prefer to cook meals by yourself."

They walked together to the lavishly decorated dining room and the kitchen equipped with machines that Mariya had never seen in her life.

"I'll show you how to use them, said Sofia, and she opened the closet doors on the wall, "Here is an elevator, which is designed to deliver to your to your floor the fresh ingredients for the dishes you are cooking. To order, you can press this button and list the meats or vegetables you need. It will be delivered to you in just a few minutes. If you prefer to eat with everybody in the main dining hall, just go to the first floor.

There are many elevators around; you can use them instead of stairs. You can also order the meals which you prefer to eat, and it will be cooked for you as if you were at a restaurant. Any other times you want to eat just go to the buffet, and you can help yourself, or you will be served."

When Sofia left, Mariya said, "I'm speechless, Vania, we have our own servants."

"But they are not slaves, Mariya, and that makes a big difference."

"For the first time we are going to have lunch at the buffet, it's less trouble and tomorrow maybe I'll cook. What about children, they need to eat too."

With a press of the button, Sofia appeared at the door.

"Sofia, the children need to be fed, they must be hungry."

"I wouldn't worry about them, Mariya, they have their own servants to feed and watch over them. But if you like, I will call them, and if you would like to see you now."

"Yes, Sofia I would like to see them."

In a few minutes, Mariya and Ivan could hear excited voices and a girl's voice that was like a silver bell echoing in the air.

"Are you hungry, children?"

"No, Mama, we ate," as Sasha rolled his hand over his stomach, "It was so good, Mama, just like what you cooked at home, but even better."

Mariya smiled, "Then Papa and I are going to eat without you."

"Can we go now, Mama? We would like to go outside to the park."

"Go enjoy the weather. It's a beautiful sunny day."

Mariya and Ivan walked down the stairs while looking at the magnificent ceiling, and the beautiful decor, and couldn't believe the luxury which was surrounding them. There saw nobody on their way. They went to the left and didn't find any buffet there. They walked through the hall, and the door to the buffet was wide open. In the middle of the spacious room was a table shaped like a snake. It was covered with white table cloth, and several trays of food were neatly arranged on it. There was a cold section with seafood; oysters, shrimp, red lobsters that were cut in half and displayed on rock ice adorned with crystal bowls filled with black and red caviar.

"The caviar was shipped from Astrakhan on the Caspian Sea, where I worked when escaped the captivity. I didn't have a chance to taste it then, now it's my turn", and he put a full spoon of black caviar on his plate.

There were poultry and fresh cut ham, many kinds of cheeses and sweet pastries, fruits, enough to feet army.

After they had tasted all of the delicious foods, they went to the garden and sat on a bench. They were alone, and it was peaceful and quiet all around. The air was full of aroma from the roses and other flowers.

272

"Tomorrow is your birthday, Vania, and we are not at home to celebrate it. I will bake a pie with blueberries for you, and we will light the candles on the center as we did for so many birthdays that we celebrated in the mountains. What about animals, have they been fed, Vania?"

"I believe Misha when he said that they would be given to people who need them and won't leave them hungry."

They got up and walked around to the back of the Mansion. The park with tropical trees, bushes with huge leaves, the carpet of green grass and flowers didn't seem to have an end. Behind the group of trees, there was a lake with many swans. Slowly gliding on the surface of the clear water, the elegant bird's image reflected on the glass, mirror like water.

"It's breathtakingly beautiful and peaceful. It must be their lake."

"Whose lake?"

"The Swans, of course, look Vania how many of them here."

The day passed fast, and at six o'clock, Michail found them in the park. He sat with them on a bench next to the lake.

"How do you like the weather here?" Michail addressed to both of them, "It's sunny every day all the year around."

"After our mosquitoes in the summer and the freeze in the winter, this is Heaven on earth, Misha," Ivan laughed.

"There are six main Canary Islands and many small islands like this one. The climate here is subtropical, but if you explore all islands, you will find the variety of climate changes. You can find spring-like temperature climate at the north of the Islands, and then high up into the mountains, some in excess of 4 kilometers, where you could find yourself enshrouded by the clouds, even snow, and yet less than an hour further drive you could journeying through the middle of volcanic wasteland that's more reminiscent of the prehistoric days, and driving down you could find yourself on sandy beach on the same day. We have plenty of time to explore it later."

"The bell, can you hear the bell?" It's time to go and have a dinner."

They got up and headed to the Mansion.

"We still have so much to talk Vania, but we have all the time for it."

They sat in the medium size dining hall at a table for 12 people, though only five of them were eating. The dinner was served by the uniformed servants, but they weren't formally dressed for dinner. They weren't accustomed to this etiquette.

Mariya and Ivan had never been served before, so they watched Misha and did as he. They both thought the same thing. "We won't be embarrassed in Michail's house as he wasn't embarrassed to eat in our home." And they enjoyed the meal in full. When one used plate was replaced with a clean one, Ivan remembered how he was served in his grave jail. But that was in the past.

After dinner, Ivan, Mariya, and Misha walked to the front of the Mansion to view the Ocean and all its beauty. The children joined them, running back and forth.

"How many days are in the year? There are so many different things we can do here. There is a lot of tropical fish in this water, and we can go scuba diving, windsurfing, and sailing. The water is warm and pleasant," said Michail with a smile.

They sat for a while and enjoined the rest of the evening breathing the clean air.

Mariya went to play with the children and Ivan asked Misha, "I've been contemplating what you told me about your family tragedy, Misha. I know that your wounds are still fresh, and I am wondering, how you stay so good-hearted, kind, and a generous human after you went through?"

"Do you remember, Vania, I asked you the same question?"

"How, after so much bitterness, do you remain such a positive and loving person?"

"I do, Misha, I do. The wounds will heal in time, but the scars will stay for many years."

They sat for a while thinking of everything that was unveiled to each other.

"The air here is clean, as in our mountains," Ivan said and got up.

"We better go to bed now. The children must be tired because much happened at once and it was a long and exciting day, Misha, thank you."

"Don't mention it. Tomorrow will be a better day. Sleep well, my friends."

Mariya and Ivan went to see their children as they went to bed and to kiss them goodnight, and found Misha there; he was doing the same.

This first night in their new home and new life; it felt like they were lying on the cloud in their bed. They used to sleep together and decided to alternate the beds for the sake of variety.

In the morning, the bright sun lit their room. Ivan walked to the balcony, to see the Ocean view in front of him; the water reflected many beautiful colors from turquoise on the coast to dark blue on the horizon. The sun was brilliant and the fresh air filled with the aroma of flowers. Ivan took a deep breath. He was happy, although, his mind was still haunted by memories of the past.

"When I was in slavery, I wished that my life would be better, but I never thought that it would be this good. I ran from people to stay alive and save Mariya and my son."

His thoughts were interrupted by his wife. She joined him on the balcony. She was incredibly beautiful in her white cotton nightgown with her wavy brown hair loose and spread over her shoulders. "I never saw Mariya look like this in Siberia," he

275

thought, and he wrapped his arm around her waist and pulling her closer to him. He softly spoke to her, "You are so beautiful, Mariya. It was worth it for me to fight to live and to have you back."

Mariya was hiding something behind her back, and Ivan's hands founded it.

"What are you hiding there, let me see?"

"Happy Birthday, Vania." Mariya gave him a small box, wrapped in plain white paper from the page from a notebook.

Ivan unwrapped the box. His eyes opened wide seeing the surprise inside, "My watch, my father's watch - you saved it. This is the most precious gift I've ever received. Thank you, Mariya, for loving me." He kissed her passionately, and they shared a kiss of love and affection for each other.

During the day were a lot of activities around. The children wanted to go to the Ocean, and Ivan, Mariya, Nana and Alfaro took them to go swimming.

For the first time in her life, Mariya walked on white sand with bare feet and stepped into the warm, crystal clear water near the coast of Africa.

"Mama, watch me," Sasha dove in the water, keeping his legs above the surface.

Mariya smiled, holding Angelica under her belly when she was trying to remove splashes of water from her eyes.

"When did my son managed to learn to dive into water? Ah, children, they grow so fast. Vania, you are like a dolphin in deep waters. I need to keep an eye on you also," but Vania didn't hear her; he was diving again and again into the turquoise water.

Forgetting about the time, most of the day they spent on the beach. There they had lunch and just enjoyed the warm water.

At three o'clock, Alfaro, who was in charge of watching the time, announced that they need to go to the Mansion for the Birthday celebration.

"Vania, Michail remembered that today is your birthday. That is so nice of him."

Angelica and Sasha ran ahead of everyone and were taken to their rooms to get ready.

Ivan and Mariya were met by Oleg and Sofia who helped with their bath. Sofia brought a long evening gown for Mariya. It was made of turquoise silk chiffon with a silver lacy design inserted throughout the gown.

Mariya looked at her image in a mirror and didn't recognize herself.

"Is it me Sofia, do I really look like this?"

"It's you Mariya, and you look stunning."

"If it's me, then I've never seen myself before," she said, and they both laugh.

Ivan never in his life had a decent suite and he was not recognizable in his elegant beige tuxedo.

When Mariya and Ivan were walking down the wide curved staircase, they saw that the sparkling hall was full of people. They all were all dressed in beautiful and colorful clothes.

"Happy Birthday, Ivan Antonovich." He heard the words, which were addressed to him. His heart started to beat very fast and almost jumped out of his chest. "Oh, God, do I deserve this?"

The crystal chandeliers hung between columns illuminating the hall with brilliant light. The women's long evening gowns were sparkling in the light, and the men in their tuxedos were extremely elegant.

Ivan and Mariya joined the crowd and recognized the some of the people. There were maybe 100 people or more. They came from the surrounding small islands to celebrate Ivan's birthday and were all looking beautiful, dressed up for the special occasion.

They talked to each other like long-time friends, and the atmosphere was very festive and exciting.

Michail asked for everyone's attention. He stood on a little platform so that everybody could see him better. The voices got quiet, and when it was completely silent, Michail started, "Today we got together to meet Ivan Antonovich and Mariya Sergeevna." A loud applause echoed in the hall.

Today we celebrate the 48th birthday of my friend, who became more than a friend. He is like a brother to me - he is my family now. I want to thank him for the greatest gift he gave me. I owe him and his wife, Mariya, my life because they not only saved me, they healed me and nursed me back to good health for two long years.

Ivan took care of my broken body from the plane crash and gave me another chance to live a healthy and productive life. Living in an isolated and remote place in cold Siberia and having limited recourses, he built a wheelchair for me with his hands."

The blanket which was covering the wheelchair was removed, and everybody could see the hand carved wooden wheels attached to a handmade chair.

"Misha values my chair after what he has." Ivan suppressed the raging wave of tears wanting to burst from his eyes.

"My brother Ivan suffered from violence and the greed of other people. After his escape from captivity for thirteen years in Chechnya, he returned to his wife, Mariya. He didn't hold anger in his heart against the people that held him; he just hid in the remote maintains, in Siberia's Taiga so he would not be hurt again. But we found each other and my time has come to thank him from my heart. Today is his Birthday, and I have a gift for him."

Michail stepped down from the improvised podium, picked up a narrow box about 40 centimeters long that was he had sat on a table next to him and handed it to Ivan.

"Happy Birthday Vania, it's my gift to you."

Ivan opened the box and on a soft pillow of red velvet was resting a gold key. Ivan looked at this large gold key and said, "This key is for a very large door, Misha. Which door I should open with this key?"

"This one," Michail pointed to the Mansion's entrance door."

"This is your key, and this is your house now. But that is not all. The entire Island is yours; it's in your name. It's not big, but it's yours."

Ivan gave the box with the key to Mariya, covered his face with his hands and lowered his head so that nobody could see his eyes filled with tears. He couldn't say a word; they stuck in his throat. Finally, he exposed his face, wet with tears on his face, and with a broken voice, said, "Misha, this is too much for a simple man like me. No amount of money in the world could be equal to what you gave me, a simple man, and that I value the most. Every person has value in this world and is shown by his conduct that he too wishes to be valued. I was a guest in your home there. Now I'll be your guest again, here, if you don't mind."

They hugged each other like two brothers and exchanged kisses on the forehead with affection for each other, just like in those days when they did in cold Siberia.

"What should I call this Island?"

"It will be your choice; you name it."

"Swan," he said, I'll call it Swan Island."

This time, Michail's eyes filled with tears, "Only a man like Vania can feel the pain of others."

Loud applause broke the silence with, "Happy birthday Ivan Antonovich," and the flutes with champagne were emptied to the bottom.

Ivan was touched so deeply, that he couldn't stand on his feet. He sat next to Mariya on the wide sofa, sinking into the soft cushion and tears once again field their eyes. Mariya cried for having her Vania back, for all missing years, and for the unexpected transformation in their life. Ivan cried with tears for the third time in his life. The first time he cried was when he was on the train and was losing Mariya. The second time was when his friend Sasha died in his hands on the train, and the third time he cried was today. But today, they were tears of happiness, tears of a celebration of human dignity, love, and gratitude. Michail sat next to them and two adorable children, eight and ten years, old joined their parents.

"I am grateful to this man. I lost my family through a tragedy, and yet another tragedy, I found a new family, and I attend to keep this one. Vania was crying. When you find a great deal of gratitude in a poor man, we take it for granted, but there would be as much generosity if he were rich." That is how Michail thought about Ivan.

The festivities continued until late evening, and after nightfall, millions of lights lit the sky with from a magnificent display of firework.

Mariya looked at the bright colors of firework for the first time in her life and said, "I remember your words, Vania, when you asked me to marry you. You said that you would take me to Heaven with you, and I see today, you kept your words. There is Heaven on earth and you brought me here."

CHAPTER 28

Michail took the whole family to discover the treasures of the island.

"Your Swan Island is not big, Vania, when you climb to the highest point of the island, you can see all its coasts. The beaches have white sand all around the island except one place in the East where there is a steep cliff and under the cliff, there is a cave."

"Angelica, Sasha, put your hiking shoes on, we are going on a trip," Mariya called the children.

Five of them gathered together and went through the garden into the subtropical forest.

There was no wall around the park, only the palm trees with emerald-green leaves and bushes with flowers surrounded the Mansion.

Michail was leading the group, and Ivan was at the rear guarding them. They walked by the narrow passes between the bushes with large size leaves and trees with fruits, not familiar to them. The bright and large flowers were growing everywhere. Suddenly Mariya turned to Ivan and said, "Vania, there is winter right now in our cold Siberia and look at these flowers."

"It will not be cold in your life any more Mariya," Michail said to her, "It will be only sun and flowers."

On their way, they passed a house where a family lived that worked in the Mansion. "This house is three times bigger than where we lived," Ivan thought as they passed it.

In the distance were two other houses. The road led them up and down the hills, and after they had walked through three-quarter of the island, they were on East side of it and could see the Ocean.

"Look," Sasha was addressing to everyone, "The ship; I see a white ship on the horizon."

"That is big Ocean liner, Sasha, and one day we will take a trip to somewhere on it."

"This is my big wish, uncle Misha," Sasha said in an exciting voice, taking Angelica's hand and holding her from sliding down on the steep side of the pass.

They walked closer to the edge, and a big panorama view of ocean opened for them.

"It's a breathtaking beauty!" Mariya exclaimed. "It's just magnificent." In her mind, she flew back to her small house in Taiga and a chill went through her body remembering the cold.

"It is winter back there and maybe a snow storm by now. Vania, did you noticed that there are no mosquitoes here. How it's possible that there are no mosquitoes?" she laughs.

They rested a little bit and then headed home.

The life on the island took over and soon the old life in Siberia was only in memory like it was in another life. Every day was new discoveries for them. They were snorkeling around the coast. For the first time, they saw the colorful tropical fish in its environment.

There was no need to have bodyguards on the island. Everybody was safe here, and the bodyguards had a different job here to watch that everyone was safe in the water. They were trained in scuba diving and gave the lessons in the pool on how to use the equipment.

In the morning after a light breakfast, the whole family and two guards descended to the coast. A little bit to the left from the front of the Mansion, there was spacious bay with a few boats.

They put on their scuba diving equipment, and the motor boat took them to small rocks not far away from the coast. But when they approached the rocks, it was much bigger than it looked from a distance. The waves were splashing on black with sharp edges rock, breaking water into millions of sparkling drops in the sun before falling back into the ocean. The boat was secured with an anchor and one by one everybody was in the clear blue water.

All of them dove at once into another world. The steep side of the rocks was covered with pink, red and purple corals. Fern looking plants were swinging in the water and black, yellow with black stripes flat fish was swimming right next to them. Purple, red, and blue fish larger in size was circling them.

"Even fish is not afraid of people, as we were afraid of our own spices," Ivan thought as he touched fish next to him.

The bodyguards were swimming next to children. There was so much to see, but the time came to get back to the boat. Michail gave the signal and bodyguards helped children to climb on the boat, and they headed to the coast.

At lunch, it was very noisy at the table. Everybody in exciting voices was expressing their impression interrupting each other by sharing their experience in the water. The children were ecstatic.

"Angelica, did you see the Porcupine?"

"No, I've only seen a Porcupine at the Zoo." And they laughed in their sonorous children's voices.

"Uncle Misha, are we going to see the cave?"

"You read my mind," exclaimed Sasha, "I just was going to tell you that tomorrow we are going to the cave."

The next day, they walked to the bay, got on a motorboat and it took them to the side of the cave.

They went inside through a small entrance and followed each other walking the narrow footpath deeper into the cave. It became darker every step they took, using their flashlight to see the road.

"What is this hanging from the ceiling?" Angelica asked.

"Those are stalagmites. They grow like icicles, little by little, and it takes them a long time to become so big," Sasha explained.

"He can always explain everything to me, my smart Sasha." Angelica already learned from him a lot and become attached to Sasha.

"Sasha, can you see the bottom in this dark water? It must be very deep like the Lake Baikal. Do you know that the Lake Baikal is 1.700 meters deep?" Angelica asked to impress Sasha with her knowledge.

"I didn't know exactly how deep it is, but I know that it's the deepest lake on the Earth."

They reached the point where the ceiling was very low, and if they wanted to continue to go ahead, they have to crouch for a few steps.

"This time we want to go farther. Let's walk through this bridge to another side. Watch your steps," Michail said, even he knew that it was secure to walk through.

"Ah, how beautiful this side of the cave is. It's sparkling like stars in the night sky, but without a Moon. Angelica's voice echoed reflecting from the walls. She heard herself, and suddenly she started to sing in her child's voice: "Memory all alone in the moonlight I can smile at the old days I was beautiful then….. "

It took Michail by surprise to hear this beautiful, strong voice. How does this powerful voice can fit in a tiny body? "When did she learn the words of the song? It sounds like her mother is singing about her not fulfilled life and only a memory remains. Yes, here underground, that was a cry for her mother, and I heard her clearly. Oh, my God, my Laura you gave me Angel, thank you, my Love. Your daughter's angelic voice is made to sing. It was so unexpected that everybody stopped.

They heard the voice of Angel. Her powerful voice filled all hidden spaces of the cave.

They were so shocked by her voice that they stood there like frozen stalagmites not breathing. She finished singing the verse and said in a quiet voice. "Only the stars here are a little bit bigger than in Mausoleum."

Michel understood that she was thinking about her mother.

"She has her mother's voice, but much stronger, more powerful. Oh, my Angel, how blessed I am to have you. You alone can fill the life of human being. I am sorry that your mama can't hear you. No, your voice can wake up the dead and your mama heard you right now." Michail was so touched by this discovery that he wanted to hug his little Angel.

"You will sing, I will give you a chance to polish your abilities. I will take you to the big city to learn and to shine."

At dinner, they shared their experiences and impressions they had throughout the day. They talked about Angelica's voice and how she impressed them. From that moment everybody knew that she would be a Big Star.

Every day was something new to discover on the island and their days were filled with enjoying and without any distress.

When Mariya and Ivan were walking through the beautiful hall filled with sunlight and rainbow colors shining all around, this beauty couldn't touch the human senses, and Ivan said, "I am glad, Mariya," that I was lucky to survive and to live to these days. You never know where your fate will bring you. I am so happy."

"The rays of happiness like those of light are colorless when unbroken."

"Oh, Mariya, she always could say something smart, it must be somebody said, like always in the past."

The turquoise water sparkled in the sunlight. Sasha and Angelica rode their horses at a fast pace on the wet sand holding kites by strings.

Angelica, catch me," Sasha gave a command to his black Mustang to run.

"Wait, Sasha, wait for me," Angelica called to him, laughing with her sonorous voice, riding without a saddle on the back of white and brown Pinto. She rode her horse on the water passing Sasha. Her Pinto made big splashes and the sprays of water that reached Sasha's face. They let go their kites and the kites' flu to the ocean and disappeared from their site.

"Catch me if you can," he laughed. His Mustang again was ahead of her Pinto.

"Sasha," she yelled as she slipped from her horse and fell in the water. The waves covered her and drug her into deeper water. He turned his horse around and hurried to rescue his friend.

"I won't let you go down," he was saying, pulling her by her dress from the water.

"I wasn't going to drown, silly one," she laughed, freeing her face from her wet hair.

They sat on the hot sand; he put his arm around her wet shoulders, and they laughed together pushing white sand with their feet.

"You are wet already," Sasha said and pulled Angelica by her hand back to the water.

They ran into the shallow water, making splashes, and at the same time, dove into an upcoming wave, and emerged on the surface at the same time.

"Let's do it again," Angelica laughed. Then they rolled on the sand and went back to the water.

Too tired to fight with the waves any longer, they climbed like two monkeys on the trunk of a palm tree leaning over the sand palm and sat close together, dangling their legs in the air.

Break time came to an end, and it was time to study again. Angelica started her fifth grade and Sasha his seventh. They had their teachers, who came to live on the island for the school season. Mariya often joined the classes and sometimes replaced teachers when they needed a break. The same teachers taught the other children of the island.

Days passed, and it was summer on the big land in Russia and Michail was planning to visit his business in Moscow.

Preparing for the trip, Michail was working in his office. His office was facing the ocean and the garden in front of the Mansion. He pulled the documents from the draw and put them on the table in front of an open window and opened the folder. The breeze from the ocean picked up the papers and they flew out of the window. Michail called his Butler to help him to collect the important documents from the ground. While they were descending, Ivan who was sitting on the bench in the park, picked up a few papers and a photograph that fell to the ground. The image he saw, shocked him; it was the wall surrounding the yellow color house. It astonished him.

"This is the wall I build and these are the stones I gathered from the quarry. How did this picture get into Michail's hands?"

Michail was approaching Ivan to collect the papers he was holding.

"Misha, this is the wall I built in Chechnya when I was in slavery for eleven years."

They both stood rooted to the spot and looked at each other in disbelieve.

"What are you saying, Vania? This is the house of my daughter-in-law. Oh, Vania," the only words came out of Michail's mouth. His legs couldn't hold him, and if Ivan didn't support him, Michail would fall onto the ground. They sat on the bench, and Michail said.

"My son, Vladimir, was married to a girl from Chechnya, Adele, she had a brother, Mansur and it is their home, where they were born and lived with their parents. This is same Mansur I told you about on the plane. That's him in the photograph with his sister Adele."

"I remember the voices of children when I was locked in the basement, while they had guests in the house and I remember the names, Mansur and Adele. They were children at that time I could say by their voices."

"So, it was their father, who kept you in slavery." Michail closed his eyes, and there not enough air for him to breathe.

They were sitting silently for a long time with dropped heads deep in their thoughts.

"How two men were leaving so far away from each other could be connected by their fate and through tragedy found each other? Aren't we, the people on the earth, one family and related to each other? Why are we hurting the members of our family, what wrong with us? Our planet is so small compared to the universe. But big compared to the population on our Earth. To every human with their birth is given the opportunity to grow, create and love. There are many religions on Earth, and every religion teaches to love each other. Some people choose the wrong path to hurt their brothers and sisters and to destroy the happiness of others. But they never win, because they fight against nature - nature is a living thing and can't be destroyed."

"Vania," Michail broke the silence. "This is the most horrible thing that could happen to people, and we are both are victims of human worth weakness. I think we have a destiny. Our fate was written before we were born and we lived our lives without understanding why we were suffering? How else we can explain why and how our lives have crossed each other?"

"It is Providence itself who had brought the five us together."

"Now I see that there is balance in nature. Innocent people will be rewarded in life, and the evil souls will be condemned."

"You are right Vania, Mansur was executed soon after his conviction and his father died shortly after his crime was exposed

288

to the world. You know the rest of my tragedy in my family. I raised my children in good faith, gave them love, the opportunity to develop themselves, and live a prosperous life, but maybe I gave them too much, and they lost the value of everything. I don't have the answer, Vania, why my innocent ones have to die? "

The same thought came to each of them, and their eyes met, they understood each other as they had expressed it in the words, saying "they live here," Ivan put his hand on his heart. Michail smiled back with bitterness on his lips.

"They are."

As much of the pain that was in their hearts in the past, so much happiness and joy filled now their souls watching their children. They were teens now but still behaved like children.

"Papa," Angelica and Sasha were calling them in one voice, when they ran toward them from Ocean, "Look what we found in the Ocean. It's a sea star," as they both dropped them on the bench next to their fathers, but just for a moment before they ran away again.

~

A couple of years passed, and Michail said, "We have an opportunity to travel. Why not to take a trip to Morocco, I have been there, and it is very exotic and interesting country. It's good for children's education to know more about the world and after all, it is very close.

"Will we ride on camels in a desert," Papa?

"It would be one of the most interesting things about our journey. I don't think that we will travel to Sahara this time, but we will make an excursion on camels. But first, we will fly to the capital of Morocco, Casablanca."

They packed for the road, and a helicopter took them to the Las Palmas. From there by commercial airline, they arrived in the

Mohamed V International Airport. Before they landed, Sasha asked Michail, "What is this huge structure which stands out on the edge of the ocean, Uncle Misha?"

"Oh, this is Hassan II Mosque, and it's an enormous structure. It can hold 25, 000 faithful. When we get closer, you will see how tall it is. It took over 3 000 craftsmen from every part of the kingdom to build this 2-hectar monument on mighty pillars to erect the world's tallest minaret (200 meters)." Sasha made a funny face to Angelica about how impressed he was, and she giggled back.

Walking through narrow streets, they saw many merchants. Here the coppersmiths forge teapots, cauldrons, candelabras, vases, lanterns and trays.

"I'll take you to the famous bazaars they are bursting from floor to ceiling with different kinds of merchandise."

"Look, Vania, this man is dressed in very colorful, must be national clothes; they are doing sewing right on the street."

"Now, Mariya, we all will develop an appetite after we visit this market. It will be a first for the eyes and nose."

"This is fresh looking fish, seafood must be straight out of the ocean," Ivan noticed.

"Look at the pyramids of fruit and vegetables," Mariya was amazed.

"And bunches of flowers," Angelica added.

"Do you know Angelica, that to make one liter of distilled rose water, the one you are using for your bath, it needs a ton of rose petals."

"Oh," she put her hands on her chicks, "That much?"

"Now is the time to have a snack, taste the oysters in this cozy place, and have a tea with the date pastries."

After they had explored Casablanca, they took the railroad to Marrakech.

"Oh, look Vania at how beautiful the snow on the mountains and how big contrast to see the palm trees in the city. I never saw so many fruits at once; this is definitely another world. Oh, I recognize these spices from my study of botanic, and here is, saffron, cumin, black paper, ginger, and cloves. It tickles my nose. All these full baskets of nuts, dates, and olives, and here is the bottles with rose extract," Mariya was wondering.

"Smell it," Angelica gave a sample of jasmine extract to Sasha.

"Umm, Angelica," Smell this piece of umber and musk.

"Misha, you promised us paradise, and I believe we are in it, and it doesn't have the end."

Angelica and Mariya choose a few pieces of Berber jewelers for themselves and the workers in Mansion. Then they ate from rounded terracotta pots an exquisite stew of mutton with spices, which was cooked slowly and buried in ashes through the night.

"I ate a lot of lamb in my captivity and thought that I would never eat it again in my life, but this is a real delicacy, Ivan said licking his lips."

They were moving south and visited the city of Agadir right on the ocean. Between the balsamic greenery of the eucalyptus, pines, tamarinds, the captivating blue sea, and the crystal blue sky where the bright sun shines every day. They spent half a day on the beach in the hot golden sun.

"Just like at home," Mariya said taking a deep breath.

"I'm so happy, that Mariya calls the island her home," Michail thought.

Then they stopped near the mosque, sat at a coffee table to take a break and to taste local sweetness, then strolled around the bazaars and watched the activities of fishermen like animated spectacle.

"This is the largest fishing port in Morocco," Michail said.

"What a contrast to the pictures of fishing in our cold country. It looks to me that they are on vacation here and not to work," Ivan said, "It is much easier to fish when the sun shines."

Michail heard him and thought. "It will always be sunny for you now, Vania."

After spending the night in a splendid hotel, they were moving closer home heading more south.

In the far South, the panoramic view is striking. The snow-capped mountains peaks, burning sand, orchards fields, the gardens reflecting in emerald waters of lakes, everything was unbelievably beautiful.

"Vania, living in our cold Siberia, I never thought that I would see bunches of golden dates like this, hanging from the palm trees. How beautiful the colors emerald greenery and ochre colored land."

"When I compare the cold and misery I saw in my life - I think that I died and gone to Heaven."

"Oh, Vania, try to forget it, it was in the past and never comes back."

After they had visited valleys, they took a ride on camels. Before getting on the camel, everybody got a lesson in camel riding.

"Sasha, this camel is so sturdy, it rides much smoother than a horse," Angelica said. "And it's as comfortable as a sofa," Mariya laughed.

"The camel able to go several days without drinking water," Sasha added.

"But not a human being," Ivan thought.

"Did you fulfill your desire, Angelica, to ride the camel?"

"That was the most magnificent trip, Papa, thank you."

"So we are going back to the city of Marrakech and from there we will fly home."

All family safely came back to their Mansion.

"After traveling, to the mainland, our island I feel more at home than before, Vania."

"Me too, Mariya, finally we are at home."

CHAPTER 29

The old say that happy people don't watch the time, and time passes fast.

Every year Michail flew to Moscow and Magadan, and every time there was a reason to celebrate. First, his safe returns and second their fortune was growing. Michail made a new 'will' a long time ago, in which the estate was divided evenly between all of them.

Sasha and Angelica were not children anymore. Instead of playing, now they often walked around the coast and on the island, sometimes disappearing for long hours and missing their meals with their parents.

She was wearing a white cotton dress down to her ankles. Her long hair was tied on the back of her head with a blue ribbon. They walked hand in hand far away to the cliff and sat on a grass tightly together and silently watched the ocean.

Sasha's hand touched Angelica's head. He pulled the end of the blue ribbon, and his fingers ran through her long large gold curls down to her waist. He wrapped his hand around her slim waist and pulled her closer to him. She dropped her head back, and he gently touched her coral lips with his. Then he opened his lips and took hers inside. The sweet bliss overcame this two young people.

"I love you, Angelica."

"I love you too, Sasha," she cooed.

"When we grow up to become adults, I want to marry you. Will you marry me?"

She hid her lips inside of his mouth, looked into his eyes, and nodded her head. He kissed her again, and she responded with all her willingness. Then they got up and walked back home.

It was their secret, but their parents knew from the beginning that this was unavoidable.

The sweet expectation of the future only enhances their desire to be together. When they were free of studying, they enjoyed the luxury of what the ocean offered them.

"Bend your head, Angelica, or the sail will hit you. Move to my side; we need to put more weight on this side." Sasha was commanding his sailboat. They leaned over the side, hanging over the water, and the wind turned their boat and tossed both of them into the water. But they were good swimmers and managed to climb back onto the boat. They guided the boat back and forth in warm wind of the summer. Another time, they placed two boats parallel to each other, and both of them were water skiing, turning 360 degrees in the air, and did it again and again. With practice, they synchronized their movements and could do it simultaneously as their parents watched them from the coast.

Parasailing was even more exciting when they flew in the air dangling their legs and laughing the entire time.

In the evening sometimes all staff together with the parents listened Angelica's singing under accompaniment on the piano by her music teacher. When she stops, they would ask her to sing more.

There were many birthdays throughout the year to celebrate. On big holidays, like New Year and the spring vacation for Sasha and Angelica, many guests were invited to the island, and their joy was prolonged for a few days.

One particular day was Angelica's day. Angelica was beautiful as a child, but now at 17, she blossomed to a beautiful flower. For this special day, the interior of Mansion was decorated with flower garlands hung between columns and big bouquets of fresh flowers were placed in antique vases around the hall. A hundred guests dressed in bright colors were in the main room waiting for her to come down.

The familiar music from Swan Lake announced her arrival. Everybody looked at the balcony. There she was standing, dressed in bright blue silk beautifully designed in Paris especially for her to fit her graceful figure. Her shiny gold hair was pulled up, and a few locks of curls were loose on the sides of her gorgeous face. Diamonds on her earrings sparkled in the brightness of the sun.

When she walked down the stairs, her father couldn't determine if she was Laura, or his daughter, Angelica. She was a splitting image of her mother when Laura was seventeen when he met her eighteen years ago.

There was sadness in his heart, "I didn't lose you my love; you came back to me.

She slowly descended the stairs and walked to her father. Michail took both her hands in his and pulled her to his chest and kissed her on her forehead.

"I wish you Happy Birthday, my Angel."

She looked in her father's eyes and smiled back with a captivating smile to him, just like her mother.

Then Sasha took her hand and walked her away from the crowd to tell her how gorgeous she looks today and how much he loves her.

They mixed with the guests, and she received a hundred or more greetings. For a moment, Sasha left her alone with the guests and then she heard his voice.

"Angelica," Sasha called her with his matured voice, "Come here," and he hid behind the door in an empty room. She slipped behind the door, and he took her in his arms to kiss her coral lips.

"You are so beautiful. I never get tired of looking at you," Sasha was whispered in her ear. She smiled at her handsome young man and said, "Let's go back before they become suspicious."

"After this kiss," and only then he let her go.

Then, like always, she sang for them with her Angel's voice, which surprised the new guests with its power and beauty.

CHAPTER 30

Good times fly fast, and Michail, returning from Russia, said, "When I turned 65, the time came for me to retire and take care of our children's education. We are going to London and Sasha will attend Oxford University."

Sasha was 19-years-old, and Angelica was seventeen. With her incredibly powerful and beautiful voice, she got accepted into the London Music Academy.

When the season to study came, the three of them flew to London and were living together in an old rented house next to Kensington Palace.

Sasha wanted to learn economics, and Michail was very pleased with his choice because he could take over the oil business.

Every day he enjoyed listening to Angelica's vocal, and each time her voice became better toned and sounded even stronger. She grew up to be an incredibly beautiful young lady. Only Michail knew how much the resemblance was with her mother. When Michail didn't watch her, two bodyguards were taking care of both of them.

During school brakes and summer vacation they visited home on Swan Island and enjoyed the blue and warm ocean. Ivan and Mariya watched these two children become two beautiful adults.

Sasha turned into a tall and very handsome man with a strong and athletic body.

It was impossible not to notice the attraction between two of them, and they didn't hide it. It was natural for these two young people growing up together to gradually fall in love. They often went to theaters, sports games and other places of attraction were young people like to be. And one day, when father and daughter were alone, Angelica told him, "Papa, when we return home to the island, Sasha and I want to get married."

"Do you love him that much, my Angel?"

"Maybe you didn't notice it, Papa, but we fell in love with each other from the first time we met."

"When was it, my Angel?"

"It was when we went to the Tretyakov Gallery to see The Swan-Princess. That time Sasha was looking at me, and the picture, and at me again. I was watching him and that time I knew that he was the one I will marry one day."

"He deserves you, my Angel, I know him very well."

They had one more year remaining for them to complete their education. Again, happy people not watching the time and it ran for them very fast.

Ivan and Mariya, Michail and Angelica and their staff were flown to London to attended Sasha's and Angelica's graduation. When they sat in the row reserved for parents to watch the ceremony, Ivan whispered into Mariya's ear, "Mariya," do you remember where we came from? Do you remember when our little son in the summer was wearing the muck to protect his face from mosquitoes with the pine branch in his hand chasing the rabbit on the grass in our yard? Do you remember how you taught him to read when he was 4-years-old?"

"I remember everything Vania, just like it was yesterday. It wasn't much to be happy about, but we were happy during that time in our own way. I was always worried about his future, and wished that he would be exposed to a better life, but I never imagined that our Sasha would be graduating from one of most prestigious universities in the world, and he is one of the honorable students. His success is our pride." Her eyes were wet from overcoming emotions.

"For all this, we have to thank the man, who fell on us from the sky..." "but happened to be that he was an Angel," Mariya finished the sentence.

When the ceremony was over, and Sasha walked down from the stage in the huge auditorium, his family congratulated him on his completion of his years as a student and with stepping into a new chapter of his life as an adult man.

There were many parties to attend for the youngsters and they enjoyed it in full.

Two weeks later, there was Angelica's graduation. All the guests from Swan Island were staying in London for another special day.

After the formal ceremony in the big theater when the diplomas were presented to the students, the concert began. One after another young people showed their talents. They played instruments and sung with beautiful voices and family members applaud to their success. But our family was waiting for her turn.

When she walked to the center of a stage in her light lavender, full skirt dress with diamonds in her hair, sparkling in the bright lights, all audience focused on her. The audience was silent when the soft music started to play. Michail stopped breathing; he was listening to the music, "She will start right now." It was not a familiar melody to him, and he was wondering what she will perform.

She began with a quiet voice the first notes, and her voice gradually grew stronger and stronger and then it acquired full power. Her voice filled all space in the vast hall, and everybody knew that one more star just emerged in their presents. They heard the voice of Angel.

Nobody could know it and feel it better than Michail. His eyes were filled with tears happiness.

Her voice on her graduation day produced such sensation that she was immediately invited to perform at concerts in Royal Opera House, London Coliseum, and South Bunk Center. That was her triumph, and she sang at the areas from famous operas as well as songs of contemporary composers. She sang the leading roles in Andrew Lloyd Weber's musicals Phantom of the Opera and Cats. Guests of the family attended all her performances, and when they heard, "Memory all alone in the moonlight. I can smile at the old days. I was beautiful then." They remembered her first performance in the cave on the Swan Island when she was only nine years old.

Her debut was an incredible success, and she became a Star from her first performance. Her Majesty, Queen Elisabeth the II attended her concert. She received a standing aviation, and flowers covered the stage floor.

She sang on many other stages in English, Russian, Italian and Spanish languages.

She shined on the stage and was adored by people. "But all of this is for them," she thought, and what I want for myself. I want my Sasha.

She completed her concerts, which were scheduled for her and the day came to return home.

There was no end of festivities in their return. Ivan and Mariya were the happiest people on earth because their Sasha found his love as he told them.

~

Finally, the two young people could be alone. Day time they disappeared from the eyes of people, and spent, as before, hours walking around the Island. They sat on the high cliff hanging their legs in the air and looked at the Ocean hearing the noise far below as waves were crashing on the black volcanic wall creating white foam and going back to the ocean. On the other side of the Island, they swam in the blue-turquoise water - the color of Angelica's eyes. They again traveled by boat and visited the other Canary Islands. They both were fluent in Spanish, English, and French, which they learned while studying in England. Here they could practice it in real life. Angelica learned more songs in different languages; they all were about love. She performed on local stages and became their Idol. A few months passed as they enjoyed their youth and freedom.

Once they were sitting on the beach, and nobody was around. Sasha held Angelica's hand.

"Now, after we prepared ourselves to take responsibility in our lives, the time has come to ask Angelica to marry me," Sasha thought as he heard Angelica's voice.

"When are you going to ask my father, Sasha, I'm melting like a snowflake, and don't you see it?"

Sasha took her in his arms and took her lips in his, and they kissed as it was the kiss of agreement to be together forever.

At the evening dinner, it was tradition to dine in the formal dining hall with full service of privileged people, Sasha, before dinner, stood on his feet and addressed Angelica's father.

"Michail Alexandrovich, Angelica and I have loved each other very much for a long time, actually from the first moment we saw each other standing at the picture of her Mother in Tretyakov Gallery. We grew up together and fell in love. Today, Michail Alexandrovich, I'm asking for your permission for daughter's hand to marry me so that I can love her forever, as you, our parents, loved and love each other."

Michail was so sensitive that things like this were hard for him to take without emotions involved. He looked at Sasha and saw him as not only an incredibly handsome and physically fit man but inside his soul was pure and beautiful.

"Come to me my son," Michail raced from his seat.

"I'll be the happiest father on the earth to trust you with my precious daughter, the last love in my life. Marry her and love her as I do."

He reached out and took the hand of his daughter and put it in Sasha's palm.

"We are the happiest parents in the whole world, aren't we Vania, Mariya?"

"This is not all I want to ask you Michail Alexandrovich. With my father's blessing, I want to ask you for the honor to carry your family name Rennin to preserve it for generations ahead."

Tears fell up Michail's eyes, and he said. "I'll be honored, Sasha, if you take it," this unexpected request stunned him. Tears rolled out of his eyes and ran down his cheeks. "I'll be so happy," he said with a broken voice, "after all, it's not such a big change from Repin to Rennin."

The servants, who were in the hall and happy parents, applaud with joy. The dinner was delightful and delicious like never before.

Three days later, they had an engagement party, when Sasha stood on one knee and said, "I love you, Angelica Rennin, and I am asking you to marry me, will you be my wife?"

"Yes, Sasha, I've wanted to marry you since I was 10."

It sounded so cute and innocent that everybody smiled.

Then Sasha put the diamond engagement ring on Angelica's finger.

The festivities began and lasted until late evening. Then the announcement was made to all household and guests that there will be wedding soon, and the preparations need to be made.

Mariya took charge to direct the jobs, and she worked her plan to separate the priorities like cleaning, from secondary jobs. Then she worked with the cooks to create the menu and special wedding cake.

Ivan took charge outside to prepare the park for the guest's to add more benches and create the arch for the ceremony. When the time comes, there will be twine around with fresh flowers.

A plan was made to build a stage for the Orchestra and the other performers. The chairs were placed in a semicircle facing the arch and the Mention.

In two weeks, there will be a lot of music and dancing. The gypsies will entertain the guests with their fiery dances and soul tortured songs.

Mariya checked that the Mansion was thoroughly cleaned for the occasion, including the crystal glass chandelier over the main hall. After cleaning, it sparkled even brighter than the sun itself. Finally, after the Mansion was cleaned and decorated, she prepared the rooms for the guests. All rooms for the guests were cleaned and ready to accommodate them. There will be many guests from Russia, including all Moscow staff and all employees from Magadan. There was guest house hotel-type built on the coast along with the Mansion a long time ago, and the guests who couldn't stay in Mansion will comfortably stay in that guest house. The Mansion employees had extra rooms in their homes and were happy to give it to the guests.

The wedding day was scheduled for the middle of July. Michail's private secretary, Sergey Sergeevich, flew to Moscow and took charges of sending the invitations for the wedding and a Russian Pope from Moscow was asked to marry the couple.

While all the preparations were being made, Michail took Angelica and Sasha to Paris to have a special gown and suite for the bride and groom.

"She will wear the diamond tiara, which her mama was wearing when she married me. It is very close to the tiara Swan-Princess was wearing on Vrubel's picture."

When they returned to the island ten days later, everything was ready.

The helicopters were busy flying to the main island to pick up the guests from the airport. A few boats were traveling back and forth caring more guests.

CHAPTER 31

The wedding was set for 1 o'clock in the afternoon on July 15. The week before, all guests arrived, and there was enough room for more than 500 guests to stay comfortably. For an entire week, they enjoyed the weather, the warm water of the ocean, swimming and tanning in the sun on white beaches of the island.

There were a few students from London, along the close friends of Sasha and Angelica, who will be the maids of honor and groom's best friends at the wedding, but the most of the guests were employees from Moscow and Magadan. Not many of them traveled abroad, and no one had been on Canary Islands before.

Two executive directors, Anton Sergeevich and Kiril Vasilevich, were walking in their shorts and bare feet in the shallow water at the beach.

"This is paradise on Earth; so much sun and light. Not like in Moscow."

"I don't need to mention Magadan. We never saw weather like this. I never thought that I'd have the chance to see it."

"As much as Michail is rich, he is so much more generous."

"Whatever he has, he did it himself. He is not only smart but has a big heart as well."

"We've never even come close to experiencing what he felt when he learned that he lost his family. I was the one, who gave him the Newspapers when he arrived in Magadan. That's when he first heard about the tragedy in his family."

"I remember his beautiful young wife, Laura, with golden hair and the face of Angel," Kiril Vasilevich said, "but wait a minute; it's her on the horse. She is alive."

"No, that is his daughter Angelica. She is a carbon copy of her mother, and she is going to marry a gorgeous man."

"You are right; it's an incredible resemblance. I'm kidding, I know the truth."

The guests watched as the young man and beautiful woman rode their horses in the morning in the shallow water of the coast. The graceful, charcoal black Mustang was running after a white Pinto, and the white dress of the rider was floating in the air, and her long gold hair was bouncing, flying together with a laughing Angel.

Leaving the horses on the beach, they ran into the water with their clothes on and swam far away from the coast playing with waves. Their guests joined them, skiing on the water and sailing in the warm wind. They snorkeled and went scuba diving.

When they visited the cave, Sasha asked Angelica to sing for them.

"Memory all alone in the moonlight I can smile at the old days I was beautiful then…"

The beautiful voice bounced off the walls, and its sheer power magnified many times. When she stopped, her last note echoed many times.

One person said, "This clean and powerful voice moved my soul."

"Her voice can not only move a soul but mountains as well."

"You are right. I remember her as a beautiful child, and I'm not surprised that she grew up to become a gorgeous young woman with incredible voice and talent."

It was one of many unexpected surprises on this island and this unusual family.

More than 500 chairs were facing the Mansion, and the arch was decorated with light pink roses in front of them. The guests took their seats while soft music was playing by a live orchestra.

Dressed in a white tuxedo, the handsome, tall and well-built groom was waiting for his bride. The Pope of the Russian Orthodox Church wore a gold embroidered rope with multi-color ornaments.

On the left, in the first row, were sitting Ivan and Mariya. On the right, was an empty chair waiting for Michail. Sitting next to him were his closest friends, Kiril Vasilevich with his family from Moscow, Anton Sergeevich from Magadan with his family, and on both sides the rest of the guests.

The traditional wedding music, the March by Mendelssohn, made the voices disappear, and everybody's eyes were on the main door. When the gold door slowly opened, they saw father and daughter were standing in the doorway. The tiara and veil that covered her face were trimmed with hundreds of diamonds that sparkled in the bright sun. The white dress was made of finest silk chiffon which was pressed with the patron and looked like feathers.

They were standing still until the music stopped, and new music from Tchaikovsky Swan Lake began to play. Under this music, they slowly moved toward the steps and descended to the ground. All guests kept their silence mesmerized by the beauty of the bride.

She was a Swan-Princess from the painting of Vrubel, which is familiar to every Russian, but she was real.

The proud father walked his daughter to the arch laced with white and pink roses where her groom was waiting for her. Michail looked at Sasha's eyes and said to him. "She is yours, Sasha."

When Michail took his seat, the Pope started the ceremony. Not many people have seen a traditional Russian marriage ceremony, but it is a very beautiful ritual.

"I wish you could see our daughter, my Love'"

"But I'm here," she answered him. "I am with you."

"She is marrying a fitting and worthy man, he is also very handsome," he smiled.

"My son from a small house in Siberia reached to the stars and took the brightest one to light his life, just like Mariya was my shining star all my life. I lived only because I had her."

"For my son, I will go to the end of the Earth," thought Mariya as she smiled.

After exchanging the rings, the Pope crossed them both and said his last words.

"And now I pronounce you husband and wife. You may kiss the bride."

Diamonds sparkled like millions of stars when the groom slowly uncovered bride's face.

Thick eyelashes rose upward and dark blue eyes like water in the ocean looked in his eyes.

"You are my Angel," he said, and his lips met her coral lips when he held her head in his hands.

Then they slowly turned around, and the bridesmaids straightened her dress and veil.

When they walked through the alley between the guests, all eyes followed them with adoration. "The diamonds, oh beautiful diamonds; "it's hard to take eyes off them."

The parents were following the couple. All guests got up from their seats as husband and wife walked through the corridor of arches laced with multicolored roses facing toward the ocean.

All the guests continued to follow them. At the coast, they stopped and saw a magnificent ocean yacht docked in front of them.

"This is your ship Capitan. When you were 10-years-old, you told me, that when you grow up, you want to be a Capitan."

"And you said to me," Sasha continued, "that one day you will have your ship, Captain." Sasha was speechless. He hugged his father-in-law and saluted him as Capitan's do.

"You were planning to go to Europe for your honeymoon, and after that, to travel to many countries. Now you can do it in style and comfort.

"What shall I call this ship, Father?"

"It's your ship, Capitan; you name it."

"Angel, I'll call it Angel."

Michail waved his hand, and the white cloth covered the name dropped.

"Oh!" Sasha exclaimed in surprise throwing his hands up, "She is Angel." Father! You read my mind before I could think. She is real, "Angel."

"He called me Father." Michail smiled. "Now, I have Son."

www.ingramcontent.com/pod-product-compliance
Lightning Source LLC
Chambersburg PA
CBHW031236090426
42742CB00007B/222